Classic
HUNTING STORIES

Classic
HUNTING STORIES

EDITED *by*
LAMAR UNDERWOOD

THE LYONS PRESS
GUILFORD, CONNECTICUT

The Lyons Press is an imprint of
The Globe Pequot Press

10 9 8 7 6 5

Printed in the United States of America

Designed by Claire Zoghb

Paperback ISBN 978-1-59228-057-5

Library of Congress Cataloging-in-Publication
Data is available on file.

Contents

CONTENTS

CONTENTS

Introduction

The oldest hunting images are familiar now, crude and strange drawings left on the walls of caves and the faces of prominent rock outcroppings. They are scenes of triumph in the face of danger—and survival in the face of starvation. The primitive ancients wrote their stories in pictures, and one can imagine the voices and gesturing that resounded from the firesides as the light weaved and danced across the scenes on the walls. The exhilarating details of the chase, the moments of suspense when failure loomed, the skills that prevailed through great difficulties—these classic elements of hunting talk were no doubt as much in evidence for the pursuers of the woolly mammoth as they are today for the pursuers of whitetail deer, and all other game.

The fireplace and hearth where today's hunter holds forth will, like the primitives', no doubt include pictures that trigger precious memories, captured today with acrylics and oils far superior to the strange mixtures the ancients used to depict their hunts. Today, artists like David Maass and Bob Kuhn preserve the action and emotions of hunting and wildlife encounters with precise and dramatic interpretation. Near these paintings in the hunter's home, probably within the light flickering from the glowing hearth, there will be books. Visit these and you will probably find useful and pragmatic treatises on whatever hunting skills you are interested in perfecting—from training a dog to training yourself to make the shot. And also present on the shelves, whether as a few scattered outriders or vast collections, there will be hunting stories.

Preserved in books, hunting stories transcend the ages for all to whom the call of the chase is irresistible and rewarding. To the brethren of the chase, the call is clear: Hunting, thinking about hunting, and talking about hunting. In this way of life, the best talk is always hunting talk, and some of the most engaging you'll ever find is gathered in books, both new and dusty.

But how does a hunting story become so enduring to a reader that he catalogues it in his mind under the exalted title, "Classic"? One would suppose that any tale that hangs around long enough, staying in print here and there, earns the "Classic" label. And certainly that distinction is shared by many stories by great hunting writers like Nash Buckingham, Archibald Rutledge, and the enduring Theodore Roosevelt. Some of their tales have been on the contents pages of scores of anthologies, and will no doubt continue to do so. Clearly, they are "Classic" stories. People want to read them, to hear the stories of the old hunts again and again.

The editors of such collections, like myself, have the opportunity to show the world the "Classic" stories of our own choosing. We are not unlike cowpunchers, rounding up a herd, picking out the best stock we can find. When our work is done, the stories we have come to love and think of as "Classic" gathered in one place, we realize in presenting them that our personal tastes and judgment may not hold up in the reader's eyes. A story we have read countless times and choose to call "Classic," might be quickly brushed aside as "boring hogwash" by a reader. That's why the editor's chair is somewhat an uneasy one. But that's the job: To make the call. To tell the world, "Hey, listen up, you hunters. You're going to love these stories. They're all classics to me."

Obviously, I hope this collection finds an audience of appreciative readers. I like to think that you've picked up the book because you're willing to trust your editor at least to the point of giving the stories a serious look. If the word "Classic" makes you nervous because it sounds rather pretentious, I apologize for pervading my literary choices upon you in such a way. If "Classic" sounds like an announcement for something from the dusty, staid corridors of academia, I urge you to fear not. For I shall not take you on such a journey. Instead we are going afield, hunting with writers whose creativity and talent bring their experiences alive on the printed page.

Through the magic of enduring prose, we will share the camaraderie of duck camps and greet the dawn from a blind. We'll follow gallant bird dogs in the uplands, stalk man-eating lions, ride into the high country for elk, duel with the elusive wild turkey, try to bring down a giant bear. And much more.

Eventually, I hope these tales come to be old friends to the reader. Yes, "Classics." Enduring not because some editor said they were "Classics." But because people love reading them.

—Lamar Underwood
May, 2003

Classic

HUNTING STORIES

The Hunt for the Man-Eaters of Tsavo

[LT. COL. J. M. PATTERSON, D.S.O.]

Editor's Note: When assigned to help supervise the building of a Uganda Railroad bridge over the Tsavo River in east Africa in March, 1898, Lt. Col. J. H. Patterson, D. S. O., had little idea of the magnitude of the adventure upon which he was embarking. The site of the bridge, which is today a part of Kenya, became the scene of savage attacks by man-eating lions preying on the workers. Col. Patterson's stirring book, "The Man-Eaters of Tsavo," remains in print to this day. The drama was also captured quite well in the film, "The Ghost and the Darkness," starring Val Kilmer and Michael Douglas.

Unfortunately this happy state of affairs did not continue for long, and our work was soon interrupted in a rude and startling manner. Two most voracious and insatiable man-eating lions appeared upon the scene, and for over nine months waged an intermittent warfare against the railway and all those connected with it in the vicinity of Tsavo. This culminated in a perfect reign of terror in December, 1898, when they actually succeeded in bringing the railway works to a complete standstill for about three weeks. At first they were not always successful in their efforts to carry off a victim, but as time went on they stopped at nothing and indeed braved any danger in order to obtain their favourite food. Their methods then became so uncanny, and their man-stalking so well-timed and so certain of success, that the workmen firmly believed that they were not real animals at all, but devils in lions' shape. Many a time the coolies solemnly assured me that it was absolutely useless to attempt to shoot them. They were quite convinced that the angry spirits of two departed native chiefs had taken this form in order to protect against a railway being made through their country, and by stopping its progress to avenge the insult thus shown to them.

I had only been a few days at Tsavo when I first heard that these brutes had been seen in the neighbourhood. Shortly afterwards one or two coolies mysteriously disappeared, and I was told that they had been carried off by night from their tents and devoured by lions. At the time I did not credit this

story, and was more inclined to believe that the
unfortunate men had been the victims of foul play at
the hands of some of their comrades. They were, as it
happened, very good workmen, and had each saved a
fair number of rupees, so I thought it quite likely that
some scoundrels from the gangs had murdered them
for the sake of their money. This suspicion, however,
was very soon dispelled. About three weeks after my
arrival, I was roused one morning about daybreak
and told that one of my *jemadars*, a fine powerful Sikh
named Ungan Singh, had been seized in his tent during the night, and dragged off and eaten.

Naturally I lost no time in making an examination
of the place, and was soon convinced that the man
had indeed been carried off by a lion, and its "pug"
marks were plainly visible in the sand, while the fur-
rows made by the heels of the victim showed the
direction in which he had been dragged away.
Moreover, the *jemadar* shared his tent with half a
dozen other workmen, and one of his bedfellows
had actually witnessed the occurrence. He graphi-
cally described how, at about midnight, the lion suddenly put its head in at the open tent door and seized
Ungan Singh—who happened to be nearest the
opening—by the throat. The unfortunate fellow
cried out *"Choro"* ("Let go"), and threw his arms up
round the lion's neck. The next moment he was
gone, and his panic-stricken companions lay help-

less, forced to listen to the terrible struggle which took place outside. Poor Ungan Singh must have died hard; but what chance had he? As a coolie gravely remarked, "Was he not fighting with a lion?"

On hearing this dreadful story I at once set out to try to track the animal, and was accompanied by Captain Haslem, who happened to be staying at Tsavo at the time, and who, poor fellow, himself met with a tragic fate very shortly afterwards. We found it an easy matter to follow the route taken by the lion, as he appeared to have stopped several times before beginning his meal. Pools of blood marked these halting-places, where he doubtless indulged in the man-eaters' habit of licking the skin off so as to get at the fresh blood. (I have been led to believe that this is their custom from the appearance of two half-eaten bodies which I subsequently rescued: the skin was gone in places, and the flesh looked dry, as if it had been sucked.) On reaching the spot where the body had been devoured, a dreadful spectacle presented itself. The ground all round was covered with blood and morsels of flesh and bones, but the unfortunate *jemadar*'s head had been left intact, save for the holes made by the lion's tusks on seizing him, and lay a short distance away from the other remains, the eyes staring wide open with a startled, horrified look in them. The place was considerably cut up, and on closer examination we found that two lions had been there and had probably struggled for possession of the body. It was the most gruesome sight I had ever seen. We collected the remains as well as we could and heaped stones on them, the head with its fixed, terrified stare seeming to watch us all the time, for it we did not bury, but took back to camp for identification before the Medical Officer.

Thus occurred my first experience of man-eating lions, and I vowed there and then that I would spare no pains to rid the neighbourhood of the brutes. I little knew the trouble that was in store for me, or how narrow were to be my own escapes from sharing poor Ungan Singh's fate.

That same night I sat up in a tree close to the late *jemadar*'s tent, hoping that the lions would return to it for another victim. I was followed to my perch by a few of the more terrified coolies, who begged to be allowed to sit up in the tree with me; all the other workmen remained in their tents, but no more doors were left open. I had with me my .303 and 12-bore shot gun, one barrel loaded with ball and the other with slug. Shortly after settling down to my vigil, my hopes of bagging one of the brutes were raised by the sound of their ominous roaring coming closer and closer. Presently this ceased, and quiet reigned for an hour or two, as lions always stalk their prey in complete silence. All at once, however, we heard a great uproar and frenzied cries coming from another camp about half a mile away; we knew then that the lions had seized a victim there, and that we should see or hear nothing further of them that night.

Next morning I found that one of the brutes had broken into a tent at Railhead Camp—whence we had heard the commotion during the night—and had made off with a poor wretch who was lying there asleep. After a night's rest, therefore, I took up my position in a suitable tree near this tent. I did not at all like the idea of walking the half-mile to the place after dark, but all the same I felt fairly safe, as one of my men carried a bright lamp close behind me. He in his turn was followed by another leading a goat, which I tied under my tree in the hope that the lion might be tempted to seize it instead of a coolie. A steady drizzle commenced shortly after I had settled down to my night of watching, and I was soon thoroughly chilled and wet. I stuck to my uncomfortable post, however, hoping to get a shot, but I well remember the feeling of impotent disappointment I experienced when about midnight I heard screams and cries and a heartrending shriek, which told me that the man-eaters had again eluded me and had claimed another victim elsewhere.

At this time the various camps for the workmen were very scattered, so that the lions had a range of some eight miles on either side of Tsavo to work upon; and as their tactics seemed to be to break into a different camp each night, it was most difficult to forestall them. They almost appeared, too, to have an extraordinary and uncanny faculty of finding out our plans beforehand, so that no matter in how likely or how tempting a spot we lay in wait for them, they invariably avoided that particular place and seized their victim for the night from some other camp. Hunting them by day moreover, in such a dense wilderness as surrounded us, was an exceedingly tiring and really foolhardy undertaking. In a thick jungle of the kind round Tsavo the hunted animal has every chance against the hunter, as however careful the latter may be, a dead twig or something of the sort is sure to crackle just at the critical moment and so give the alarm. Still I never gave up hope of some day finding their lair, and accordingly continued to devote all my spare time to crawling about through the undergrowth. Many a time when attempting to force my way through this bewildering tangle I had to be released by my gun-bearer from the fast clutches of the "wait-a-bit"; and often with immense pains I succeeded in tracing the lions to the river after they had seized a victim, only to lose the trail from there onwards, owing to the rocky nature of the ground which they seemed to be careful to choose in retreating to their den.

At this early stage of the struggle, I am glad to say,

the lions were not always successful in their efforts to capture a human being for their nightly meal, and one or two amusing incidents occurred to relieve the tension from which our nerves were beginning to suffer. On one occasion an enterprising *bunniah* (Indian trader) was riding along on his donkey late one night, when suddenly a lion sprang out on him knocking over both man and beast. The donkey was badly wounded, and the lion was just about to seize the trader, when in some way or other his claws became entangled in a rope by which two empty oil tins were strung across the donkey's neck. The rattle and clatter made by these as he dragged them after him gave him such a fright that he turned tail and bolted off into the jungle, to the intense relief of the terrified *bunniah*, who quickly made his way up the nearest tree and remained there, shivering with fear, for the rest of the night.

Shortly after this episode, a Greek contractor named Themistocles Pappadimitrini had an equally marvellous escape. He was sleeping peacefully in his tent one night, when a lion broke in, and seized and made off with the mattress on which he was lying. Though rudely awakened, the Greek was quite unhurt and suffered from nothing worse than a bad fright. This same man, however, met with a melancholy fate not long afterwards. He had been to the Kilima N'jaro district to buy cattle, and on the return journey attempted to take a short cut across country to the railway, but perished miserably of thirst on the way.

On another occasion fourteen coolies who slept together in a large tent were one night awakened by a lion suddenly jumping on to the tent and breaking through it. The brute landed with one claw on a coolie's shoulder, which was badly torn; but instead of seizing the man himself, in his hurry he grabbed a large bag of rice which happened to be lying in the tent, and made off with it, dropping it in disgust some little distance away when he realised his mistake.

These, however, were only the earlier efforts of the man-eaters. Later on, as will be seen, nothing flurried or frightened them in the least, and except as food they showed a complete contempt for human beings. Having once marked down a victim, they would allow nothing to deter them from securing him, whether he were protected by a thick fence, or inside a closed tent, or sitting round a brightly burning fire. Shots, shouting and firebrands they alike held in derision.

THE ATTACK ON THE GOODS-WAGON

All this time my own tent was pitched in an open clearing, unprotected by a fence of any kind round it. One night when the medical officer, Dr. Rose, was staying with me, we were awakened about midnight by hearing something tumbling about among the tent ropes, but on going out with a lantern we could discover nothing. Daylight, however, plainly revealed the "pug" marks of a lion, so that on that occasion I fancy one or other of us had a narrow escape. Warned by this experience, I at once arranged to move my quarters, and went to join forces with Dr. Brock, who had just arrived at Tsavo to take medical charge of the district. We shared a hut of palm leaves and boughs, which we had constructed on the eastern side of the river, close to the old caravan route leading to Uganda; and we had it surrounded by a circular *boma*, or thorn fence, about seventy yards in diameter, well made and thick and high. Our personal servants also lived within the enclosure, and a bright fire was always kept up throughout the night. For the sake of coolness, Brock and I used to sit out under the verandah of this hut in the evenings; but it was rather trying to our nerves to attempt to read or write there, as we never knew when a lion might spring over the *boma*, and be on us before we were aware. We therefore kept our rifles within easy reach, and cast many an anxious glance out into the inky darkness beyond the circle of the firelight. On one or two occasions, we found in the morning that the lions had come quite close to the fence; but fortunately they never succeeded in getting through.

By this time, too, the camps of the workmen had also been surrounded by thorn fences; nevertheless the lions managed to jump over or to break through some one or other of these, and regularly every few nights a man was carried off, the reports of the disappearance of this or that workman coming in to me with painful frequency. So long, however, as Railhead Camp—with its two or three thousand men, scattered over a wide area—remained at Tsavo, the coolies appeared not to take much notice of the dreadful deaths of their comrades. Each man felt, I suppose, that as the man-eaters had such a large number of victims to choose from, the chances of their selecting him in particular were very small. But when the large camp moved ahead with the railway, matters altered considerably. I was then left with only some few hundred men to complete the permanent works; and as all the remaining workmen were naturally camped together the attentions of the lions became more apparent and made a deeper impression. A regular panic consequently ensued, and it required all my powers of persuasion to induce the men to stay on. In fact, I succeeded in doing so only by allowing them to knock off all regular work until they had built exceptionally thick and high *bomas* round each camp. Within these enclosures fires were kept burning all night, and it was also the duty of the night-watchman to keep clattering half a dozen empty oil tins suspended from a convenient tree. These he manipulated by means of a long rope, while sitting in the hopes of terrifying away the man-eaters. In spite of all these precautions, however, the lions would not be denied, and men continued to disappear.

When the railhead workmen moved on, their hospital camp was left behind. It stood rather apart from the other camps, in a clearing about three-quarters of a mile from my hut, but was protected by a good thick fence and to all appearance was quite secure. It seemed, however, as if barriers were of no avail against the "demons", for before very long one of them found a weak spot in the *boma* and broke through. On this occasion the Hospital Assistant had a marvellous escape. Hearing a noise outside, he opened the door of his tent and was horrified to see a great lion standing a few yards away looking at him. The beast made a spring towards him, which gave the Assistant such a fright that he jumped backwards, and in doing so luckily upset a box containing medical stores. This crashed down with such a loud clatter of breaking glass that the lion was startled for the moment and made off to another part of the enclosure. Here, unfortunately, he was more successful, as he jumped on to and broke through a tent in which eight patients were lying. Two of them were badly wounded by his spring, while a third poor wretch was seized and dragged off bodily through the thorn fence. The two wounded coolies were left where they lay; a piece of torn tent having fallen over them; and in this position the doctor and I found them on our arrival soon after dawn next morning. We at once decided to move the hospital closer to the main camp; a fresh site was prepared, a stout hedge built round the enclosure, and all the patients were moved in before nightfall.

As I had heard that lions generally visit recently deserted camps, I decided to sit up all night in the vacated *boma* in the hope of getting an opportunity of bagging one of them; but in the middle of my lonely vigil I had the mortification of hearing shrieks and cries coming from the direction of the new hospital, telling me only too plainly that our dreaded foes had once more eluded me. Hurrying to the place at daylight I found that one of the lions had jumped over the newly erected fence and had carried off the hospital *bhisti* (water-carrier), and that several other coolies had been unwilling witnesses of the terrible scene which took place within the circle of light given by the big camp fire. The *bhisti*, it appears, had been lying on the floor, with his head towards the centre of the tent and his feet nearly touching the side. The lion managed to get its head in below the canvas, seized him by the foot and pulled him out. In desperation the unfortunate water-carrier clutched hold of a heavy box in a vain attempt to prevent himself being carried off, and dragged it with him until he was forced to let go by its being stopped by the side of the tent. He then caught hold of a tent rope, and clung tightly to it until it broke. As soon as the lion managed to get him clear of the tent, he sprang at his throat and after a few vicious shakes the poor *bhisti*'s agonising cries were silenced for ever. The brute then seized him in his mouth, like a huge cat with a mouse, and ran up and down the *boma* looking for a weak spot to break through. This he presently found and plunged into, dragging his victim with him and leaving shreds of torn cloth and flesh as ghastly evidences of his passage through the thorns. Dr. Brock and I were easily able to follow his track, and soon found the remains about four hundred yards away in the bush. There was the usual horrible sight. Very little was left of the unfortunate *bhisti*—only the skull, the jaws, a few of the larger bones and a portion of the palm with one or two fingers attached. On one of these was a silver ring, and this, with the teeth (a relic much prized by certain castes), was sent to the man's widow in India.

Again it was decided to move the hospital; and again, before nightfall, the work was completed, including a still stronger and thicker *boma*. When the patients had been moved, I had a covered goods-wagon placed in a favourable position on a siding which ran close to the site which had just been abandoned, and in this Brock and I arranged to sit up that night. We left a couple of tents still standing within the enclosure, and also tied up a few cattle in it as bait for the lions, who had been seen in no less than three different places in the neighbourhood during the afternoon (April 23). Four miles from Tsavo they had attempted to seize a coolie who was walking along the line. Fortunately, however, he had just time to escape up a tree, where he remained, more dead than alive, until he was rescued by the Traffic Manager, who caught sight of him from a passing train. They next appeared close to Tsavo Station, and a couple of hours later some workmen saw one of the lions stalking Dr. Brock as he was returning about dusk from the hospital.

In accordance with our plan, the doctor and I set out after dinner for the goods-wagon, which was about a mile away from our hut. In the light of subsequent events, we did a very foolish thing in taking up our position so late; nevertheless, we reached our destination in safety, and settled down to our watch about ten o'clock. We had the lower half of the door of the wagon closed, while the upper half was left wide open for observation: and we faced, of course, in the direction of the abandoned *boma*, which, however, we were unable to see in the inky darkness. For an hour or two everything was quiet, and the deadly silence was becoming very monotonous and oppressive, when suddenly, to our right, a dry twig snapped, and we knew that an animal of some sort was about. Soon afterwards we heard a dull thud, as if some heavy body had jumped over the *boma*. The cattle, too, became very uneasy, and we could hear them moving about restlessly. Then again came dead silence. At this juncture I proposed to my companion that I should get out of the wagon and lie on the ground close to it, as I could see better in that position should the lion come in our direction with his prey. Brock, however, persuaded me to remain where I was; and a few seconds afterwards I was heartily glad that I had taken his advice, for at that very moment one of the man-eaters—although we did not know it—was quietly stalking us, and was even then almost within springing distance. Orders had been given for the entrance to the *boma* to be blocked up, and accordingly we were listening in the expectation of hearing the lion force his way out through the bushes with his prey. As a matter of fact, however, the doorway had not been properly closed, and while we were wondering what the lion could be doing inside the *boma* for so long, he was outside all the time, silently reconnoitring our position.

Presently I fancied I saw something coming very stealthily towards us. I feared however, to trust to my eyes, which by that time were strained by prolonged staring through the darkness, so under my breath I asked Brock whether he saw anything, at the same time covering the dark object as well as I could with my rifle. Brock did not answer; he told me afterwards that he, too, thought he had seen something move, but was afraid to say so lest I should fire and it turn out to be nothing after all. After this there was intense silence again for a second or two, then with a sudden bound a huge body sprang at us. "The lion!" I shouted, and we both fired almost simultaneously— not a moment too soon, for in another second the brute would assuredly have landed inside the wagon. As it was, he must have swerved off in his spring, probably blinded by the flash and frightened by the noise of the double report which was increased a hundredfold by the reverberation of the hollow iron roof of the truck. Had we not been very much on the alert, he would undoubtedly have got one of us, and we realised that we had had a very lucky and very narrow escape. The next morning we found Brock's bullet embedded in the sand close to a foot-print; it could not have missed the lion by more than an inch or two. Mine was nowhere to be found.

Thus ended my first direct encounter with one of the man-eaters.

THE REIGN OF TERROR

The lions seemed to have got a bad fright the night Brock and I sat up in wait for them in the goods-wagon, for they kept away from Tsavo and did not molest us in any way for some considerable time—not, in fact, until long after Brock had left me and gone on *safari* (a caravan journey) to Uganda. In this breathing space which they vouchsafed us, it occurred to me that should they renew their attacks, a trap would perhaps offer the best chance of getting at them, and that if I could construct one in which a couple of coolies might be used as bait without being subjected to any danger, the lions would be quite daring enough to enter it in search of them and thus be caught. I accordingly set to work at once, and in a short time managed to make a suffi-ciently strong trap out of wooden sleepers, tram-rails, pieces of telegraph wire, and a length of heavy chain. It was divided into two compartments—one for the men and one for the lion. A sliding door at one end admitted the former, and once inside this compartment they were perfectly safe, as between them and the lion, if he entered the other, ran a cross wall of iron rails only three inches apart, and embed-ded both top and bottom in heavy wooden sleepers. The door which was to admit the lion, of course, at the opposite end of the structure, but otherwise the whole thing was very much on the principle of the ordinary rat-trap, except that it was not necessary for the lion to seize the bait in order to send the door clattering down. This part of the contrivance was arranged in the following manner. A heavy chain was secured along the top part of the lion's doorway, the ends hanging down to the ground on either side of the opening; and to these were fastened, strongly secured by stout wire, short lengths of rails placed about six inches apart. This made a sort of flexible door which could be packed into a small space when not in use, and which abutted against the top of the doorway when lifted up. The door was held in this position by a lever made of a piece of rail, which in turn was kept in its place by a wire fastened to one end and passing down to a spring concealed in the ground inside the cage. As soon as the lion entered sufficiently far into the trap, he would be bound to tread on the spring; his weight on this would release the wire, and in an instant down would come the door behind him; and he could not push it out in any way, as it fell into a groove between two rails firmly embedded in the ground.

In making this trap, which cost us a lot of work, we were rather at a loss for want of tools to bore holes in the rails for the doorway, so as to enable them to be fastened by the wire to the chain. It occurred to me, however, that a hard-nosed bullet from my .303 would penetrate the iron, and on making the experiment I was glad to find that a hole was made as cleanly as if it had been punched out.

When the trap was ready I pitched a tent over it in order further to deceive the lions, and built an exceedingly strong *boma* round it. One small entrance was made at the back of the enclosure for the men, which they were to close on going in by pulling a bush after them; and another entrance just in front of the door of the cage was left open for the lions. The wiseacres to whom I showed my invention were generally of the opinion that the man-eaters would be too cunning to walk into my parlour; but, as will be seen later, their predictions proved false. For the first few nights I baited the trap myself, but nothing happened except that I had a very sleepless and uncomfortable time, and was badly bitten by mosquitoes.

As a matter of fact, it was some months before the lions attacked us again, though from time to time we heard of their depredations in other quarters. Not long after our night in the goods-wagon, two men were carried off from railhead, while another was taken from a place called Engomani, about ten miles away. Within a very short time, this latter place was again visited by the brutes, two more men being seized, one of whom was killed and eaten, and the other so badly mauled that he died within a few days. As I have said, however, we at Tsavo enjoyed complete immunity from attack, and the coolies, believing that their dreaded foes had permanently deserted the district, resumed all their usual habits and occupations, and life in the camps returned to its normal routine.

At last we were suddenly startled out of this feeling of security. One dark night the familiar terror-stricken cries and screams awoke the camps, and we knew that the "demons" had returned and had commenced a new list of victims. On this occasion a number of men had been sleeping outside their tents for the sake of coolness, thinking, of course, that the lions had gone for good, when suddenly in the middle of the night one of the brutes was discovered forcing its way through the *boma*. The alarm was at once given, and sticks, stones and firebrands were hurled in the direction of the intruder. All was of no avail, however, for the lion burst into the midst of the terrified group, seized an unfortunate wretch amid the cries and shrieks of his companions, and dragged him off through the thick thorn fence. He was joined outside by the second lion, and so daring had the two brutes become that they did not trouble to carry their victim any further away, but devoured him within thirty yards of the tent where he had been seized. Although several shots were fired in their direction by the *jemadar* of the gang to which the coolie belonged, they took no notice of these and did not attempt to move until their horrible meal was finished. The few scattered fragments that remained of the body I would not allow to be buried at once, hoping that the lions would return to the spot the following night; and on the chance of this I took up my station at nightfall in a convenient tree. Nothing occurred to break the monotony of my watch, however, except that I had a visit from a hyena, and the next morning I learned that the lions had attacked another camp about two miles from Tsavo—for by this time the camps were again scattered, as I had works in progress all up and down the line. There the man-eaters had been successful in obtaining a victim, whom, as in the previous instance, they devoured quite close to the camp. How they forced their way through the *bomas* without making a noise was, and still is, a mystery to me; I should have thought that it was next to impossible for an animal to get through at all. Yet they continually did so, and without a sound being heard.

After this occurrence, I sat up every night for over a week near likely camps, but all in vain. Either the lions saw me and then went elsewhere, or else I was unlucky, for they took man after man from different places without ever once giving me a chance of a shot at them. This constant night watching was most dreary and fatiguing work, but I felt that it was a duty that had to be undertaken, as the men naturally looked to me for protection. In the whole of my life I have never experienced anything more nerve-shaking than to hear the deep roars of these dreadful monsters growing gradually nearer and nearer, and to know that some one or other of us was doomed to be their victim before morning dawned. Once they reached the vicinity of the camps, the roars completely ceased, and we knew that they were stalking for their prey. Shouts would then pass from camp to camp, *"Khabar dar, bhaieon, shaitan ata"* ("Beware, brothers, the devil is coming"), but the warning cries would prove of no avail, and sooner or later agonising shrieks would break the silence and another man would be missing from roll-call next morning.

I was naturally very disheartened at being foiled in this way night after night, and was soon at my wits' end to know what to do; it seemed as if the lions were really "devils" after all and bore a charmed life. As I have said before, tracking them through the jungle was a hopeless task; but as something had to be done to keep up the men's spirits, I spent many a wry day crawling on my hands and knees through the dense undergrowth of the exasperating wilderness around us. As a matter of fact, if I had come up with the lions on any of these expeditions, it was much more likely that they would have added me to their list of victims than that I should have succeeded in killing either of them, as everything would have been in their favour. About this time, too, I had many helpers, and several officers—civil, naval and military—came to Tsavo from the coast and sat up night after night in order to get a shot at our daring foes. All of us, however, met with the same lack of success, and the lions always seemed capable of avoiding the watchers, while succeeding at the same time in obtaining a victim.

I have a very vivid recollection of one particular night when the brutes seized a man from the railway station and brought him close to my camp to devour. I could plainly hear them crunching the bones, and the sound of their dreadful purring filled the air and rang in my ears for days afterwards. The terrible thing was to feel so helpless; it was useless to attempt to go out, as of course the poor fellow was dead, and in addition it was so pitch dark as to make it impossible to see anything. Some half a dozen workmen, who lived in a small enclosure close to mine, became so terrified on hearing the lions at their meal that they shouted and implored me to allow them to come inside my *boma*. This I willingly did, but soon afterwards I remembered that one man had been lying ill in their camp, and on making enquiry I found that they had callously left him behind alone. I immediately took some men with me to bring him to my *boma*, but on entering his tent I saw by the light of the lantern that the poor fellow was beyond need of safety. He had died of shock at being deserted by his companions.

From this time matters gradually became worse and worse. Hitherto, as a rule, only one of the man-eaters had made the attack and had done the foraging, while the other waited outside in the bush; but now they began to change their tactics, entering the *bomas* together and each seizing a victim. In this way two Swahili porters were killed during the last week of November, one being immediately carried off and devoured. The other was heard moaning for a long time, and when his terrified companions at last summoned up sufficient courage to go to his assistance, they found him stuck fast in the bushes of the *boma* through which for once the lion had apparently been unable to drag him. He was still alive when I saw him next morning, but so terribly mauled that he died before he could be got to the hospital.

Within a few days of this the two brutes made a most ferocious attack on the largest camp in the section, which for safety's sake was situated within a stone's throw of Tsavo Station and close to a Permanent Way Inspector's iron hut. Suddenly in the dead of night the two man-eaters burst in among the terrified workmen, and even from my *boma*, some distance away, I could plainly hear the panic-stricken shrieking of the coolies. Then followed cries of "They've taken him; they've taken him," as the brutes carried off their unfortunate victim and began their horrible feast close beside the camp. The Inspector, Mr. Dalgairns, fired over fifty shots in the direction in which he heard the lions, but they were not to be frightened and calmly lay there until their meal was finished. After examining the spot in the morning, we at once set out to follow the brutes, Mr. Dalgairns feeling confident that he had wounded one of them, as there was a trail on the sand like that of the toes of a broken limb. After some careful stalking, we suddenly found ourselves in the vicinity of the lions, and were greeted with ominous growlings. Cautiously advancing and pushing the bushes aside, we saw in the gloom what we at first took to be a lion cub; closer inspection, however, showed it to be the remains of the unfortunate coolie, which the man-eaters had evidently abandoned at our approach. The legs, one arm and half the body had been eaten, and it was the stiff fingers of the other arm trailing along the sand which had left the marks we had taken to be the trail of a wounded lion. By this time the beasts had retired far into the thick jungle where it was impossible to follow them, so we had the remains of the coolie buried and once more returned home disappointed.

Now the bravest men in the world, much less the ordinary Indian coolie, will not stand constant terrors of this sort indefinitely. The whole district was by this time thoroughly panic-stricken, and I was not at all surprised, therefore, to find on my return to camp that same afternoon (December 1) that the men had all struck work and were waiting to speak to me. When I sent for them, they flocked to my *boma* in a body and stated that they would not remain at Tsavo any longer for anything or anybody; they had come from India on an agreement to work for the government, not to supply food for either lions or "devils." No sooner had they delivered this ultimatum than a regular stampede took place. Some hundreds of them stopped the first passing train by throwing themselves on the rails in front of the engine, and then, swarming on to the trucks and throwing in their possessions anyhow, they fled from the accursed spot.

After this the railway works were completely stopped; and for the next three weeks practically nothing was done but build "lion-proof" huts for those workmen who had had sufficient courage to remain. It was a strange and amusing sight to see these shelters perched on the top of water-tanks, roofs and girders—anywhere for safety—while some even went so far as to dig pits inside their tents, into which they descended at night, covering the top over with heavy logs of wood. Every good-sized tree in the camp had as many beds lashed on to it as its branches would bear—and sometimes more. I remember that one night when the camp was attacked, so many men swarmed on to one particular tree that down it came with a crash, hurling its terror-stricken load of shrieking coolies close to the very lions they were trying to avoid. Fortunately for them, a victim had already been secured, and the brutes were too busy devouring him to pay attention to anything else.

THE DISTRICT OFFICER'S NARROW ESCAPE

Some little time before the flight of the workmen, I had written to Mr. Whitehead, the District Officer, asking him to come up and assist me in my campaign against the lions, and to bring with him any of his *askaris* (native soldiers) that he could spare. He replied accepting the invitation, and told me to expect him about dinner-time on December 2, which turned out to be the day after the exodus. His train was due at Tsavo about six o'clock in the evening, so I sent my "boy" up to the station to meet him and to help in carrying his baggage to the camp. In a very short time, however, the "boy" rushed back trembling with terror, and informed me that there was no sign of the train or of the railway staff, but that an enormous lion was standing on the station platform. This extraordinary story I did not believe in the least, as by this time the coolies—never remarkable for bravery—were in such a state of fright that if they caught sight of a hyena, or a baboon, or even a dog, in the bush, they were sure to imagine it was a lion; but I found out next day that it was an actual fact, and that both stationmaster and signalman had been obliged to take refuge from one of the man-eaters by locking themselves in the station building.

I waited some little time for Mr. Whitehead, but eventually, as he did not put in an appearance, I concluded that he must have postponed his journey until the next day, and so had my dinner in my customary solitary state. During the meal I heard a couple of shots, but paid no attention to them, as rifles were constantly being fired off in the neighbourhood of the camp. Later in the evening, I went out as usual to watch for our elusive foes, and took up my position in a crib made of sleepers which I had built on a big girder close to a camp which I thought was likely to be attacked. Soon after settling down at my post, I was surprised to hear the man-eaters growling and purring and crunching up bones about seventy yards from the crib. I could not understand what they had found to eat, as I had heard no commotion in the camps, and I knew by bitter experience that every meal the brutes obtained from us was announced by shrieks and uproar. The only conclusion I could come to was that they had pounced upon some poor unsuspecting native traveller. After a time I was able to make out their eyes glowing in the darkness, and I took as careful aim as was possible in the circumstances and fired; but the only notice they paid to the shot was to carry off whatever they were devouring and to retire quietly over a slight rise, which prevented me from seeing them. There they finished their meal at their ease.

As soon as it was daylight, I got out of my crib and went towards the place where I had last heard them. On the way, whom should I meet but my missing guest, Mr. Whitehead, looking very pale and ill, and generally dishevelled.

"Where on earth have you come from?" I exclaimed. "Why didn't you turn up to dinner last night?"

"A nice reception you give a fellow when you invite him to dinner," was his only reply.

"Why, what's up?" I asked.

"That infernal lion of yours nearly did for me last night," said Whitehead.

"Nonsense, you must have dreamed it!" I cried in astonishment.

For answer he turned round and showed me his back. "That's not much of a dream, is it?" he asked.

His clothing was rent by one huge tear from the nape of the neck downwards, and on the flesh there were four great claw marks, showing red and angry through the torn cloth. Without further parley, I hurried him off to my tent, and bathed and dressed his wounds; and when I had made him considerably more comfortable, I got from him the whole story of the events of the night.

It appeared that his train was very late, so that it was quite dark when he arrived at Tsavo Station, from which the track to my camp lay through a small cutting. He was accompanied by Abdullah, his sergeant of *askaris*, who walked close behind him carrying a lighted lamp. All went well until they were about half-way through the gloomy cutting, when one of the lions suddenly jumped down upon them from the high bank, knocking Whitehead over like a ninepin, and tearing his back in the manner I had seen. Fortunately, however, he had his carbine with him, and instantly fired. The flash and the loud report must have dazed the lion for a second or two, enabling Whitehead to disengage himself; but the next instant the brute pounced like lightning on the unfortunate Abdullah, with whom he at once made off. All that the poor fellow could say was: *"Eh,*

Bwana, simba" ("Oh, Master, a lion"). As the lion was dragging him over the bank, Whitehead fired again, but without effect, and the brute quickly disappeared into the darkness with his prey. It was, of course, this unfortunate man whom I had heard the lions devouring during the night. Whitehead himself had a marvellous escape; his wounds were happily not very deep, and caused him little or no inconvenience afterwards.

On the same day, December 3, the forces arrayed against the lions were further strengthened. Mr. Farquhar, the Superintendent of Police, arrived from the coast with a score of sepoys to assist in hunting down the man-eaters, whose fame had by this time spread far and wide, and the most elaborate precautions were taken, his men being posted on the most convenient trees near every camp. Several other officials had also come up on leave to join in the chase, and each of these guarded a likely spot in the same way, Mr. Whitehead sharing my post inside the crib on the girder. Further, in spite of some chaff, my lion trap was put in thorough working order, and two of the sepoys were installed as bait.

Our preparations were quite complete by nightfall, and we all took up our appointed positions. Nothing happened until about nine o'clock, when to my great satisfaction the intense stillness was suddenly broken by the noise of the door of the trap clattering down. "At last," I thought, "one at least of the brutes is done for." But the sequel was an ignominious one.

The bait-sepoys had a lamp burning inside their part of the cage, and were each armed with a Martini rifle, with plenty of ammunition. They had also been given strict orders to shoot at once if a lion should enter the trap. Instead of doing so, however, they were so terrified when he rushed in and began to lash himself madly against the bars of the cage, that they completely lost their heads and were actually too unnerved to fire. Not for some minutes—not, indeed, until Mr. Farquhar, whose post was close by, shouted at them and cheered them on—did they at all recover themselves. Then when at last they did begin to fire, they fired with a vengeance—anywhere, anyhow. Whitehead and I were at right angles to the direction in which they should have shot, and yet their bullets came whizzing all round us. Altogether they fired over a score of shots, and in the end succeeded only in blowing away one of the bars of the door, thus allowing our prize to make good his escape. How they failed to kill him several times over is, and always will be, a complete mystery to me, as they could have put the muzzles of their rifles absolutely touching his body. There was, indeed, some blood scattered about the trap, but it was small consolation to know that the brute, whose capture and death seemed so certain, had only been slightly wounded.

Still we were not unduly dejected, and when morning came, a hunt was at once arranged. Accordingly we spent the greater part of the day on our hands and knees following the lions through the dense thickets of thorny jungle, but though we heard their growls from time to time, we never succeeded in actually coming up with them. Of the whole party, only Farquhar managed to catch a momentary glimpse of one as it bounded over a bush. Two days more were spent in the same manner, and with equal unsuccess; and then Farquhar and his sepoys were obliged to return to the coast. Mr. Whitehead also departed for his district, and once again I was left alone with the man-eaters.

THE DEATH OF THE
FIRST MAN-EATER

A day or two after the departure of my allies, as I was leaving my *boma* soon after dawn on December 9, I saw a Swahili running excitedly towards me, shouting out *"Simba! Simba!"* ("Lion! Lion!"), and every now and again looking behind him as he ran. On questioning him I found that the lions had tried to snatch a man from the camp by the river, but being foiled in this had seized and killed one of the donkeys, and were at that moment busy devouring it not far off. Now was my chance.

I rushed for the heavy rifle which Farquhar had kindly left with me for use in case an opportunity such as this should arise, and, led by the Swahili, I started most carefully to stalk the lions, who, I devoutly hoped, were confining their attention strictly to their meal. I was getting on splendidly, and could just make out the outline of one of them through the dense bush, when unfortunately my guide snapped a rotten branch. The wily beast heard the noise, growled his defiance, and disappeared in a moment into a patch of even thicker jungle close by. In desperation at the thought of his escaping me once again, I crept hurriedly back to the camp, summoned the available workmen and told them to bring all the tom-toms, tin cans and other noisy instruments of any kind that could be found. As quickly as possible I posted them in a half-circle round the thicket, and gave the head *jemadar* instructions to start a simultaneous beating of the tom-toms and cans as soon as he judged that I had had time to get round to the other side. I then crept round by myself and soon found a good position and one which the lion was most likely to retreat past, as it was in the middle of a broad animal path leading straight from the place where he was concealed. I lay down behind a small ant hill, and waited expectantly. Very soon I heard a tremendous din being raised by the advancing line of coolies, and almost immediately, to my intense joy, out into the open path stepped a huge maneless lion. It was the first occasion during all these trying months upon which I had had a fair chance at one of these brutes, and my satisfaction at the prospect of bagging him was unbounded.

Slowly he advanced along the path, stopping every few seconds to look round. I was only partially concealed from view, and if his attention had not been so fully occupied by the noise behind him, he must have observed me. As he was oblivious to my presence, however, I let him approach to within about fifteen yards of me, and then covered him with my rifle. The moment I moved to do this, he caught sight of me, and seemed much astonished at my sudden appearance, for he stuck his forefeet into the ground, threw himself back on his haunches and growled savagely. As I covered his brain with my rifle, I felt that at last I had him absolutely at my mercy, but . . . never trust an untried weapon! I pulled the trigger, and to my horror heard the dull snap that tells of a misfire.

Worse was to follow. I was so taken aback and disconcerted by this untoward accident that I entirely forgot to fire the left barrel, and lowered the rifle from my shoulder with the intention of reloading—if I should be given time. Fortunately for me, the lion was so distracted by the terrific din and uproar of the coolies behind him that instead of springing on me, as might have been expected, he bounded aside into the jungle again. By this time I had collected my wits, and just as he jumped I let him have the left barrel. An answering angry growl told me that he had been hit; but nevertheless he succeeded once more in getting clear away, for although I tracked him for some little distance, I eventually lost his trail in a rocky patch of ground.

Bitterly did I anathematise the hour in which I had relied on a borrowed weapon, and in my disappointment and vexation I abused owner, maker, and rifle with fine impartiality. On extracting the unexploded cartridge, I found that the needle had not struck home, the cap being only slightly dented; so that the whole fault did indeed lie with the rifle, which I later returned to Farquhar with polite compliments. Seriously, however, my continued ill-luck was most exasperating; and the result was that the Indians were more than ever confirmed in their belief that the lions were really evil spirits, proof against mortal weapons. Certainly, they did seem to bear charmed lives.

After this dismal failure there was, of course, nothing to do but to return to camp. Before doing so, however, I proceeded to view the dead donkey, which I found to have been only slightly devoured at the quarters. It is a curious fact that lions always begin at the tail of their prey and eat upwards towards the head. As their meal had thus been interrupted evidently at the very beginning, I felt pretty sure that one or other of the brutes would return to the carcase at nightfall. Accordingly, as there was no tree of any kind close at hand, I had a staging erected some ten feet away from the body. This *machan* was about twelve feet high and was composed of four poles stuck into the ground and inclined toward each other at the top, where a plank was lashed to serve as a seat. Further, as the nights were still pitch dark, I had the donkey's carcase secured by strong wires to a neighbouring stump, so that the lions might not be able to drag it away before I could get a shot at them.

At sundown, therefore, I took up my position on my airy perch, and much to the disgust of my gun-bearer, Mahina, I decided to go alone. I would gladly have taken him with me, indeed, but he had a bad cough, and I was afraid lest he should make any involuntary noise or movement which might spoil all. Darkness fell almost immediately, and everything became extraordinarily still. The silence of an African jungle on a dark night needs to be experienced to be realised; it is most impressive, especially when one is absolutely alone and isolated from one's fellow creatures, as I was then. The solitude and stillness, and the purpose of my vigil, all had their effect on me, and from a condition of strained expectancy I gradually fell into a dreamy mood which harmonised well with my surroundings. Suddenly I was startled out of my reverie by the snapping of a twig; and, straining my ears for a further sound, I fancied I could hear the rustling of a large body forcing its way through the bush. "The man-eater," I thought to myself; "surely to-night my luck will change and I shall bag one of the brutes." Profound silence again succeeded; I sat on my eyrie like a statue, every nerve tense with excitement. Very soon, however, all doubts as to the presence of the lion was dispelled. A deep long-drawn sigh—sure sign of hunger—came up from the bushes, and the rustling commenced again as he cautiously advanced. In a moment or two a sudden stop, followed by an angry growl, told me that my presence had been noticed; and I began to fear that disappointment awaited me once more.

But no; matters quickly took an unexpected turn. The hunter became the hunted; and instead of either making off or coming for the bait prepared for him, the lion began stealthily to stalk *me*! For about two hours he horrified me by slowly creeping round and round my crazy structure, gradually edging his way nearer and nearer. Every moment I expected him to rush it; and the staging had not been constructed with an eye to such a possibility. If one of the rather flimsy poles should break, or if the lion could spring the twelve feet which separated me from the ground . . . the thought was scarcely a pleasant one. I began to feel distinctly "creepy," and heartily repented my folly in having placed myself in such a dangerous position. I kept perfectly still, however, hardly daring even to blink my eyes: but the long continued strain was telling on my nerves, and my feelings may be better imagined than described when about midnight suddenly something came flop and struck me on the back of the head. For a moment I was so terrified that I nearly fell off the plank, as I thought that the lion had sprung on me from behind. Regaining my senses in a second or two, I realised that I had been hit by nothing more formidable than an owl, which had doubtless mistaken me for the branch of a tree—not a very alarming thing to happen in ordinary circumstances, I admit, but coming at the time it did, it almost paralysed me. The involuntary start which I could not help giving was immediately answered by a sinister growl from below.

After this I again kept as still as I could, though absolutely trembling with excitement; and in a short while I heard the lion begin to creep stealthily towards me. I could barely make out his form as he crouched among the whitish undergrowth; but I saw enough for my purpose and before he could come any nearer, I took careful aim and pulled the trigger. The sound of the shot was at once followed by a most terrific roar, and then I could hear him leaping about in all directions. I was no longer able to see him, however, as his first bound had taken him into the thick bush; but to make assurance doubly sure, I kept blazing away in the direction in which I heard him plunging about. At length came a series of mighty groans, gradually subsiding into deep sighs, and finally ceasing altogether; and I felt convinced that one of the "devils" who had so long harried us would trouble us no more.

As soon as I ceased firing, a tumult of inquiring voices was borne across the dark jungle from the men in camp about a quarter of a mile away. I shouted back that I was safe and sound, and that one of the lions was dead: whereupon such a mighty cheer went up from all the camps as must have astonished the denizens of the jungle for miles around. Shortly I saw scores of lights twinkling through the bushes: every man in camp turned out, and with tom-toms beating and horns blowing came running to the scene. They surrounded my eyrie, and to my amazement prostrated themselves on the ground before me, saluting me with cries of *"Mabarak!*

Mabarak!" which I believe means "blessed one" or "saviour." All the same, I refused to allow any search to be made that night for the body of the lion, in case his companion might be close by; besides, it was possible that he might be still alive, and capable of making a last spring. Accordingly we all returned in triumph to the camp, where great rejoicings were kept up for the remainder of the night, the Swahili and other African natives celebrating the occasion by an especially wild and savage dance.

For my part, I anxiously awaited the dawn; and even before it was thoroughly light I was on my way to the eventful spot, as I could not completely persuade myself that even yet the "devil" might not have eluded me in some uncanny and mysterious way. Happily my fears proved groundless, and I was relieved to find that my luck—after playing me so many exasperating tricks—had really turned at last. I had scarcely traced the blood for more than a few paces when, on rounding a bush, I was startled to see a huge lion right in front of me, seemingly alive and crouching for a spring. On looking closer, however, I satisfied myself that he was really and truly stone-dead, whereupon my followers crowded round, laughed and danced and shouted with joy like children, and bore me in triumph shoulder-high round the dead body. These thanksgiving ceremonies being over, I examined the body and found that two bullets had taken effect—one close behind the left shoulder, evidently penetrating the heart, and the other in the off hind leg. The prize was indeed one to be proud of; his length from tip of nose to tip of tail was nine feet eight inches, he stood three feet nine inches high, and it took eight men to carry him back to camp. The only blemish was that the skin was much scored by the *boma* thorns through which he had so often forced his way in carrying off his victims.

The news of the death of one of the notorious man-eaters soon spread far and wide over the country: telegrams of congratulations came pouring in, and scores of people flocked from up and down the railway to see the skin for themselves.

THE DEATH OF THE SECOND MAN-EATER

It must not be imagined that with the death of this lion our troubles at Tsavo were at an end; his companion was still at large, and very soon began to make us unpleasantly aware of the fact. Only a few nights elapsed before he made an attempt to get at the Permanent Way Inspector, climbing up the steps of his bungalow and prowling round the verandah. The Inspector, hearing the noise and thinking it was a drunken coolie, shouted angrily "Go away!" but, fortunately for him, did not attempt to come out or to open the door. Thus disappointed in his attempt to obtain a meal of human flesh, the lion seized a couple of the Inspector's goats and devoured them there and then.

On hearing of this occurrence, I determined to sit up the next night near the Inspector's bungalow. Fortunately there was a vacant iron shanty close at hand, with a convenient loophole in it for firing from; and outside this I placed three full-grown goats as bait, tying them to a half-length of rail, weighing about 250 lbs. The night passed uneventfully until just before daybreak, when at last the lion turned up, pounced on one of the goats and made off with it, at the same time dragging away the others, rail and all. I fired several shots in his direction, but it was pitch dark and quite impossible to see anything, so I only succeeded in hitting one of the goats. I often longed for a flashlight on such occasions.

Next morning I started off in pursuit and was joined by some others from the camp. I found that the trail of the goats and rail was easily followed, and we soon came up, about a quarter of a mile away, to where the lion was still busy at his meal. He was concealed in some thick bush and growled angrily on hearing our approach; finally, as we got closer, he suddenly made a charge, rushing through the bushes at a great pace. In an instant, every man of the party scrambled hastily up the nearest tree, with the exception of one of my assistants, Mr. Winkler, who stood steadily by me throughout. The brute, however, did not press his charge home: and on throwing stones into the bushes where we had last seen him, we guessed by the silence that he had slunk off. We therefore advanced cautiously, and on getting up to the place discovered that he had indeed escaped us, leaving two of the goats scarcely touched.

Thinking that in all probability the lion would return as usual to finish his meal, I had a very strong scaffolding put up a few feet away from the dead goats, and took up my position on it before dark. On this occasion I brought my gun-bearer, Mahina, to take a turn at watching, as I was by this time worn out for want of sleep, having spent so many nights on the look-out. I was just dozing off comfortably when suddenly I felt my arm seized, and on looking up saw Mahina pointing in the direction of the goats. *"Sher!"* ("Lion!") was all he whispered. I grasped my double smooth-bore, which I had charged with slug, and waited patiently. In a few moments I was rewarded, for as I watched the spot where I expected the lion to appear, there was a rustling among the bushes and I saw him stealthily emerge into the open and pass almost directly beneath us. I fired both barrels practically together into his shoulder, and to my joy could see him go down under the force of the blow. Quickly I reached for the magazine rifle, but before I could use it, he was out of sight among the bushes, and I had to fire after him quite at random. Nevertheless I was confident of getting him in the morning, and accordingly set out as soon as it was light. For over a mile there was no difficulty in following the blood-trail, and as he had rested several times I felt sure that he had been badly wounded. In the end, however, my hunt proved fruitless, for after a time the traces of blood ceased and the surface of the ground became rocky, so that I was no longer able to follow the spoor.

About this time Sir Guilford Molesworth, K. C. I. E., late Consulting Engineer to the Government of India for State Railways, passed through Tsavo on a tour of inspection on behalf of the Foreign Office. After examining the bridge and other works and expressing his satisfaction, he took a number of photographs, one or two of which he has kindly allowed me to reproduce in this book. He thoroughly sympathised with us in all the trials we had endured from the man-eaters, and was delighted that one at least was dead. When he asked me if I expected to get the second lion soon, I well remember his half-doubting smile as I rather too confidently asserted that I hoped to bag him also in the course of a few days.

As it happened, there was no sign of our enemy for about ten days after this, and we began to hope that he had died of his wounds in the bush. All the same we still took every precaution at night, and it was fortunate that we did so, as otherwise at least one more victim would have been added to the list. For on the night of December 27, I was suddenly aroused by terrified shouts from my trolley men, who slept in a tree close outside my *boma* to the effect that a lion was trying to get at them. It would have been madness to have gone out, as the moon was hidden by dense clouds and it was absolutely impossible to see anything more than a yard in front of one; so all I could do was to fire off a few rounds just to frighten the brute away. This apparently had the desired effect, for the men were not further molested that night; but the man-eater had evidently prowled about for some time, for we found in the morning that he had gone right into every one of their tents, and round the tree was a regular ring of his footmarks.

The following evening I took up my position in this same tree, in the hope that he would make another attempt. The night began badly, as while climbing up to my perch I very nearly put my hand on a venomous snake which was lying coiled round one of the branches. As may be imagined, I came down again very quickly, but one of my men managed to despatch it with a long pole. Fortunately the night was clear and cloudless, and the moon made every thing almost as bright as day. I kept watch until about 2 a.m., when I roused Mahina to take his turn. For about an hour I slept peacefully with my back to the tree, and then woke suddenly with an uncanny feeling that something was wrong. Mahina, however, was on the alert, and had seen nothing; and although I looked carefully round us on all sides, I too could discover nothing unusual. Only half satisfied, I was about to lie back again, when I fancied I saw something move a little way off among the low bushes. On gazing intently at the spot for a few seconds, I found I was not mistaken. It was the man-eater, cautiously stalking us.

The ground was fairly open round our tree, with only a small bush every here and there; and from our position it was a most fascinating sight to watch this great brute stealing stealthily round us, taking advantage of every bit of cover as he came. His skill showed that he was an old hand at the terrible game of man-hunting: so I determined to run no undue risk of losing him this time. I accordingly waited until he got quite close—about twenty yards away—and then fired my .303 at his chest. I heard the bullet strike him, but unfortunately it had no knockdown effect, for with a fierce growl he turned and made off with great long bounds. Before he disappeared from sight, however, I managed to have three more shots at him from the magazine rifle, and another growl told me that the last of these had also taken effect.

We awaited daylight with impatience, and at the first glimmer of dawn we set out to hunt him down. I took a native tracker with me, so that I was free to keep a good look-out, while Mahina followed immediately behind with a Martini carbine. Splashes of blood being plentiful, we were able to get along quickly; and we had not proceeded more than a quarter of a mile through the jungle when suddenly a fierce warning growl was heard right in front of us. Looking cautiously through the bushes, I could see the man-eater glaring out in our direction, and showing his tusks in an angry snarl. I at once took careful aim and fired. Instantly he sprang out and made a most determined charge down on us. I fired again and knocked him over; but in a second he was up once more and coming for me as fast as he could in his crippled condition. A third shot had no apparent effect, so I put out my hand for the Martini, hoping to stop him with it. To my dismay, however, it was not there. The terror of the sudden charge had proved too much for Mahina, and both he and the carbine were by this time well on their way up a tree. In the circumstances there was nothing to do but follow suit, which I did without loss of time: and but for the fact that one of my shots had broken a hind leg, the brute would most certainly have had me. Even as it was, I had barely time to swing myself up out of his reach before he arrived at the foot of the tree.

When the lion found he was too late, he started to limp back to the thicket; but by this time I had seized the carbine from Mahina, and the first shot I fired from it seemed to give him his quietus, for he fell over and lay motionless. Rather foolishly, I at once scrambled down from the tree and walked up towards him. To my surprise and no little alarm he jumped up and attempted another charge. This time, however, a Martini bullet in the chest and another in the head finished him for good and all; he dropped in his tracks not five yards away from me, and died gamely, biting savagely at a branch which had fallen to the ground.

By this time all the workmen in camp, attracted by the sound of the firing, had arrived on the scene, and so great was their resentment against the brute who had killed such numbers of their comrades that it was only with the greatest difficulty that I could restrain them from tearing the dead body to pieces. Eventually, amid the wild rejoicings of the natives and coolies, I had the lion carried to my *boma*, which was close at hand. On examination we found no less than six bullet holes in the body, and embedded only a little way in the flesh of the back was the slug which I had fired into him from the scaffolding about ten days previously. He measured nine feet six inches from tip of nose to tip of tail, and stood three feet eleven and a half inches high; but, as in the case of his companion, the skin was disfigured by being deeply scored all over by the *boma* thorns.

The news of the death of the second "devil" soon spread far and wide over the country, and natives actually travelled from up and down the line to have a look at my trophies and at the "devil-killer," as they called me. Best of all, the coolies who had absconded came flocking back to Tsavo, and much to my relief work was resumed and we were never again troubled by man-eaters. It was amusing, indeed, to notice the change which took place in the attitude of the workmen towards me after I had killed the two lions. Instead of wishing to murder me, as they once did, they could not now do enough for me, and as a token of their gratitude they presented me with a beautiful silver bowl, as well as with a long poem written in Hindustani describing all our trials and my ultimate victory. As the poem relates our troubles in somewhat quaint and biblical language, I have given a translation of it in the appendix. The bowl I shall always consider my most highly prized and hardest won trophy. The inscription on it reads as follows:—

Sir,—We, your Overseer, Timekeepers, *Mistaris* and Workmen, present you with this bowl as a token of our gratitude to you for your bravery in killing two man-eating lions at great risk to your own life, thereby saving us from the fate of being devoured by these terrible monsters who nightly broke into our tents and took our fellow-workers from our side. In presenting you with this bowl, we all add our prayers for your long life, happiness and prosperity. We shall ever remain, Sir, Your grateful servants,

> *Baboo* Purshotam Hurjee Purmar, *Overseer and Clerk of the Works, on behalf of your Workmen.*
> Dated at Tsavo, *January* 30, 1899.

Before I leave the subject of "The Man-Eaters of Tsavo," it may be of interest to mention that these two lions possess the distinction, probably unique among wild animals, of having been specifically referred to in the House of Lords by the Prime Minister of the day. Speaking of the difficulties which had been encountered in the construction of the Uganda Railway, the late Lord Salisbury said:—

> "The whole of the works were put a stop to for three weeks because a party of man-eating lions appeared in the locality and conceived a most unfortunate taste for our porters. At last the labourers entirely declined to go on unless they were guarded by an iron entrenchment. Of course it is difficult to work a railway under these conditions, and until we found an enthusiastic sportsman to get rid of these lions, our enterprise was seriously hindered."

Also, *The Spectator* of March 3, 1900, had an article entitled "The Lions that Stopped the Railway," from which the following extracts are taken:—

"The parallel to the story of the lions which stopped the rebuilding of Samaria must occur to everyone, and if the Samaritans had quarter as good cause for their fears as had the railway coolies, their wish to propitiate the local deities is easily understood. If the whole body of lion anecdote, from the days of the Assyrian Kings till the last year of the nineteenth century, were collated and brought together, it would not equal in tragedy or atrocity, in savageness or in sheer insolent contempt for man, armed or unarmed, white or black, the story of these two beasts. . . .

"To what a distance the whole story carries us back, and how impossible it becomes to account for the survival of primitive man against this kind of foe! For fire—which has hitherto been regarded as his main safeguard against the carnivora—these cared nothing. It is curious that the Tsavo lions were not killed by poison, for strychnine is easily used, and with effect.★ Poison may have been used early in the history of man, for its powers are employed with strange skill by the men in the tropical forest, both in American and West Central Africa. But there is no evidence that the old inhabitants of Europe, or if Assyria or Asia Minor, ever killed lions or wolves by this means. They looked to the King or chief, or some champion, to kill these monsters for them. It was not the sport but the duty of Kings, and was in itself a title to be a ruler of men. Theseus, who cleared the roads of beasts and robbers; Hercules, the lion killer; St. George, the dragon-slayer, and all the rest of their class owed to this their everlasting fame. From the story of the Tsavo River we can appreciate their services to man even at this distance of time. When the jungle twinkled with hundreds of lamps, as the shout went on from camp to camp that the first lion was dead, as the hurrying crowds fell prostrate in the midnight forest, laying their heads on his feet, and the Africans danced savage and ceremonial dances of thanksgiving, Mr. Patterson must have realised in no common way what it was to have been a hero and deliverer in the days when man was not yet undisputed lord of the creation, and might pass at any moment under the savage dominion of the beasts."

(*I may mention that poison *was* tried, but without effect. The poisoned carcases of transport animals which had died from the bite of the tsetse fly were placed in likely spots, but the wily man-eaters would not touch them, and much preferred live men to dead donkeys.)

Well had the two man-eaters earned all this fame; they had devoured between them no less than twenty-eight Indian coolies, in addition to scores of unfortunate African natives of whom no official record was kept.

An Elk Hunt at Two-Ocean Pass

[THEODORE ROOSEVELT]

In September, 1891, with my ranch-partner, Ferguson, I made an elk-hunt in northwestern Wyoming among the Shoshone Mountains, where they join the Hoodoo and Absoraka ranges. There is no more beautiful game-country in the United States. It is a park land, where glades, meadows, and high mountain pastures break the evergreen forest; a forest which is open compared to the tangled density of the woodland farther north. It is a high, cold region of many lakes and clear rushing streams. The steep mountains are generally of the rounded form so often seen in the ranges of the Cordilleras of the United States; but the Hoodoos, or Goblins, are carved in fantastic and extraordinary shapes; while the Tetons, a group of isolated rock-

peaks, show a striking boldness in their lofty outlines.

This was one of the pleasantest hunts I ever made.
As always in the mountains, save where the country
is so rough and so densely wooded that one must go
a-foot, we had a pack-train; and we took a more
complete outfit than we had ever before taken on
such a hunt, and so travelled in much comfort. Usually when in the mountains I have merely had one
companion, or at most a couple, and two or three
pack-ponies; each of us doing his share of the packing, cooking, fetching water, and pitching the small
square of canvas which served as tent. In itself packing is both an art and a mystery, and a skilful professional packer, versed in the intricaies of the "diamond
hitch," packs with a speed which no non-professional
can hope to rival, and fixes the side packs and top
packs with such scientific nicety, and adjusts the
doubles and turns of the lash-rope so accurately, that
everything stays in place under any but the most
adverse conditions. Of course, like most hunters, I
can myself in case of need throw the diamond hitch
after a fashion, and pack on either the off or near
side. Indeed, unless a man can pack it is not possible
to make a really hard hunt in the mountains, if
alone, or with only a single companion. The mere
fair-weather hunter, who trusts entirely to the exertions of others, and does nothing more than ride or

walk about under favorable circumstances, and shoot at what somebody else shows him, is a hunter in name only. Whoever would really deserve the title must be able at a pinch to shift for himself, to grapple with the difficulties and hardships of wilderness life unaided, and not only to hunt, but at times to travel for days, whether on foot or on horseback, alone. However, after one has passed one's novitiate, it is pleasant to be comfortable when the comfort does not interfere with the sport; and although a man sometimes likes to hunt alone, yet often it is well to be with some old mountain hunter, a master of woodcraft, who is a first-rate hand at finding game, creeping upon it, and tracking it when wounded. With such a companion one gets much more game, and learns many things by observation instead of by painful experience.

On this trip we had with us two hunters, Tazewell Woody and Elwood Hofer, a packer who acted as cook, and a boy to herd the horses. Of the latter, there were twenty; six saddle-animals and fourteen for the packs—two or three being spare horses, to be used later in carrying the elk-antlers, sheep-horns, and other trophies. Like most hunters' pack-animals, they were either half broken, or else broken down; tough, unkempt; jaded-looking beasts of every color—sorrel, buckskin, pinto, white, bay, roan. After the day's work was over, they were turned loose to shift for themselves; and about once a week they strayed, and all hands had to spend the better part of the day hunting for them. The worst ones for straying, curiously enough, were three broken-down old "bear-baits," which went by themselves, as is generally the case with the cast-off horses of a herd. There were two sleeping-tents, another for the provisions,—in which we ate during bad weather,—and a canvas tepee, which was put up with lodge-poles, Indian fashion, like a wigwam. A tepee is more difficult to put up than an ordinary tent; but it is very convenient when there is rain or snow. A small fire kindled in the middle keeps it warm, the smoke escaping through the open top—that is, when it escapes at all; strings are passed from one pole to another, on which to hang wet clothes and shoes, and the beds are made around the edges. As an offset to the warmth and shelter, the smoke often renders it impossible even to sit upright. We had a very good camp-kit, including plenty of cooking-and eating-utensils; and among our provisions were some canned goods and sweetmeats, to give a relish to our meals of meat and bread. We had fur coats and warm clothes,—which are chiefly needed at night,—and plenty of bedding, including water-proof canvas sheeting and a couple of caribou-hide sleeping-bags, procured from the survivors of a party of arc-

tic explorers. Except on rainy days I used my buckskin hunting-shirt or tunic; in dry weather I deem
it, because of its color, texture, and durability, the
best possible garb for the still-hunter, especially in
the woods.

Starting a day's journey south of Heart Lake, we
travelled and hunted on the eastern edge of the great
basin, wooded and mountainous, wherein rise the
head-waters of the mighty Snake River. There was
not so much as a spotted line—that series of blazes
made with the axe, man's first highway through the
hoary forest,—but this we did not mind, as for most
of the distance we followed well-worn elk-trails.
The train travelled in Indian file. At the head, to pick
the path, rode tall, silent old Woody, a true type of the
fast-vanishing race of game hunters and Indian
fighters, a man who had been one of the California
forty-niners, and who ever since had lived the restless, reckless life of the wilderness. Then came Ferguson and myself; then the pack-animals, strung out
in line; while from the rear rose the varied oaths of
our three companions, whose miserable duty it was
to urge forward the beasts of burden.

It is heart-breaking work to drive a pack-train
through thick timber and over mountains, where
there is either a dim trail or none. The animals have
a perverse faculty for choosing the wrong turn at
critical moments; and they are continually scraping

under branches and squeezing between tree-trunks, to the jeopardy or destruction of their burdens. After having been laboriously driven up a very steep incline, at the cost of severe exertion both to them and to the men, the foolish creatures turn and run down to the bottom, so that all the work has to be done over again. Some travel too slow; others travel too fast. Yet one cannot but admire the toughness of the animals, and the surefootedness with which they pick their way along the sheer mountain sides, or among boulders and over fallen logs.

As our way was so rough, we found that we had to halt at least once every hour to fix the packs. Moreover, we at the head of the column were continually being appealed to for help by the unfortunates in the rear. First it would be "that white-eyed cayuse; one side of its pack's down!" then we would be notified that the saddle-blanket of the "lopeared Indian buckskin" had slipped back; then a shout "Look out for the pinto!" would be followed by that pleasing beast's appearance, bucking and squealing, smashing dead timber, and scattering its load to the four winds. It was no easy task to get the horses across some of the boggy places without miring; or to force them through the denser portions of the forest, where there was much down timber. Riding with a pack-train, day in and day out, becomes both monotonous and irritating, unless one is upheld by the hope of a game-country ahead, or by the delight of exploration of the unknown. Yet when buoyed by such a hope, there is pleasure in taking a train across so beautiful and wild a country as that which lay on the threshold of our hunting grounds in the Shoshones. We went over mountain passes, with ranges of scalped peaks on either hand; we skirted the edges of lovely lakes, and of streams with boulder-strewn beds; we plunged into depths of sombre woodland, broken by wet prairies. It was a picturesque sight to see the loaded pack-train stringing across one of these high mountain mead-ows, the motley colored line of ponies winding round the marshy spots through the bright green grass, while beyond rose the dark line of frowning forest, with lofty peaks towering in the background. Some of the mead-ows were beautiful with many flowers—goldenrod, purple aster, bluebells, white immortelles, and here and there masses of blood-red Indian pinks. In the park-country, on the edges of the evergreen forest, were groves of delicate quaking-aspen, the trees often growing to quite a height; their tremulous leaves were already changing to bright green and yellow, occa-sionally with a reddish blush. In the Rocky Moun-tains the aspens are almost the only deciduous trees, their foliage offering a pleasant relief to the eye after the monotony of the unending pine and spruce woods, which afford so striking a contrast to the hard-wood forest east of the Mississippi.

For two days our journey was uneventful, save that we came on the camp of a squawman—one Beaver Dick, an old mountain hunter, living in a skin tepee, where dwelt his comely Indian wife and half-breed children. He had quite a herd of horses, many of them mares and colts; they had evidently been well treated, and came up to us fearlessly.

The morning of the third day of our journey was gray and lowering. Gusts of rain blew in my face as I rode at the head of the train. It still lacked an hour of noon, as we were plodding up a valley beside a rapid brook running through narrow willow-flats, the dark forest crowding down on either hand from the low foot-hills of the mountains. Suddenly the call of a bull elk came echoing down through the wet woodland on our right, beyond the brook, seemingly less than half a mile off; and was answered by a faint, far-off call from a rival on the mountain beyond. Instantly halting the train, Woody and I slipped off our horses, crossed the brook, and started to still-hunt the first bull.

In this place the forest was composed of the western tamarack; the large, tall trees stood well apart, and there was much down timber, but the ground was covered with deep wet moss, over which we trod silently. The elk was travelling up-wind, but slowly, stopping continually to paw the ground and thresh the bushes with his antlers. He was very noisy, challenging every minute or two, being doubtless much excited by the neighborhood of his rival on the mountain. We followed, Woody leading, guided by the incessant calling.

It was very exciting as we crept toward the great bull, and the challenge sounded nearer and nearer. While we were still at some distance the pealing notes were like those of a bugle, delivered in two bars, first rising, then abruptly falling; as we drew nearer they took on a harsh squealing sound. Each call made our veins thrill; it sounded like the cry of some huge beast of prey. At last we heard the roar of the challenge not eighty yards off. Stealing forward three or four yards, I saw the tips of the horns through a mass of dead timber and young growth, and I slipped to one side to get a clean shot. Seeing us, but not making out what we were, and full of fierce and insolent excitement, the wapiti bull stepped boldly toward us with a stately swinging gait. Then he stood motionless, facing us, barely fifty yards away, his handsome twelve-tined antlers tossed aloft, as he held his head with the lordly grace of his kind. I fired into his chest, and as he turned I raced forward and shot him in the flank; but the second bullet was not needed, for the first wound was mortal, and he fell before going fifty yards.

The dead elk lay among the young evergreens. The huge, shapely body was set on legs that were as strong as steel rods, and yet slender, clean, and smooth; they were in color a beautiful dark brown, contrasting well with the yellowish of the body. The neck and throat were garnished with a mane of long hair; the symmetry of the great horns set off the fine, delicate lines of the noble head. He had been wallowing, as elk are fond of doing, and the dried mud clung in patches to his flank; a stab in the haunch showed that he had been overcome in battle by some master bull who had turned him out of the herd.

We cut off the head, and bore it down to the train. The horses crowded together, snorting, with their ears pricked forward, as they smelt the blood. We also took the loins with us, as we were out of meat, though bull elk in the rutting season is not very good. The rain had changed to a steady downpour when we again got under way. Two or three miles farther we pitched camp, in a clump of pines on a hillock in the bottom of the valley, starting hot fires of pitchy stumps before the tents, to dry our wet things.

Next day opened with fog and cold rain. The drenched pack-animals, when driven into camp, stood mopingly, with drooping heads and arched backs; they groaned and grunted as the loads were placed on their backs and the cinches tightened, the packers bracing one foot against the pack to get a purchase as they hauled in on the lash-rope. A stormy morning is a trial to temper; the packs are wet and heavy, and the cold makes the work even more than usually hard on the hands. By ten we broke camp. It needs between two and three hours to break camp and get such a train properly packed; once started, our day's journey was six to eight hours, making no halt. We started up a steep, pine-clad mountain side, broken by cliffs. My hunting-shoes, though comfortable, were old and thin, and let the water through like a sieve. On the top of the first plateau, where black spruce groves were strewn across the grassy surface, we saw a band of elk, cows and calves, trotting off through the rain. Then we plunged down into a deep valley, and, crossing it, a hard climb took us to the top of a great bare table-land, bleak and wind-swept. We passed little alpine lakes, fringed with scattering dwarf evergreens. Snow lay in drifts on the north sides of the gullies; a cutting wind blew the icy rain in our faces. For two or three hours we travelled toward the farther edge of the table-land. In one place a spike bull elk stood half a mile off, in the open; he travelled to and fro, watching us.

As we neared the edge the storm lulled, and pale, watery sunshine gleamed through the rifts in the low-scudding clouds. At last our horses stood on the brink of a bold cliff. Deep down beneath our feet lay the wild and lonely valley of Two-Ocean Pass, walled in on either hand by rugged mountain chains, their flanks scarred and gashed by precipice and chasm. Beyond, in a wilderness of jagged and barren peaks, stretched the Shoshones. At the middle point of the pass, two streams welled down from either side. At first each flowed in but one bed, but soon divided into two; each of the twin branches then joined the like branch of the brook opposite, and swept one to the east and one to the west, on their long journey to the two great oceans. They ran as rapid brooks, through wet meadows and willow-flats, the eastern to the Yellowstone, the western to the Snake. The dark pine forests swept down from the flanks and lower ridges of the mountains to the edges of the marshy valley. Above them jutted gray rock peaks, snow-drifts lying in the rents that seamed their northern faces. Far below us, from a great basin at the foot of the cliff, filled with the pine forest, rose the musical challenge of a bull elk; and we saw a band of cows and calves looking like mice as they ran among the trees.

It was getting late, and after some search we failed to find any trail leading down; so at last we plunged over the brink at a venture. It was very rough scrambling, dropping from bench to bench, and in places it was not only difficult but dangerous for the loaded pack-animals. Here and there we were helped by well-beaten elk-trails, which we could follow for several hundred yards at a time. On one narrow pine-clad ledge, we met a spike bull face to face; and in scrambling down a very steep, bare, rock-strewn shoulder the loose stones started by the horses' hoofs, bounding in great leaps to the forest below, dislodged two cows.

As evening fell, we reached the bottom, and pitched camp in a beautiful point of open pine forest, thrust out into the meadow. There was good shelter, and plenty of wood, water, and grass; we built a huge fire and put up our tents, scattering them in likely places among the pines, which grew far apart and without undergrowth. We dried our steaming clothes, and ate a hearty supper of elk-meat; then we turned into our beds, warm and dry, and slept soundly under the canvas, while all night long the storm roared without. Next morning it still stormed fitfully; the high peaks and ridges round about were all capped with snow. Woody and I started on foot for an all-day tramp; the amount of game seen the day before showed that we were in a good elk-country, where the elk had been so little disturbed that they were travelling, feeding, and whistling in daylight. For three hours we walked across the forest-clad spurs of the foot-hills. We roused a small band of elk in thick timber; but they rushed off before we saw them, with much smashing of dead branches. Then we climbed to the summit of the range. The wind was light and baffling; it blew from all points, veering every few minutes. There were occasional rain-squalls; our feet and legs were well soaked; and we became chilled through whenever we sat down to listen. We caught a glimpse of a big bull feeding up-hill, and followed him; it needed smart running to overtake him, for an elk, even while feeding, has a ground-covering gait. Finally we got within a hundred and twenty-five yards, but in very thick timber, and all I could see plainly was the hip and the after-part of the flank. I waited for a chance at the shoulder, but the bull got my wind and was off before I could pull trigger. It was just one of those occasions when there are two courses to pursue, neither very good, and when one is apt to regret whichever decision is made.

At noon we came to the edge of a deep and wide gorge, and sat down shivering to await what might turn up, our fingers numb, and our wet feet icy. Suddenly the love-challenge of an elk came pealing across the gorge, through the fine, cold rain, from the heart of the forest opposite. An hour's stiff climb, down and up, brought us nearly to him; but the wind forced us to advance from below through a series of open glades. He was lying on a point of the cliff-shoulder, surrounded by his cows; and he saw us and made off. An hour afterward, as we were trudging up a steep hill-side dotted with groves of fir and spruce, a young bull of ten points, roused from his day-bed by our approach, galloped across us some sixty yards off. We were in need of better venison than can be furnished by an old rutting bull; so I instantly took a shot at the fat and tender young ten-pointer. I aimed well ahead and pulled trigger just as he came to a small gully; and he fell into it in a heap with a resounding crash. This was on the birthday of my eldest small son; so I took him home the horns, "for his very own." On the way back that afternoon I shot off the heads of two blue grouse, as they perched in the pines.

That evening the storm broke, and the weather became clear and very cold, so that the snow made the frosty mountains gleam like silver. The moon was full, and in the flood of light the wild scenery round our camp was very beautiful. As always where we camped for several days, we had fixed long tables and settles, and were most comfortable; and when we came in at nightfall, or sometimes long afterward, cold, tired, and hungry, it was sheer physical delight to get warm before the roaring fire of pitchy stumps, and then to feast ravenously on bread and beans, on stewed or roasted elk venison, on grouse and sometimes trout, and flapjacks with maple syrup.

Next morning dawned clear and cold, the sky a glorious blue. Woody and I started to hunt over the great table-land, and led our stout horses up the mountain-side, by elk-trails so bad that they had to climb like goats. All these elk-trails have one striking peculiarity. They lead through thick timber, but every now and then send off short, well-worn branches to some cliff-edge or jutting crag, commanding a view far and wide over the country beneath. Elk love to stand on these lookout points, and scan the valleys and mountains round about.

Blue grouse rose from beside our path; Clarke's crows flew past us, with a hollow, flapping sound, or lit in the pine-tops, calling and flirting their tails; the gray-clad whisky-jacks, with multitudinous cries, hopped and fluttered near us. Snow-shoe rabbits scuttled away, the big furry feet which give them their name already turning white. At last we came out on the great plateau, seamed with deep, narrow ravines. Reaches of pasture alternated with groves and open forests of varying size. Almost immediately we heard the bugle of a bull elk, and saw a big band of cows and calves on the other side of a valley. There were three bulls with them, one very large, and we tried to creep up on them; but the wind was baffling and spoiled our stalk. So we returned to our horses, mounted them, and rode a mile farther, toward a large open wood on a hill-side. When within two hundred yards we heard directly ahead the bugle of a bull, and pulled up short. In a moment I saw him walking through an open glade;

he had not seen us. The slight breeze brought us down his scent. Elk have a strong characteristic smell; it is usually sweet, like that of a herd of Alderney cows; but in old bulls, while rutting, it is rank, pungent, and lasting. We stood motionless till the bull was out of sight, then stole to the wood, tied our horses, and trotted after him. He was travelling fast, occasionally calling; whereupon others in the neighborhood would answer. Evidently he had been driven out of some herd by the master bull.

He went faster than we did, and while we were vainly trying to overtake him we heard another very loud and sonorous challenge to our left. It came from a ridge-crest at the edge of the woods, among some scattered clumps of the northern nut-pine or pinyon—a queer conifer, growing very high on the mountains, its multiforked trunk and wide-spreading branches giving it the rounded top, and, at a distance, the general look of an oak rather than a pine. We at once walked toward the ridge, up-wind. In a minute or two, to our chagrin, we stumbled on an outlying spike bull, evidently kept on the outskirts of the herd by the master bull. I thought he would alarm all the rest; but, as we stood motionless, he could not see clearly what we were. He stood, ran, stood again, gazed at us, and trotted slowly off. We hurried forward as fast as we dared, and with too little care; for we suddenly came in view of two cows. As they raised their heads to look, Woody squatted down where he was, to keep their attention fixed, while I cautiously tried to slip off to one side unobserved. Favored by the neutral tint of my buckskin hunting-shirt, with which my shoes, leggings, and soft hat matched, I succeeded. As soon as I was out of sight I ran hard and came up to a hillock crested with pinyons, behind which I judged I should find the herd. As I approached the crest, their strong, sweet smell smote my nostrils. In another moment I saw the tips of a pair of mighty antlers, and I peered over the crest with my rifle at the ready. Thirty yards off, behind a clump of pinyons, stood a huge bull, his head thrown back as he rubbed his shoulders with his horns. There were several cows around him, and one saw me immediately, and took alarm. I fired into the bull's shoulder, inflicting a mortal wound; but he went off, and I raced after him at top speed, firing twice into his flank; then he stopped, very sick, and I broke his neck with a fourth bullet. An elk often hesitates in the first moments of surprise and fright, and does not get really under way for two or three hundred yards; but, when once fairly started, he may go several miles, even though mortally wounded; therefore, the hunter, after his first shot, should run forward as fast as he can, and shoot again and again until the quarry drops. In this way many animals that would otherwise be lost are obtained, especially by the man who has a repeating-rifle. Nevertheless the hunter should beware of being led astray by the ease with which he can fire half a dozen shots from his repeater; and he should aim as carefully with each shot as if it were his last. No possible rapidity of fire can atone for habitual carelessness of aim with the first shot.

The elk I thus slew was a giant. His body was the size of a steer's, and his antlers, though not unusually long, were very massive and heavy. He lay in a glade, on the edge of a great cliff. Standing on its brink we overlooked a most beautiful country, the home of all homes for the elk: a wilderness of mountains, the immense evergreen forest broken by park and glade, by meadow and pasture, by bare hill-side and barren table-land. Some five miles off lay the sheet of water known to the old hunters as Spotted Lake; two or three shallow, sedgy places, and spots of geyser formation, made pale green blotches on its wind-rippled surface. Far to the southwest, in daring beauty and majesty, the grand domes and lofty spires of the Tetons shot into the blue sky. Too sheer for the snow to rest on their sides, it yet filled the rents in their rough flanks, and lay deep between the towering pinnacles of dark rock.

That night, as on more than one night afterward, a bull elk came down whistling to within two or three hundred yards of the tents, and tried to join the horse herd. The moon had set, so I could not go after it. Elk are very restless and active throughout the night in the rutting season; but where undisturbed they feed freely in the daytime, resting for two or three hours about noon.

Next day, which was rainy, we spent in getting in the antlers and meat of the two dead elk; and I shot off the heads of two or three blue grouse on the way home. The following day I killed another bull elk, following him by the strong, not unpleasing, smell, and hitting him twice as he ran, at about eighty yards. So far I had had good luck, killing everything I had shot at; but now the luck changed, through no fault of mine, as far as I could see, and Ferguson had his innings. The day after I killed this bull he shot two fine mountain rams; and during the remainder of our hunt he killed five elk,—one cow, for meat, and four good bulls. The two rams were with three others, all old and with fine horns; Ferguson peeped over a lofty precipice and saw them coming up it only fifty yards below him. His two first and finest bulls were obtained by hard running and good shooting; the herds were on the move at the time, and only his speed of foot and soundness of wind enabled him to get near enough for a shot. One herd started before he got close, and he killed the master bull by a shot right through the heart, as it trotted past, a hundred and fifty yards distant.

As for me, during the next ten days I killed nothing save one cow for meat; and this though I hunted hard every day from morning till night, no matter what the weather. It was stormy, with hail and snow almost every day; and after working hard from dawn until nightfall, laboriously climbing the slippery mountain-sides, walking through the wet woods, and struggling across the bare plateaus and cliff-shoulders, while the violent blasts of wind drove the frozen rain in our faces, we would come in after dusk wet through and chilled to the marrow. Even when it rained in the valleys it snowed on the mountaintops, and there was no use trying to keep our feet dry. I got three shots at bull elk, two being very hurried snap-shots at animals running in thick timber, the other a running-shot in the open, at over two hundred yards; and I missed all three. On most days I saw no bull worth shooting; the two or three I did see or hear we failed to stalk, the light, shifty wind baffling us, or else an outlying cow which we had not seen giving the alarm. There were many blue and a few ruffed grouse in the woods, and I occasionally shot off the heads of a couple on my way homeward in the evening. In racing after one elk, I leaped across a gully and so bruised and twisted my heel on a rock that, for the remainder of my stay in the mountains, I had to walk on the fore part of that foot. This did not interfere much with my walking, however, except in going down-hill.

Our ill success was in part due to sheer bad luck; but the chief element therein was the presence of a great hunting-party of Shoshone Indians. Split into bands of eight or ten each, they scoured the whole country on their tough, sure-footed ponies. They always hunted on horseback, and followed the elk at full speed wherever they went. Their method of hunting was to organize great drives, the riders strung in lines far apart; they signalled to one another by means of willow whistles, with which they also imitated the calling of the bull elk, thus tolling the animals to them, or making them betray their whereabouts. As they slew whatever they could, but by preference cows and calves, and as they were very persevering, but also very excitable and generally poor shots, so that they wasted much powder, they not only wrought havoc among the elk, but also scared the survivors out of all the country over which they hunted.

Day in and day out we plodded on. In a hunting-trip the days of long monotony in getting to the ground, and the days of unrequited toil after it has been reached, always far outnumber the red-letter days of success. But it is just these times of failure that really test the hunter. In the long run, common-sense and dogged perseverance avail him more than any other qualities. The man who does not give up, but hunts steadily and resolutely through the spells of bad luck until the luck turns, is the man who wins success in the end.

After a week at Two-Ocean Pass, we gathered our pack-animals one frosty morning, and again set off across the mountains. A two-days' jaunt took us to the summit of Wolverine Pass, near Pinyon Peak, beside a little mountain tarn; each morning we found its surface skimmed with black ice, for the nights were cold. After three or four days, we shifted camp to the mouth of Wolverine Creek, to get off the hunting grounds of the Indians. We had used up our last elk-meat that morning, and when we were within a couple of hours' journey of our intended halting-place, Woody and I struck off on foot for a hunt. Just before sunset we came on three or four elk; a spike bull stood for a moment behind some thick evergreens a hundred yards off. Guessing at his shoulder, I fired, and he fell dead after running a few rods. I had broken the luck, after ten days of ill success.

Next morning Woody and I, with the packer, rode to where this elk lay. We loaded the meat on a pack-horse, and let the packer take both the loaded animal and our own saddle-horses back to camp, while we made a hunt on foot. We went up the steep, forest-clad mountain-side, and before we had walked an hour heard two elk whistling ahead of us. The woods were open, and quite free from undergrowth, and we were able to advance noiselessly; there was no wind, for the weather was still, clear, and cold. Both of the elk were evidently very much excited, answering each other continually; they had probably been master bulls, but had become so exhausted that their rivals had driven them from the herds, forcing them to remain in seclusion until they regained their lost strength. As we crept stealthily forward, the calling grew louder and louder, until we could hear the grunting sounds with which the challenge of the nearest ended. He was in a large wallow, which was also a lick. When we were still sixty yards off, he heard us, and rushed out, but wheeled and stood a moment to gaze, puzzled by my buckskin suit. I fired into his throat, breaking his neck, and down he went in a heap. Rushing in and turning, I called to Woody, "He's a twelve-pointer, but the horns are small!" As I spoke I heard the roar of the challenge of the other bull not two hundred yards ahead, as if in defiant answer to my shot.

Running quietly forward, I speedily caught a glimpse of his body. He was behind some fir-trees about seventy yards off, and I could not see which way he was standing, and so fired into the patch of flank which was visible, aiming high, to break the back. My aim was true, and the huge beast crashed down-hill through the evergreens, pulling himself on his fore legs for fifteen or twenty rods, his hind quarters trailing. Racing forward, I broke his neck. His antlers were the finest I ever got. A couple of whisky-jacks appeared at the first crack of the rifle with their customary astonishing familiarity and heedlessness of the hunter; they followed the wounded bull as he dragged his great carcass down the hill, and pounced with ghoulish blood-thirstiness on the gouts of blood that were sprinkled over the green herbage.

These two bulls lay only a couple of hundred yards apart, on a broad game-trail, which was as well beaten as a good bridle-path. We began to skin out the heads; and as we were finishing we heard another bull challenging far up the mountain. He came nearer and nearer, and as soon as we had ended our work we grasped our rifles and trotted toward him along the game-trail. He was very noisy, uttering his loud, singing challenge every minute or two. The trail was so broad and firm that we walked in perfect silence. After going only five or six hundred yards, we got very close indeed, and stole forward on tiptoe, listening to the roaring music. The sound came from a steep, narrow ravine, to one side of the trail, and I walked toward it with my rifle at the ready. A slight puff gave the elk my wind, and he dashed out of the ravine like a deer; but he was only thirty yards off, and my bullet went into his shoulder as he passed behind a clump of young spruce. I plunged into the ravine, scrambled out of it, and raced after him. In a minute I saw him standing with drooping head, and two more shots finished him. He also bore fine antlers. It was a great piece of luck to get three such fine bulls at the cost of half a day's light work; but we had fairly earned them, having worked hard for ten days, through rain, cold, hunger, and fatigue, to no purpose. That evening my home-coming to camp, with three elk-tongues and a brace of ruffed grouse hung at my belt, was most happy.

Next day it snowed, but we brought a pack-pony to where the three great bulls lay, and took their heads to camp; the flesh was far too strong to be worth taking, for it was just the height of the rut.

This was the end of my hunt; and a day later Hofer and I, with two pack-ponies, made a rapid push for the Upper Geyser Basin. We travelled fast. The first day was gray and overcast, a cold wind blowing strong in our faces. Toward evening we came on a bull elk in a willow thicket; he was on his knees in a hollow, thrashing and beating the willows with his antlers. At dusk we halted and went into camp, by some small pools on the summit of the pass north of Red Mountain. The elk were calling all around us. We pitched our cozy tent, dragged great stumps for the fire, cut evergreen boughs for our beds, watered the horses, tethered them to improvised picket-pins in a grassy glade, and then set about getting supper ready. The wind had gone down, and snow was falling thick in large, soft flakes; we were evidently at the beginning of a heavy snowstorm. All night we slept soundly in our snug tent. When we arose at dawn there was a foot and a half of snow on the ground, and the flakes were falling as fast as ever. There is no more tedious work than striking camp in bad weather; and it was over two hours from the time we rose to the time we started. It is sheer misery to untangle picket-lines and to pack animals when the ropes are frozen; and by the time we had loaded the two shivering, wincing pack-ponies, and had bridled and saddled our own riding-animals, our hands and feet were numb and stiff with cold, though we were really hampered by our warm clothing. My horse was a wild, nervous roan, and as I swung carelessly into the saddle, he suddenly began to buck before I got my right leg over, and threw me off. My thumb was put out of joint. I pulled it in again, and speedily caught my horse in the dead timber. Then I treated him as what the cowboys call a "mean horse," and mounted him carefully, so as not to let him either buck or go over backward. However, his preliminary success had inspirited him, and a dozen times that day he began to buck, usually choosing a down grade, where the snow was deep, and there was much fallen timber.

All day long we pushed steadily through the cold, blinding snowstorm. Neither squirrels nor rabbits were abroad; and a few Clarke's crows, whisky-jacks, and chickadees were the only living things we saw. At nightfall, chilled through, we reached the Upper Geyser Basin. Here I met a party of railroad surveyors and engineers, coming in from their summer's field-work. One of them lent me a saddle-horse and a pack-pony, and we went on together, breaking our way through the snow-choked roads to the Mammoth Hot Springs, while Hofer took my own horses back to Ferguson.

I have described this hunt at length because, though I enjoyed it particularly on account of the comfort in which we travelled and the beauty of the land, yet, in point of success in finding and killing game, in value of trophies procured, and in its alternations of good and bad luck, it may fairly stand as the type of a dozen such hunts I have made. Twice I have been much more successful; the difference being due to sheer luck, as I hunted equally hard in all three instances. Thus on this trip I killed and saw nothing but elk; yet the other members of the party either saw, or saw fresh signs of, not only blacktail deer, but sheep, bear, bison, moose, cougar, and wolf. Now in 1889 I hunted over almost precisely similar country, only farther to the northwest, on the boundary between Idaho and Montana, and, with the exception of sheep, I stumbled on all the animals mentioned, and white goat in addition, so that my bag of twelve head actually included eight species— much the best bag I ever made, and the only one that could really be called out of the common. In 1884, on a trip to the Bighorn Mountains, I killed three bear, six elk and six deer. In laying in the winter stock of meat for my ranch I often far excelled these figures as far as mere numbers went; but on no other regular hunting trip, where the quality and not the quantity of the game was the prime consideration, have I ever equalled them; and on several where I worked hardest I hardly averaged a head a week. The occasional days or weeks of phenomenal luck, are more than earned by the many others where no luck whatever follows the very hardest work. Yet, if a man hunts with steady resolution he is apt to strike enough lucky days amply to repay him.

On this Shoshone trip I fired fifty-eight shots. In preference to using the knife I generally break the neck of an elk which is still struggling; and I fire at one as long as it can stand, preferring to waste a few extra bullets, rather than see an occasional head of game escape. In consequence of these two traits the nine elk I got (two running at sixty and eighty yards, the others standing, at from thirty to a hundred) cost me twenty-three bullets; and I missed three shots— all three, it is but fair to say, difficult ones. I also cut off the heads of seventeen grouse, with twenty-two shots; and killed two ducks with ten shots—fifty-eight in all. On the Bighorn trip I used a hundred and two cartridges. On no other trip did I use fifty.

To me still-hunting elk in the mountains, when they are calling, is one of the most attractive of sports, not only because of the size and stately beauty of the quarry and the grand nature of the trophy, but because of the magnificence of the scenery, and the stirring, manly, exciting nature of the chase itself. It yields more vigorous enjoyment than does lurking stealthily through the grand but gloomy monotony of the marshy woodland where dwells the moose. The climbing among the steep forest-clad and glade-strewn mountains is just difficult enough thoroughly to test soundness in wind and limb, while without the heart-breaking fatigue of white goat hunting. The actual grapple with an angry grisly is of course far more full of strong, eager pleasure; but bear hunting is the most uncertain, and usually the least productive, of sports.

As regards strenuous, vigorous work, and pleasurable excitement the chase of the bighorn alone stands higher. But the bighorn, grand beast of the chase though he be, is surpassed in size, both of body and of horns, by certain of the giant sheep of Central Asia; whereas the wapiti is not only the most stately and beautiful of American game—far more

so than the bison and moose, his only rivals in size—
but is also the noblest of the stag kind throughout
the world. Whoever kills him has killed the chief of
his race; for he stands far above his brethren of Asia
and Europe.

De Shootinest Gent'man

[NASH BUCKINGHAM]

Supper was a delicious memory. In the matter of a certain goose stew, Aunt Molly had fairly outdone herself. And we, in turn, had jolly well done her out of practically all the goose. It may not come amiss to explain frankly and aboveboard the entire transaction with reference to said goose. Its breast had been deftly detached, lightly grilled and sliced into ordinary "mouth-size" portions. The remainder of the dismembered bird, back, limbs and all parts of the first part thereunto pertaining were put into an iron pot. Keeping company with the martyred fowl, in due proportion of culinary wizardry, were sundry bell peppers, two cans of mock turtle soup, diced roast pork, scrambled ham rinds, peas, potatoes, some corn and dried garden okra, shredded onions and pretty much anything and everything that wasn't tied down or that Molly had lying loose around her kitchen. This stew, served right royally, and attended by outriders of "cracklin' bread," was flanked by a man-at-arms in the form of a saucily flavored brown gravy. I recall a dish of broiled teal and some country puddin' with ginger pour-over, but merely mention these in passing.

So the Judge and I, in rare good humor (I forgot to add that there had been a dusty bottle of the Judge's famous port), as becomes sportsmen blessed with a perfect day's imperfect duck shooting, had discussed each individual bird brought to bag, with reasons, pro and con, why an undeniably large quota had escaped uninjured. We bordered upon that indecisive moment when bedtime should be imminent, were it not for the delightful trouble of getting started in that direction. As I recollect it, ruminating upon our sumptuous repast, the Judge had just countered upon my remark that I had never gotten enough hot turkey hash and beaten biscuits, by stating decisively that his craving for smothered quail remained inviolate, when the door opened softly and in slid "Ho'ace"! He had come, following a custom of many years, to tale final breakfast instructions before packing the embers in "Steamboat Bill," the stove, and dousing our glim.

Seeing upon the center table, t'wixt the Judge and me, a bottle and the unmistakable ingredients and tools of the former's ironclad rule for a hunter's nightcap, Ho'ace paused in embarrassed hesitation and seated himself quickly upon an empty shell case. His attitude was a cross between that of a timid gazelle's scenting danger and a wary hunter's sighting game and effacing himself gently from the landscape.

Long experience in the imperative issue of securing an invitation to "get his'n" had taught Ho'ace that it were ever best to appear humbly disinterested and thoroughly foreign to the subject until negotiations, if need be even much later, were opened with him directly or indirectly. With old-time members he steered along the above lines. But with newer ones or their uninitiated guests, he believed in quicker campaigning, or, conditions warranting, higher pressure sales methods. The Judge, reaching for the sugar bowl, mixed his sweetening water with adroit twirl and careful scrutiny as to texture; fastening upon Ho'ace meanwhile a melting look of liquid mercy. In a twinkling, however, his humor changed and the darky found himself in the glare of a forbidding menace, creditable in his palmiest days to the late Mister Chief Justice Jeffries himself.

"Ho'ace," demanded the Judge, tilting into his now ready receptacle a gurgling, man-size libation, "who is the best shot—the best duck-shot—you have ever paddled on this lake—barring—of course—a-h-e-m-m—myself?" Surveying himself with the coyness of a juvenile, the Judge stirred his now beading toddy dreamily and awaited the encore. Ho'ace squirmed a bit as the closing words of the Judge's query struck home with appalling menace upon his ears. He plucked nervously at his battered headpiece. His eyes, exhibiting a vast expanse of white, roamed pictured walls and smoke-dimmed ceiling in furtive, reflective, helpless quandry. Then speaking slowly and gradually warming to his subject, he fashioned the following alibi.

"Jedge, y' know, suh, us all has ouh good an' ouh bad days wid de ducks. Yes, my Lawdy, us sho' do. Dey's times whin de ducks flies all ovah ev'ything an' ev'ybody, an' still us kain't none o' us hit nuthin'—lak me an' you wuz dis mawnin'." At this juncture the Judge interrupted, reminding Ho'ace that he meant when the Judge—and *not* the Judge and Ho'ace—was shooting.

"An' den deys times whin h'it look lak dey ain't no shot too hard nur nary a duck too far not t'be kilt. But Mister Buckin'ham yonder—Mister Nash—he brung down de shootin'est gent'man what took all de cake. H'it's lots o' d' members here whut's darin' shooters, but dat fren' o' Mister Nash's—uummppphhh—don't never talk t' me 'bout him whur de ducks kin hear. 'Cause dey'll leave de laik ef dey hears he's even comin' dis way.

"Dat gent'man rode me jes' lak I wuz' er saddle,

an' he done had on rooster spurs. Mister Nash he brung him on down here an' say, 'Ho'ace,' he say, 'here's a gent'man frum Englan',' 'he say, 'Mister Money—Mister Harol' Money—an' say I wants you t' paddle him tomorrow an' see dat he gits er gran' shoot—unnerstan'?' I say, 'Yaas, suh, Mister Nash,' I say, 'dat I'll sho'ly do, suh. Mister Money gwi' hav' er fine picnic ef I has t' see dat he do my sef—but kin he shoot, suh?'

"Mister Nash, he say, 'Uh—why—uh—yaas, Ho'ace, Mister Money he's—uh—ve'y fair shot—'bout lak Mister Immitt Joyner or Mister Hal Howard.' I say t' mysef, I say, 'Uuummmpphhh—huuummmppphhh—well—he'ah now—ef dats d' case, me an' Mister Money gwi' *do* some shootin' in d' mawnin.'

"Mister Money he talk so kin'er queer an' brief like, dat I hadda pay clos't inspection t' whut he all de time asayin'. But nex' mawnin', whin me an' him goes out in de bote, I seen he had a gre't big ol' happy bottle o' Brooklyn Handicap in dat shell box so I say t' m'sef, I say, 'W-e-l-l-l—me an' Mister Money gwi' got erlong someway, us is.'

"I paddles him on up de laik an' he say t' me, say, 'Hawrice—uh—hav yo'—er—got anny wager,' he say, 'or proposition t' mek t' me, as regards," he say, 't' shootin' dem dar eloosive wil'fowls?' he say.

"I kinder studies a minit, 'cause, lak I done say, he

talk so brief. Den I says, 'I guess you is right 'bout dat, suh.'

"He say, 'Does you follow me, Hawrice, or is I alone?' he say.

"I says, 'Naw, suh, Mister, I'm right wid you in dis bote.'

" 'You has no proposition t' mek wid me den?' he say.

"S' I, 'Naw, suh, Boss, I leaves all dat wid you, suh, trustin' t' yo' gin'rosity, suh.'

" 'Ve'y good, Hawrice,' he say, 'I sees you doan grasp de principul. Now I will mek you de proposition,' he say. I jes' kep' on paddlin'. He say, 'Ev'y time I miss er duck you gits er dram frum dis hu'ah bottle—ev'y time I kills er duck—I gits de drink—which is h'it—come—come—speak up, my man.'

"I didn' b'lieve I done heard Mister Money rightly, an' I say, 'Uh—Mister Money,' I say, 'suh, does you mean dat I kin d' chice whedder you misses or kills ev'y time an' gits er drink?'

"He say, 'Dat's my defi',' he say.

"I says, 'Well, den—w-e-l-l—den—ef dat's de case, I gwi' choose ev'y time yo' misses, suh.' Den I say t'm'sef, I say, 'Ho'ace, right hu'ah whar you gotta be keerful, 'ginst you fall outa d' bote an' git fired frum d' lodge; 'cause ef'n you gits er drink ev'y time dis gent'man misses an' he shoot lak Mister Hal

Howard, you an' him sho' gwi' drink er worl' o' liquah—er worl' o' liquah.'

"I pushes on up nurly to de Han'werker stan', an' I peeks in back by da li'l pocket whut shallers off'n de laik, an' sees some sev'ul blackjacks—four on 'em—settin' in dar. Dey done seen us, too. An' up come dey haids. I spy 'em twis'in', an' turnin'—gittin' raidy t' pull dey freight frum dar. I says, 'Mister Money,' I says, 'yawnder sets some ducks—look out now, suh, 'cause dey gwi' try t' rush on out pas' us whin dey come outa dat pocket.' Den I think, 'W-e-l-l-l, hu'ah whar I knocks d' gol' fillin' outa d' mouf' o' Mister Money's bottle o' Brooklyn Handi-cap!'

"I raised de lid o' d' shell box an' dar laid dat ol' bottle—still dar. I say, 'Uuummmppphhh—hum-mmph.' Jus' 'bout dat time up goes dem black-haids an' outa dar dey come—dey did—flyin' low t' d' watah—an' sorta raisin' lak—y' knows how dey does h'it, Jedge?'

"Mister Money he jus' pick up dat fas' feedin' gun—t'war er pump—not one o' dese hu'ah new afromatics—an' whin he did, I done reach f' d' bot-tle, 'cause I jes' natcherly know'd dat my time had done come. Mister Money he swings down on dem bullies. Ker-py—ker-py-powie-powie—splamp-splamp-splamp—ker-splash—Lawdy mussy—gent'-

mans—fo' times, right in d' same place, h'it sounded lak—an' d' las' duck fell ker-flop almos' in ouh bote.

"I done let go d' bottle, an' Mister Money say—mighty cool lak—say, 'Hawrice, say, kin'ly to examine dat las' chap clos'ly,' he say, 'an' obsurve,' he say, 'ef'n he ain' shot thru de eye.'

"I rakes in dat blackjack, an' sho' nuff—bofe eyes done shot plum out—yaas, suh, bofe on 'em right on out. Mister Money say, 'I wuz—er—slightly afraid,' he say, 'dat I had unknowin'ly struck dat fella er trifle too far t' win'ward,' he say. 'A ve'y fair start, Hawrice,' he say. 'You'd bettah place me in my station, so we may continue on wid'out interruption,' he say.

" 'Yaas, suh,' I say. 'I'm on my way right dar now, suh, 'an I say t' m'sef, I say, 'Mek haste, Man, an' put dis gent'man in his bline an' giv' him er proper chanc't to miss er duck. I didn' hones'ly b'lieve but whut killin' all four o' dem other ducks so peart lak wuz er sorter accident. So I put him on de Han' werker bline. He seen I kep' de main shell bucket an' d' liquah, but he never said nuthin'. I put out d' m 'coys an' den creep back wid d' bote into d' willows t' watch.

"Pretty soon, hu'ah come er big ole drake flyin' mighty high. Ouh ole hen bird she holler t' him, an' d' drake he sorter twis' his haid an' look down.

'Warn't figurin' nuthin' but whut Mister Money gwi' let dat drake circle an' come 'mongst d' m 'coys—but—aw—aw! All uv er sudden he jus' raise up sharp lak an'—kerzowie! Dat ole drake jus' throw his haid on his back an' ride on down—looked t' me lak he fell er mile—an' whin he hit he thow'd watah fo' feet. Mister Money he nuvver said er word—jus' sot dar!

"Hu'ah come another drake—way off t' d' lef'— up over back o' me. He turn eroun'—quick lak—he did an'—kerzowie—he cut him on down, too. Dat drake fall way back in d' willows an' cose I hadda wade after 'im.

"Whilst I wuz gone, Mister Money shoot twice. An' whin I come stumblin' back, dar laid two mo' ducks wid dey feets in de air. Befo' I hav' time t' git in de bote again he done knock down er hen away off in d' elbow brush.

"I say, 'Mister Money, suh, I hav' behin' some far-knockin' guns in my time an' I'se er willin' worker, shoe—but ef you doan, please suh, kill dem ducks closer lak, you gwi' kill yo' willin' supporter Ho'ace in de mud.' He say, 'Da's all right 'bout dat,' he say. 'Go git d' bird—he kain't git er-way 'cause h'its dead ez er wedge.'

"Whin I crawls back t' d' bote dat las' time—it done got mighty col'. Dar us set—me in one en' ashiverin' an' dat ole big bottle wid de gol' haid in de far en'. Might jus' ez well bin ten miles so far ez my chances had done gone.

"Five mo' ducks come in—three singles an' er pair o' sprigs. An' Mister Money he chewed 'em all up lak good eatin'. One time, tho' he had t' shoot one o' them high-flyin' sprigs twice, an' I done got halfway in de bote reachin' fer dat bottle—but de las' shot got 'im. Aftah while, Mister Money say— 'Hawrice,' he say, 'how is you hittin' off—my man?'

" 'Mister Money,' I say, 'I'se pow'ful col', suh, an' ef you wants er 'umble, no 'count paddler t' tell you d' truth, suh, I b'lieves I done made er pow'ful po' bet.' He say 'Poss'bly so, Hawrice, poss'bly so.' But dat 'poss'bly' didn' git me nuthin'.

"Jedge, y' Honor, you know dat gent'man sot dar an' kill ev'ry duck come in, an' had his limit long befo' de eight-o'clock train runned. I done gone t' watchin' an' de las' duck whut come by wuz one o' dem lightnin'-express teals. Hu'ah he come—er greenwing drake—look lak' somebody done blowed er buckshot pas' us. I riz' up an' hollered, 'Fly fas', ole teal, do yo' bes'—caus' Ho'ace needs er drink.' But Mister Money jus' jumped up an' thow'd him forty feet—skippin' 'long d' watah. I say, 'Hol' on, Mister Money, hol' on—you done kilt d' limit.'

" 'Oh,' he say, 'I hav'—hav' I?'

"I say, 'Yaas, suh, an' you ain't bin long 'bout h'it—neither.

"He say, 'What are you doin' gittin' so col' then?'

"I say, 'I spec' findin' out dat I hav' done made er bad bet had er lot t' do wid d' air.'

"An' dar laid dat Brooklyn Handicap all dat time—he nuvver touched none—an' me neither. I paddles him on back to de house, an' he comes er stalkin' on in hu'ah, he did—lookin' kinda mad lak—never said nuthin' 'bout no drink. Finally he say, 'Hawrice,' he say, 'git me a bucket o' col' watah.' I say t' m'sef, I say, 'W-e-l-l-l, das mo' lak h'it—ef he wants er bucket o' watah. Boy—you gwi' *see* some real drinkin' now.'

"Whin I come in wid d' pail, Mister Money took offin all his clothes an' step out onto d' side po'ch an' say, 'Th'ow dat watah ovah me, Hawrice. I am lit'rully compel,' he say, 't' have my col' tub ev'y mawnin'.' M-a-n-n-n-n! I sho' tow'd dat ice col' watah onto him wid all my heart an' soul. But he jus' gasp an' hollah, an' jump up an' down an' slap hisse'f. Den he had me rub him red wid er big rough towel. I sho' rubbed him, too. Come on in d' club-room hu'ah, he did, an' mek hisse'f comfort'ble in dat big ol' rockin' chair yonder—an' went t' readin'. I brought in his shell bucket an' begin cleanin' his gun. But I seen him kinder smilin' t' hisse'f. Atta while, he says 'Hawrice,' he say, 'you hav' done los' yo' bet?'

"I kinder hang my haid lak, an' 'low, 'Yaas, suh, Mister Money, I don' said farewell t' d' liquah!'

"He say, 'Yo' admits den dat you hav' done los' fair an' square—an' dat yo' realizes h'it?'

" 'Yaas, suh!'

"He say, 'Yo' judgmint,' he say, 'wuz ve'y fair, considerin',' he say, 'de great law uv' av'ridge—but circumstance,' he say, 'has done render de ult'mate outcome subjec' t' d' mighty whims o' chance?'

"I say, 'Yaas, suh,' ve'y mournful lak.

"He say, 'In so far as realizin' on anything 'ceptin' de mercy o' d' Cote—say—you is absolutely non-est—eh, my man?'

"I say, 'Yaas, suh, barrin' yo' mercy, suh.'

"Den he think er moment, an' say, 'Verrree—ver-ree—good!'

"Den he 'low, 'Sence you acknowledges d' cawn, an' admits dat you hav' done got grabbed,' he say, 'step up,' he say, 'an' git you a tumbler—po' yo'sef er drink—po' er big one, too.'

"I never stopped f' nuthin' den—jes' runned an' got me a glass outa de kitchen. Ole Molly, she say, 'Whur you goin' so fas'?' I say, 'Doan stop me now ole 'ooman—I got business—p'ticler business—an' I sho' poh'd me er big bait o' liquah—er whole sloo' o' liquah. Mister Money say, 'Hawrice—de size o' yo' po'tion,' he say, 'is primus facious ev'dence,' he say, 'dat you gwi' spout er toast in honor,' he say, 'o' d' occasion.'

"I say, 'Mister Money, suh,' I say, 'all I got t' say, suh, is dat you is de kingpin, champeen duck shotter so far as I hav' done bin' in dis life—an' ve'y prob'ly as far as I'se likely t' keep on goin', too.' He sorter smile t' hisse'f!

" 'Now, suh, please, suh, tell me dis—is you *ever* missed er duck—anywhar'—anytime—anyhow— suh?'

"He say 'Really, Hawrice,' he say, 'you embarrasses me,' he say, 'so hav' another snifter—there is mo', considerably mo',' he say, 'in yo' system what demands utt'rance,' he say.

"I done poh'd me another slug o' Brooklyn Handicap an' say, 'Mister Money,' I say, 'does you expec' t' *ever* miss another duck ez long ez you lives, suh?'

"He say, 'Hawrice,' he say, 'you embarrasses me,' he say, 'beyon' words—you overwhelms me,' he say. 'Git t' hell outa hu'ah befo' you gits us bofe drunk.' "

That Twenty-Five-Pound Gobbler

[ARCHIBALD RUTLEDGE]

I suppose that there are other things which make a hunter uneasy, but of one thing I am very sure: that is to locate and to begin to stalk a deer or a turkey, only to find that another hunter is doing precisely the same thing at the same time. The feeling I had was worse than uneasy. It is, in fact, as inaccurate as if a man should say, after listening to a comrade swearing roundly, "Bill is expressing himself uneasily."

To be frank, I was jealous; and all the more so because I knew that Dade Saunders was just as good a turkey-hunter as I am—and maybe a good deal better. At any rate, both of us got after the same whopping gobbler. We knew this turkey and we knew each other; and I am positive that the wise old bird knew both of us far better than we knew him.

But we hunters have ways of improving our

acquaintance with creatures that are over-wild and shy. Both Dade and I saw him, I suppose, a dozen times; and twice Dade shot at him. I had never fired at him, for I did not want to cripple, but to kill; and he never came within a hundred yards of me. Yet I felt that the gobbler ought to be mine; and for the simple reason that Dade Saunders was a shameless poacher and a hunter-out-of-season.

I have in mind the day when I came upon him in the pine-lands in mid-July, when he had in his wagon *five* bucks in the velvet, all killed that morning. Now, this isn't a fiction story; this is fact. And after I have told you of those bucks, I think you'll want me to beat Dade to the great American bird.

This wild turkey had the oddest range that you could imagine. You hear of turkeys ranging "original forests," "timbered wilds," and the like. Make up your mind that if wild turkeys have a chance they are going to come near civilization. The closer they are to man, the farther they are away from their other enemies. Near civilization they at least have (but for the likes of Dade Saunders) the protection of the law. But in the wilds what protection do they have from wildcats, from eagles, from weasels (I am thinking of young turkeys as well as old), and from all their other predatory persecutors?

Well, as I say, time and again I have known wild

turkeys to come, and to seem to enjoy coming, close to houses. I have stood on the porch of my plantation home and have watched a wild flock feeding under the great live-oaks there. I have repeatedly flushed wild turkeys in an autumn cornfield. I have shot them in rice stubble.

Of course they do not come for sentiment. They are after grain. And if there is any better wild game than a rice-field wild turkey, stuffed with peanuts, circled with browned sweet potatoes, and fragrant with a rich gravy that plantation cooks know how to make, I'll follow you to it.

The gobbler I was after was a haunter of the edges of civilization. He didn't seem to like the wild woods. I think he got hungry there. But on the margins of fields that had been planted he could get all he wanted to eat of the things he most enjoyed. He particularly liked the edges of cultivated fields that bordered either on the pinewoods or else on the marshy rice-lands.

One day I spent three hours in the gaunt chimney of a burned rice-mill, watching this gobbler feeding on such edges. Although I was sure that sooner or later he would pass the mouth of the chimney, giving me a chance for a shot, he kept just that distance between us that makes a gun a vain thing in a man's hands. But though he did not give me my chance, he let me watch him all I pleased. This I did through certain dusty crevices between the bricks of the old chimney.

If I had been taking a post-graduate course in caution, this wise old bird would have been my teacher. Whatever he happened to be doing, his eyes and his ears were wide with vigilance. I saw him first standing beside a fallen pine log on the brow of a little hill where peanuts had been planted. I made the shelter of the chimney before he recognized me. But he must have seen the move I made.

I have hunted turkeys long enough to be thoroughly rid of the idea that a human being can make a motion that a wild turkey cannot see. One of my woodsman friends said to me, "Why, a gobbler can see anything. He can see a jaybird turn a somersault on the verge of the horizon." He was right.

Watching from my cover I saw this gobbler scratching for peanuts. He was very deliberate about this. Often he would draw back one huge handful (or footful) of viney soil, only to leave it there while he looked and listened. I have seen a turkey do the same thing while scratching in leaves. Now, a buck while feeding will alternately keep his head up and down; but a turkey gobbler keeps his down very little. That bright black eye of his, set in that sharp bluish head, is keeping its vision on every object on the landscape.

My gobbler (I called him mine from the first time I saw him) found many peanuts, and he relished them. From that feast he walked over into a patch of autumn-dried crabgrass. The long pendulous heads of this grass, full of seeds, he stripped skilfully. When satisfied with this food, he dusted himself beside an old stump. It was interesting to watch this; and while he was doing it I wondered if it was not my chance to leave the chimney, make a detour, and come up behind the stump. But of course just as I decided to do this, he got up, shook a small cloud of dust from his feathers, stepped off into the open, and there began to preen himself.

A short while thereafter he went down to a marshy edge, there finding a warm sandy hole on the sunny side of a briar patch, where he continued his dusting and loafing. I believe that he knew the stump, which shut off his view of what was behind it, was no place to choose for a midday rest.

All this time I waited patiently; interested, to be sure, but I would have been vastly more so if the lordly old fellow had turned my way. This I expected him to do when he got tired of loafing. Instead, he deliberately walked into the tall ranks of the marsh, which extended riverward for half a mile. At that I hurried forward, hoping to flush him on the margin; but he had vanished for that day. But though he had escaped me, the sight of him had made me keen to follow him until he expressed a willingness to accompany me home.

Just as I was turning away from the marsh I heard a turkey call from the shelter of a big live-oak beside the old chimney. I knew that it was Dade Saunders, and that he was after my gobbler. I walked over to where he was making his box-call plead. He expressed no surprise on seeing me. We greeted each other as two hunters, who are not over-friendly, greet when they find themselves after the same game.

"I seen his tracks," said Dade. "I believe he limps in the one foot since I shot him last Sunday will be a week."

"He must be a big bird," I said; "you were lucky to have a shot."

Dade's eyes grew hungrily bright.

"He's the biggest in these woods, and I'll git him yet. You jest watch me."

"I suppose you will, Dade. You are the best turkey-hunter of these parts."

I hoped to make him overconfident; and praise is a great corrupter of mankind. It is not unlikely to make a hunter miss a shot. I remember that a friend of mine once said laughingly: "If a man tells me I am a good shot, I will miss my next chance, as sure as guns; but if he cusses me and tells me I'm not worth a darn, then watch me shoot!"

Dade and I parted for the time. I went off

toward the marsh, whistling an old song. I wanted to have the gobbler put a little more distance between himself and the poacher. Besides, I felt that it was right of me to do this: for while I was on my own land, my visitor was trespassing. I hung around in the scrub–oak thickets for awhile; but no gun spoke out, I knew that the old gobbler's intelligence plus my whistling game had "foiled the relentless" Dade. It was a week later that the three of us met again.

Not far from the peanut field there is a plantation corner. Now, most plantation corners are graveyards; that is, cemeteries of the old days, where slaves were buried. Occasionally now Negroes are buried there, but pathways have to be cut through the jungle-like growths to enable the cortege to enter.

Such a place is a wilderness for sure. Here grow towering pines, mournful and moss-draped. Here are hollies, canopied with jasmine-vines; here are thickets of myrtle, sweet gum, and young pines. If a covey of quail goes into such a place, you might as well whistle your dog off and go after another lot of birds.

Here deer love to come in the summer, where they can hide from the heat and the gauze-winged flies. Here in the winter is a haunt for woodcock, a good range (for great live-oaks drop their sweet acorns) for wild turkeys, and a harbor for foxes. In those great pines and oaks turkeys love to roost. It was on the borders of just such a corner that I roosted the splendid gobbler.

It was a glowing December sunset. I had left the house an hour before to stroll the plantation roads, counting (as I always do) the number of deer and turkey tracks that had recently been made in the soft damp sand. Coming near the dense corner, I sat against the bole of a monster pine. I love to be a mere watcher in woodlands as well as a hunter.

About two hundred yards away there was a little sunny hill, grown to scrub-oaks. They stood sparsely; that enabled me to see well what I now saw. Into my vision, with the rays of the sinking sun gleaming softly on the bronze of his neck and shoulders, the great gobbler stepped with superb beauty. Though he deigned to scratch once or twice in the leaves, and peck indifferently at what he thus uncovered, I knew he was bent on roosting; for not only was it nearly his bedtime, but he seemed to be examining with critical judgment every tall tree in his neighborhood.

He remained in my sight ten minutes; then he stepped into a patch of gallberries. I sat where I was. I tried my best to be as silent and as motionless as the bodies lying in the ancient graves behind me. The big fellow kept me on the anxious bench for five minutes. Then he shot his great bulk into the air, beating his ponderous way into the huge pine that seemed to sentry that whole wild tract of woodland.

I marked him when he came to his limb. He sailed up to it and alighted with much scraping of bark with his No. 10 shoes. There was my gobbler poised against the warm red sky of that winter twilight. It was hard to take my sight from him; but I did so in order to get my bearings in relation to his position. His flight had brought him nearer to me than he had been on the ground. But he was still far out of gun-range.

There was no use for me to look into the graveyard, for a man cannot see a foot into such a place. I glanced down the dim pinewood road. A moving object along its edge attracted my attention. It skulked. It seemed to flit like a ghostly thing from pine to pine. But, though I was near a cemetery, I knew I was looking at no "haunt." It was Dade Saunders.

He had roosted the gobbler, and he was trying to get up to him. Moreover, he was at least fifty yards closer to him than I was. I felt like shouting to him to get off my land; but then a better thought came. I pulled out my turkey call.

The first note was good, as was intended. But after that there came some heart-stilling squeaks and shrills. In the dusk I noted two things; I saw Dade make a furious gesture, and at almost the same instant the old gobbler launched out from the pine, winging a lordly way far across the graveyard thicket. I walked down slowly and peeringly to meet Dade.

"Your call's broke," he announced.

"What makes you think so?" I asked.

"Sounds awful funny to me," he said; "more than likely it might scare a turkey. Seen him lately?" he asked.

"You are better at seeing that old bird than I am, Dade."

Thus I put him off; and shortly thereafter we parted. He was sure that I had not seen the gobbler; and that suited me all right.

Then came the day of days. I was up at dawn, and when certain red lights between the stems of the pines announced daybreak, I was at the far southern end of the plantation, on a road on either side of which were good turkey woods. I just had a notion that my gobbler might be found there, as he had of late taken to roosting in a tupelo swamp near the river, and adjacent to these woodlands.

Where some lumbermen had cut away the big timber, sawing the huge short-leaf pines close to the ground, I took my stand (or my seat) on one of these big stumps. Before me was a tangle of undergrowth; but it was not very thick or high. It gave me the screen I wanted; but if my turkey came out through it, I could see to shoot.

It was just before sunrise that I began to call. It

was a little early in the year (then the end of February) to lure a solitary gobbler by a call; but otherwise the chance looked good. And I am vain enough to say that my willow box was not broken that morning. Yet it was not I but two Cooper's hawks that got the old wily rascal excited.

They were circling high and crying shrilly over a certain stretch of deep woodland; and the gobbler, undoubtedly irritated by the sounds, or at least not to be outdone by two mere marauders on a domain which he felt to be his own, would gobble fiercely every time one of the hawks would cry. The hawks had their eye on a building site; wherefore their excited maneuvering and shrilling continued; and as long as they kept up their screaming, so long did the wild gobbler answer in rivalry or provoked superiority, until his wattles must have been fiery red and near to bursting.

I had an idea that the hawks were directing some of their crying at the turkey, in which case the performance was a genuine scolding match of the wilderness. And before it was over, several gray squirrels had added to the already raucous debate their impatient coughing barks. This business lasted nearly an hour, until the sun had begun to make the thickets "smoke off" their shining burden of morning dew.

I had let up on my calling for awhile; but when

the hawks had at last been silenced by the distance, I began once more to plead. Had I had a gobbler-call, the now enraged turkey would have come to me as straight as a surveyor runs a line. But I did my best with the one I had. I had answered by one short gobble, then by silence.

I laid down my call on the stump and took up my gun. It was in such a position that I could shoot quickly without much further motion. It is a genuine feat to shoot a turkey on the ground *after* he has made you out. I felt that a great moment was coming.

But you know how hunter's luck sometimes turns. Just as I thought it was about time for him to be in the pine thicket ahead of me, when, indeed, I thought I had heard his heavy but cautious step, from across the road, where lay the companion tract of turkey-woods to the one I was in, came a delicately pleading call from a hen turkey. The thing was irresistible to the gobbler; but I knew it to be Dade Saunders. What should I do?

At such a time a man has to use all the headwork he has. And in hunting I had long since learned that that often means not to do a darn thing but to sit tight. All I did was to put my gun to my face. If the gobbler was going to Dade, he might pass me. I had started him coming; if Dade kept him going, he might run within hailing distance. Dade was farther back in the woods than I was. I waited.

No step was heard. No twig was snapped. But suddenly, fifty yards ahead of me, the great bird emerged from the thicket of pines. For an instant the sun gleamed on his royal plumage. My gun was on him, but the glint of the sun along the barrel dazzled me. I stayed my finger on the trigger. At that instant he made me out. What he did was smart. He made himself so small that I believed it to be a second turkey. Then he ran crouching through the vines and huckleberry bushes.

Four times I thought I had my gun on him, but his dodging was that of an expert. He was getting away; moreover, he was making straight for Dade. There was a small gap in the bushes sixty yards from me, off to my left. He had not yet crossed that. I threw my gun in the opening. In a moment he flashed into it, running like a racehorse. I let him have it. And I saw him go down.

Five minutes later, when I had hung him on a scrub-oak, and was admiring the entire beauty of him, a knowing, cat-like step sounded behind me.

"Well, sir," said Dade, a generous admiration for the beauty of the great bird overcoming other less kindly emotions, "so you beat me to him."

There was nothing for me to do but to agree. I

then asked Dade to walk home with me so that we might weigh him. He carried the scales well down at the 25-pound mark. An extraordinary feature of his manly equipment was the presence of three separate beards, one beneath the other, no two connected. And his spurs were respectable rapiers.

"Dade," I said, "what am I gong to do with this gobbler? I am alone here on the plantation."

The pineland poacher did not solve my problem for me.

"I tell you," said I, trying to forget the matter of the five velveted bucks, "some of the boys from down the river are going to come up on Sunday to see how he tastes. Will you join us?"

You know Dade Saunders' answer; for when a hunter refuses an invitation to help eat a wild turkey, he can be sold to a circus.

Tige's Lion

[ZANE GREY]

Sportsmen who have hunted mountain lions are familiar with the details. The rock-ribbed ravines and spear-pointed pines, the patches of snow on the slopes, and the dry stone dust under the yellow cliffs with its pungent animal odor—these characterize the home of the big cat. The baying of the hounds, the cautious pursuit on foot or the long thrilling chase on horseback, ending before a dark cave or under a pine, and the "stand and deliver" with a heavy rifle—these are the features.

I have a story to tell of a hunt that was different.

The time was in May. With Buffalo Jones, the old plainsman, and his cowboys, I was camped on the northern rim of the Grand Canyon of Arizona, in what the Indians once named the Siwash. This heavily timbered plateau, bounded on three sides by the desert and on the fourth side by that strange delusive cleft called the canyon, is as wild and lonely, and as beautiful a place as was ever visited by man. Buckskin Mountain surmounts the plateau, and its innumerable breaks or ravines slope gently into the canyon. Here range thousands of deer and wild mustangs, and mountain lions live fat and unmolested.

On the morning of May 12, when Jones routed us out at five o'clock, as was his custom, a white frost, as deep as a light snow, clothed the forest. The air was nipping. An eager, crackling welcome came from the blazing campfire. Jim raked the hot coals over the lid of his oven. Frank and Lawson trooped in with the horses. Jones, as usual, had trouble with his hounds, particularly the ever-belligerent Tige.

Hounds in that remote section of Arizona retain a majority of their primitive instincts. Most of the time the meat they get they "rustle" for. So, taking the hard life into consideration, Jones' dogs were fairly well-behaved. Tige, a large-framed yellow bloodhound, was young, intractable, and as fierce as a tiger—whence his name. According to the cowboys, Tige was a cross between a locoed coyote and a maverick; in Jones' idea he had all the points of a great lion dog, only he needed his spirit curbed. Tige chased many a lion; he got tongue lashings and lashings of other kind, and even charge of fine shot; but his spirit remained untamed.

We had a captive lion in camp—one Jones had lassoed and brought in a few days before—and Tige had taken the matter as a direct insult to himself. Fight he would, and there was no use to club him. And on this morning when Jones slipped his chain he made for the lion again. After sundry knocks and scratches we dragged Tige to the campfire while we ate breakfast. Even then, with Jones' powerful grasp on his collar, he vented his displeasure and growled. The lion crouched close behind the pine and watched the hound with somber fiery eyes.

"Hurry, boys!" called Jones, in his sharp voice. "We'll tie up a lion this morning, sure as you're born. Jim, you and Lawson stick with us to-day. Yesterday, if we hadn't split, and lost each other, we'd have got one of those lions. If we get separated, keep yelling our signal."

Then he turned to me and shook his big finger: "Listen. I want you to hold in that black demon of a horse you're riding. He'll kill you if you are not careful. He hasn't been broke long. A year ago he was leading a band of wild mustangs over the mountain. Pull him in; hold him tight!"

"Which way?" asked Frank, as he swung into his saddle.

"I reckon it doesn't much matter," replied Jones, with his dry, grim chuckle. "We run across lion sign everywhere, don't we? Let's circle through the woods while the frost stays on."

We rode out under the stately silvered pines, down the long white aisles, with the rising sun tingeing the forest a delicate pink. The impatient hounds, sniffing and whining, trotted after Jones. They crossed fresh deer tracks with never a sign. Here and there deer, a species of mule deer almost as large as elk, bounded up the slopes. A mile or more from camp we ran over a lion trail headed for the mountain.

Sounder, the keenest hound we had, opened up first and was off like a shot. Tige gave tongue and leaped after him; then old Mose, with his short bark, led the rest of the pack. Our horses burst into action like a string of racers at the post. With Frank on his white mustang setting the pace, we drove through the forest glades swift as the wind.

"A hot trail, boys! Hi! Hi! Hi!" yelled Jones.

No need was there to inspire us. The music of the hounds did that. We split the cold air till it sang in our ears; we could scarcely get our breath, and no longer smelt the pine. The fresh and willing horses stretched lower and lower. The hounds passed out of sight into the forest, but their yelps and bays, now low, now clear, floated back to us. Either I forgot Jones' admonition or disregarded it, for I gave my horse, Satan, free rein and, without my realizing it at the time, he moved out ahead of the bunch. Compared to the riders in my rear I was a poor horseman, but as long as I could stick on, what did I care for that? Riding Satan was like sailing on a feather in a storm. Something wild in my blood leaped. My greatest danger lay in the snags and branches of the pines. Half the time I hugged Satan's neck to miss them. Many a knock and a brush I got. Looking backward once I saw I was leaving my companions, and grimly recalling former chases, in the finish of which I had not shown, I called to Satan.

"On! On! On, old fellow! This is our day!"

Then it seemed he had not been running at all. How he responded! His light, long powerful stride was a beautiful thing. The cold, sweet pine air, cutting between my teeth, left a taste in my mouth, and it had the exhilaration of old wine. I rejoiced in the wildness of movement and the indescribable blurred black and white around me; in sheer madness of sensorial perception I let out ringing yells. It was as if I were alone in the woods; it was all mine, and there was joy of chase, of action and of life.

The trail began to circle to the southwest, and in the next mile turned in the direction from which it had come. This meant the lion had probably been close at hand when we struck his trail, and hearing the hounds he had made for the canyon. Down the long, slightly swelling slope Satan thundered, and the pines resembled fence-pickets from a coasting sled. Often I saw gray, bounding flashes against the white background, and knew I had jumped deer. I wondered if any of the hounds were at fault, for sometimes they became confused at the crossing of a fresher scent. Satan kept a steady gait for five miles down the forest slope, and then raced out of the pines into a growth of scrubby oak. I knew I was not now far from the rim of the canyon, and despaired of coming up with the lion. Suddenly I realized I was not following a trail, as the frost had disappeared in the open. Neither did I hear the baying of the hounds. I hauled Satan up and, listening, heard no sound.

"Waa-hoo! Waa-hoo!" I yelled our signal cry. No answer came: only the haunting echo. While I was vainly trying to decide what to do, the dead silence was sharply broken by the deep bay of a hound. It was Tige's voice. In another second I had Satan plunging through the thicket of short oaks. Soon we were among the piñons near the rim of the canyon. Again I reined Satan to a standstill. From this point I could see out into the canyon, and as always, even under the most exciting circumstances, I drew a sharp breath at the wonder, the mystery, the sublimity of the scene. The tips of yellow crags and gray mesas and red turrets rose out of the blue haze of distance. The awful chasm, eighteen miles wide and more than a mile deep, stretched away clear and vividly outlined in the rare atmosphere for a hundred miles. The canyon seemed still wrapped in slumber, and a strange, vast silence that was the silence of ages, hung over the many-hued escarpments and sculptured domes.

Tige's bay, sounding close at hand, startled me and made Satan jump. I slid to the ground, and pulling my little Remington from the saddle, began hunting in the piñons for the hound.

Presently I sighted him, standing with his front paws against a big piñon. Tige saw me, wagged his tail, howled and looked up. Perhaps twenty feet from the ground a full-grown lion stood on branches that were swaying with his weight. He glared down at Tige and waved his long tail. He had a mean face, snarling, vicious. His fat sides heaved and I gathered he was not used to running, and had been driven to his limit.

"Tige, old boy, you're the real thing!" I yelled. "Keep him there!" For an instant I fingered the safety catch on my automatic. I did not much fancy being alone with that old fellow. I had already seen a grim, snarling face and outstretched claws in the air before my eyes—and once was enough! Still I did not want to kill him. Finally I walked cautiously to within fifty feet of him, and when he showed resentment in a slowly crouching movement I hastily snapped a picture of him. Hardly had I turned the film round when he leaped from the tree and bounded away. Knowing he would make for the rim and thus escape I dropped my camera and grabbed up the rifle. But I could not cut loose on him, because Tige kept nipping him, and I feared I might shoot the hound. Tige knew as well as I the intention of the lion and—brave fellow!—he ran between the beast and the canyon and turned him towards the woods. At this great work on the part of Tige I yelled frantically and dashed for my horse. Though the lion had passed close, Satan had not moved from his tracks.

"Hi! Hi! Hi! Take him, Tige!" I screamed, as the black launched out like an arrow.

On the open flat I spied Tige and his quarry, resembling yellow flashes in the scrub oak; and twice the hound jumped the lion. I swore in my teeth. The brave and crazy dog was going to his death. Satan fairly crashed through the thicket and we gained. I saw we were running along a cut-in from the main rim wall, and I thought the lion was making for a break where he could get down. Suddenly I saw him leap high into a pine on the edge of the forest. When I came up Tige was trying to climb the tree.

"Tige, old boy, I guess Jones had you sized up

right," I cried, as I dismounted. "If that brute jumps again it will be his last."

At this moment I heard a yell, and I sent out three "Waa-hoos," which meant "come quickly!" In a few moments Sounder burst out of the forest, then Don, then Mose. How they did yelp! I heard the pounding of hoofs, more yells, and soon Frank dashed into the open, followed by the others. The big tawny lion was in plain sight, and as each hunter saw him a wild yell pealed out.

"Hi! Hi! There he is! Tige, you're the stuff!" cried Jones, whirling off his horse. "You didn't split on deer trails, like the rest of these blasted long-eared canines. You stuck to him, old dog! Well, he's your lion. Boys, spread out now and surround the tree. This is a good tree and I hope we can hold him here. If he jumps he'll get over the rim, sure. Make all the racket you can, and get ready for work when I rope him."

Sounder, Mose, Ranger and Don went wild while Jones began climbing the tree, and as for Tige, he went through antics never before seen in a dog. Jones climbed slowly, laboriously, with his lasso trailing behind him, his brawny arms bare. How grim and cool he looked! I felt sorry for the lion.

"Look out!" called Jim. "Shore thet lion means biz."

"Jones, he's an old cuss, an' won't stand no foolin'," said Frank.

The old buffalo hunter climbed just the same, calmly and deliberately, as if he were unaware of danger.

Lawson, who was afraid of nothing on earth except lions, edged farther and farther from under the pine. The lion walked back up the limb he had gone down, and he hissed and growled. When Jones reached the first fork, the lion spat. His eyes emitted flames; his sharp claws dug into the bark of the limb; he began to show restlessness and fear. All at once he made a quick start, apparently to descend and meet Jones. We yelled like a crew of demons, and he slipped back a bit.

"Far enough!" yelled Frank, and his voice rang.

"Cut me a pole," called Jones.

In a twinkling Frank procured a long sapling and handed it up. Jones hung the noose of his lasso on it, and slowly extended it toward the lion. I snapped a picture here, and was about to take another when Jim yelled to me.

"Here, you with the rifle! Be ready. Shore we'll have hell in a minute."

Hell there was, in less time. With the dexterity of a conjuror Jones slipped the noose over the head of the lion and tightened it. Spitting furiously the lion bit, tore and clawed at the rope.

"Pull him off, boys! Now! Hurry, while the rope is over that short limb. Then we'll hang him in the air for a minute while I come down and lasso his paws. Pull! Pull!"

The boys pulled with all their might but the lion never budged.

"Pull him off, dang it! Pull!" impatiently yelled Jones, punching the lion with the pole.

But the powerful beast would not be dislodged. His long body lengthened on the limb and his great muscles stood out in ridges. There was something grand in his defiance and his resistance. Suddenly Jones grasped the lasso and slid down it, hand over hand.

I groaned in my spirit. What a picture to miss! There I was with a rifle, the only one in the party, and I had to stand ready to protect life if possible— and I had to watch a rare opportunity, one in a life-time, pass without even a try. It made me sick.

The men strained on the lasso, and shouted; the hounds whined, quivered and leaped into the air; the lion hugged the branch with his brawny paws.

"Throw your weight on the rope," ordered Jones.

For an instant the lion actually held the men off the ground; then with a scratching and tearing of bark he tumbled. But Jones had not calculated on the strength of the snag over which he expected to hang the lion. The snag was rotten; it broke. The lion whirled in the air. Crash! He had barely missed Lawson.

In a flash the scene changed from one of half-comic excitement to one of terrible danger and probably tragedy. There was a chorus of exclamation, and snarls and yelps, all coming from a cloud of dust. Then I saw a yellow revolving body in the midst of furry black whirling objects. I dared not shoot for fear of hitting my friends. Out of this snarling melee the lion sprang towards freedom. Jones pounced upon the whipping lasso, Frank and Jim were not an instant behind him, and the dogs kept at the heels of the lion. He turned on them like an exploding torpedo; then, giving a tremendous bound, straightened the lasso and threw the three men flat on their faces. But they held on.

Suddenly checked, the lion took a side jump bringing the tight lasso in connection with Lawson's flying feet. The frightened fellow had been trying to get out of the way. The lasso tripped him, giving him a hard fall. I tried to bring my rifle to bear just as the lion savagely turned on Lawson. But the brute was so quick, the action of the struggling men so confused and fast that it was impossible. I heard Jones bawl out some unintelligible command; I heard Lawson scream; I saw the flaming-eyed brute, all instinct with savage life, reach out with both huge paws.

It was at this critical instant that Tige bowled pell-mell into the very jaws of the lion. Then began a terrific wrestling combat. The lasso flew out of the hands of Frank and Jim, but the burly Jones, like his great dog, held on. Tige and the lion, fighting tooth and claw, began to roll down the incline. Jones was pulled to his feet, thrown flat again and dragged.

"Grab the rope!" he roared.

But no one could move. Jones rose to his knees, then fell, and lost the lasso.

Hound and lion in a savage clutch of death whirled down, nearer and nearer to the rim wall of the canyon. As they rolled I heard the rend and tear of hide. I knew Tige would never let go, even if he could, and I opened up with the automatic.

I heard the spats of the bullets, and saw fur, blood and gravel fly. On the very verge of the precipice the lion stretched out convulsively. Tige clung to his neck with a grim hold. Then they slipped over the wall.

Silence for a long second—then crash! There came up the rattle of stones, silence for a palpitating second—then crash! It was heavier, farther down and followed by a roar of sliding stones. Silence for a long, long moment. Finally a faint faraway sound which died instantly. The lion king lay at the foot of his throne and Tige lay with him.

Red Letter Days in British Columbia

[LIEUTENANT TOWNSEND WHELEN]

In the month of July, 1901, my partner, Bill Andrews, and I were at a small Hudson Bay post in the northern part of British Columbia, outfitting for a long hunting and exploring trip in the wild country to the North. The official map showed this country as "unexplored," with one or two rivers shown by dotted lines. This map was the drawing card which had brought us thousands of miles by rail, stage and pack train to this out-of-the-way spot. By the big stove in the living room of the factor's house we listened to weird tales of this north country, of its enormous mountains and glaciers, its rivers and lakes and of the quantities of game and fish. The factor told us of three men who had tried to get through there in the Klondike rush several years before and had not been heard from yet. The trappers and Siwashes could tell us of trails which ran up either side of the Scumscum, the river on which the post stood, but no one knew what lay between that and the Yukon to the north.

We spent two days here outfitting and on the morning of the third said goodbye to the assembled population and started with our pack train up the east bank of the Scumscum. We were starting out to live and travel in an unknown wilderness for over six months, and our outfit may perhaps interest my readers: We had two saddle horses, four pack horses and a dog. A small tent formed one pack cover. We had ten heavy army blankets, which we used for saddle blankets while traveling, they being kept clean by using canvas sweat pads under them. We were able to pack 150 pounds of grub on each horse, divided up as nearly as I can remember as follows: One hundred and fifty pounds flour, 50 pounds sugar, 30 pounds beans, 10 pounds rice, 10 pounds dried apples, 20 pounds prunes, 30 pounds corn meal, 20 pounds oatmeal, 30 pounds potatoes, 10 pounds onions, 50 pounds bacon, 25 pounds salt, 1 pound pepper, 6 cans baking powder, 10 pounds soap, 10 pounds tobacco, 10 pounds tea, and a few little incidentals weighing probably 10 pounds. We took two extra sets of shoes for each horse, with tools for shoeing, 2 axes, 25 boxes of wax matches, a large can of gun oil, canton flannel for gun rags, 2 cleaning rods, a change of underclothes, 6 pairs of socks and 6 moccasins each, with buckskin for resoling, toilet articles, 100 yards of fishing line, 2 dozen fish hooks, an oil stove, awl, file, screw-driver, needles and thread, etc.

For cooking utensils we had 2 frying pans, 3 kettles to nest, 2 tin cups, 3 tin plates and a gold pan. We took 300 cartridges for each of our rifles. Bill carried a .38-55 Winchester, model '94, and I had my old .40-72 Winchester, model '95, which had proved too reliable to relinquish for a high-power small bore. Both rifles were equipped with Lyman sights and carefully sighted. As a precaution we each took along extra front sights, firing pins and main-springs, but did not have a chance to use them. I loaded the ammunition for both rifles myself, with black powder, smokeless priming, and lead bullets. Both rifles proved equal to every emergency.

Where the post stood the mountains were low and covered for the most part with sage brush, with here and there a grove of pines or quaking aspen. As our pack train wound its way up the narrow trail above the river bank we saw many Siwashes spearing salmon, a very familiar sight in that country. These gradually became fewer and fewer, then we passed a miner's cabin and a Siwash village with its little log huts and its hay fields, from which grass is cut for the winter consumption of the horses. Gradually all signs of civilization disappeared, the mountains rose higher and higher, the valley became a canon, and the roar of the river increased, until finally the narrowing trail wound around an outrageous corner with the river a thousand feet below, and looming up in front of us appeared a range of snow-capped mountains, and thus at last we were in the haven where we would be.

That night we camped on one of the little pine-covered benches above the canon. My, but it was good to get the smell of that everlasting sage out of our nostrils, and to take long whiffs of the balsam-ladened air! Sunset comes very late at this latitude in July, and it was an easy matter to wander up a little draw at nine in the evening and shoot the heads of three grouse. After supper it was mighty good to lie and smoke and listen to the tinkle of the horse bells as they fed on the luscious mountain grass. We were old campmates, Bill and I, and it took us back to many trips we had had before, which were, however, to be surpassed many times by this one. I can well remember how as a boy, when I first took to woods loafing, I used to brood over a little work which we all know so well, entitled, "Woodcraft," by that grand old man, "Nessmuk," and particularly that part where he relates about his eight-day tramp through the then virgin wilderness of Michigan. But here we were, starting out on a trip which was to take over half a year, during which time we were destined to cover over 1,500 miles of unexplored mountains, without the sight of a human face or an axe mark other than our own.

The next day after about an hour's travel, we passed the winter cabin of an old trapper, now deserted, but with the frames for stretching bear skins and boards for marten pelts lying around— betokening the owner's occupation. The dirt roof was entirely covered with the horns of deer and mountain sheep, and we longed to close our jaws on some good red venison. Here the man-made trails came to an end, and henceforth we used the game trails entirely. These intersect the country in every direction, being made by the deer, sheep and caribou in their migrations between the high and low altitudes. In some places they were hardly discernible, while in others we followed them for days, when they were as plainly marked as the bridle paths in a city park. A little further on we saw a whole family of goats sunning themselves on a high bluff across the river, and that night we dined on the ribs of a fat little spike buck which I shot in the park where we pitched our tent.

To chronicle all the events which occurred on that glorious trip would, I fear, tire my readers, so I will choose from the rich store certain ones which have made red-letter days in our lives. I can recollect but four days when we were unable to kill enough game or catch enough fish to keep the table well supplied, and as luck would have it, those four days came together, and we nearly starved. We had been camped for about a week in a broad wooded valley, having a glorious loaf after a hard struggle across a mountain pass, and were living on trout from a little stream alongside camp, and grouse which were in the pine woods by the thousands. Tiring of this diet we decided to take a little side trip and get a deer or two, taking only our three fattest horses and leaving the others behind to fatten up on the long grass in the valley, for they had become very poor owing to a week's work high up above timber line. The big game here was all high up in the mountains to escape the heat of the valley. So we started one morning, taking only a little tea, rice, three bannocks, our bedding and rifles, thinking that we would enjoy living on meat straight for a couple of days. We had along with us a black mongrel hound named Lion, belonging to Bill. He was a fine dog on grouse but prone to chase a deer once in a while.

About eight miles up the valley could be seen a high mountain of green serpentine rock and for many days we had been speculating on the many fine bucks which certainly lay in the little ravines around the base, so we chose this for our goal. We made the top of the mountain about three in the afternoon, and gazing down on the opposite side we saw a little lake with good horse feed around it and determined to camp there. About half way down we jumped a doe and as it stood on a little hummock Bill blazed away at it and undershot. This was too much for Lion, the hound, and he broke after the deer, making the mountainside ring with his baying for half an hour. Well, we hunted all the next day, and the next, and never saw a hair. That dog had chased the deer all out of the country with his barking.

By this time our little grub-stake of rice, bannocks and tea was exhausted, and, to make things worse, on the third night we had a terrific hail storm, the stones covering the ground three inches deep. Breakfast the next morning consisted of tea alone and we felt pretty glum as we started out, determining that if we did not find game that day we would pull up stakes for our big camp in the valley. About one o'clock I struck a fresh deer trail and had not followed it long before three or four others joined it, all traveling on a game trail which led up a valley. This valley headed up about six miles from our camp in three little ravines, each about four miles long. When I got to the junction of these ravines it was getting dark and I had to make for camp. Bill was there before me and had the fire going and some tea brewing, but nothing else. He had traveled about twenty miles that day and had not seen a thing. I can still see the disgusted look on his face when he found

I had killed nothing. We drank our tea in silence, drew our belts tighter and went to bed.

The next morning we saddled up our horses and pulled out. We had not tasted food for about sixty hours and were feeling very faint and weak. I can remember what an effort it was to get into the saddle and how sick and weak I felt when old Baldy, my saddle horse, broke into a trot. Our way back led near the spot where I had left the deer trail the night before, and we determined to ride that way hoping that perhaps we might get a shot at them. Bill came first, then Loco, the pack horse, and I brought up the rear. As we were crossing one of the little ravines at the head of the main valley Loco bolted and Bill took after him to drive him back into the trail. I sat on my horse idly watching the race, when suddenly I saw a mouse-colored flash and then another and heard the thump, thump of cloven feet. Almost instantly the whole ravine seemed to be alive with deer. They were running in every direction. I leaped from my horse and cut loose at the nearest, which happened to be a doe. She fell over a log and I could see her tail waving in little circles and knew I had her. Then I turned on a big buck on the other side of the ravine and at the second shot he stumbled and rolled into the little stream. I heard Bill shooting off to the left and yelled to him that we had enough, and he soon joined me, saying he had a spike buck down. It was the work of but a few minutes to dress the deer and soon we had a little fire going and the three livers hanging in little strips around it. Right here we three, that is, Bill, the dog and myself, disposed of a liver apiece, and my! how easily and quickly it went—the first meat in over a week. Late that night we made our horse camp in the lower valley, having to walk all the way as our horses packed the meat. The next day was consumed entirely with jerking meat, cooking and eating. We consumed half the spike buck that day. When men do work such as we were doing their appetites are enormous, even without a fast of four days to sharpen them up.

One night I well remember after a particularly hard day with the pack train through a succession of wind-falls. We killed a porcupine just before camping and made it into a stew with rice, dough balls, onions and thick gravy, seasoned with curry. It filled the kettle to within an inch of the top and we ate the whole without stopping, whereat Bill remarked that it was enough for a whole boarding-house. According to the catalogue of Abercrombie and Fitch that kettle held eight quarts.

We made it the rule while our horses were in condition, to travel four days in the week, hunt two and rest one. Let me chronicle a day of traveling; it may interest some of you who have never traveled with a pack train. Arising at the first streak of dawn, one man cooked the breakfast while the other drove in the horses. These were allowed to graze free at every camping place, each horse having a cow bell around its neck, only Loco being hobbled, for he had a fashion of wandering off on an exploring expedition of his own and leading all the other horses with him. The horses were liable to be anywhere within two miles of camp, and it was necessary to get behind them to drive them in. Four miles over these mountains would be considered a pretty good day's work in the East. Out here it merely gave one an appetite for his breakfast. If you get behind a pack of well-trained horses they will usually walk right straight to camp, but on occasions I have walked, thrown stones and cussed from seven until twelve before I managed to get them in. Sometimes a bear will run off a pack of horses. This happened to us once and it took two days to track them to the head of a canon, fifteen miles off, and then we had to break Loco all over again.

Breakfast and packing together would take an hour, so we seldom got started before seven o'clock. One of us rode first to pick out the trail, then followed the four pack horses and the man in the rear, whose duty it was to keep them in the trail and going along. Some days the trail was fine, running along the grassy south hillsides with fine views of the snowcapped ranges, rivers, lakes and glaciers; and on others it was one continual struggle over fallen logs, boulders, through ice-cold rivers, swifter than the Niagara rapids, and around bluffs so high that we could scarcely distinguish the outlines of the trees below. Suppose for a minute that you have the job of keeping the horses in the trail. You ride behind the last horse, lazily watching the train. You do not hurry them as they stop for an instant to catch at a whiff of bunch grass beside the trail. Two miles an hour is all the speed you can hope to make. Suddenly one horse will leave the trail enticed by some particularly green grass a little to one side, and leaning over in your saddle you pick up a stone and hurl it at the delinquent, and he falls into line again. Then everything goes well until suddenly one of the pack horses breaks off on a faint side trail going for all he is worth. You dig in your spurs and follow him down the mountain side over rocks and down timber until he comes to a stop half a mile below in a thicket of quaking aspen. You extricate him and drive him back. The next thing you know one of the horses starts to buck and you notice that his pack is turning; then everything starts at once. The pack slides between the horse's legs, he bucks all the harder, the frying pan comes loose, a side pack comes off and the other horses fly in every direction. Perhaps in an hour you have corralled the horses, repacked the cause of your troubles and are hitting the trail again. In another day's travel the trail may lead over down timber and big boulders and for eight solid hours you are whipping the horses to make them jump the obstructions, while your companion is pulling at the halters.

Rustling with a pack train is a soul-trying occupation. Where possible we always aimed to go into camp about three in the afternoon. Then the horses got a good feed before dark—they will not feed well at night—and we had plenty of time to make a comfortable camp and get a good supper. We seldom pitched our tent on these one-night camps unless the weather looked doubtful, preferring to make a bed of pine boughs near the fire. The blankets were laid on top of a couple of pack sheets and the tent over all.

For several days we had been traveling thus, looking for a pass across a long snow-capped mountain range which barred our way to the north. Finally we found a pass between two large peaks where we thought we could get through, so we started up. When we got up to timber-line the wind was blowing so hard that we could not sit on our horses. It would take up large stones the size of one's fist and hurl them down the mountain side. It swept by us cracking and roaring like a battery of rapid-fire guns. To cross was impossible, so we back-tracked a mile to a spot where a little creek crossed the trail, made camp and waited. It was three days before the wind went down enough to allow us to cross.

The mountain sheep had made a broad trail through the pass and it was easy to follow, being mostly over shale rock. That afternoon, descending the other side of the range, we camped just below timber line by a little lake of the most perfect emerald hue I have ever seen. The lake was about a mile long. At its head a large glacier extended way up towards the peaks. On the east was a wall of bright red rock, a thousand feet high, while to the west the hillside was covered with dwarf pine trees, some of them being not over a foot high and full-grown at that. Below our camp the little stream, the outlet of the lake, bounded down the hillside in a succession of waterfalls. A more beautiful picture I have yet to see. We stayed up late that night watching it in the light of the full moon and thanked our lucky stars that we were alive. It was very cold; we put on all the clothes we owned and turned in under seven blankets. The heavens seemed mighty near, indeed, and the stars crackled and almost exploded with the still silver mountains sparkling all around. We could hear the roar of the waterfalls below us and the bells of the horses on the hillside above. Our noses were very cold. Far off a coyote howled and so we went to sleep—and instantly it was morning.

I arose and washed in the lake. It was my turn to cook, but first of all I got my telescope and looked around for signs of game. Turning the glass to the top of the wooded hillside, I saw something white moving, and getting a steady position, I made it out to be the rump of a mountain sheep. Looking carefully I picked out four others. Then I called Bill. The sheep were mine by right of discovery, so we traded the cook detail and I took my rifle and belt, stripped to trousers, moccasins and shirt, and started out, going swiftly at first to warm up in the keen mountain air. I kept straight up the hillside until I got to the top and then started along the ridge toward the sheep. As I crossed a little rise I caught sight of them five hundred yards ahead, the band numbering about fifty. Some were feeding, others were bedded down in some shale. From here on it was all stalking, mostly crawling through the small trees and bushes which were hardly knee-high. Finally, getting within one hundred and fifty yards, I got a good, steady prone position between the bushes, and picking out the largest ram, I got the white Lyman sight nicely centered behind his shoulder and very carefully and gradually I pressed the trigger. The instant the gun went off I knew he was mine, for I could call the shot exactly. Instantly the sheep were on the move. They seemed to double up, bunch and then vanish. It was done so quickly that I doubt if I could have gotten in another shot even if I had wished it. The ram I had fired at was knocked completely off its feet, but picked himself up instantly and started off with the others; but after he had run about a hundred yards I saw his head drop and turning half a dozen somersaults, he rolled down the hill and I knew I had made a heart shot. His horns measured 16½ inches at the base, and the nose contained an enormous bump, probably caused in one of his fights for the supremacy of the herd.

I dressed the ram and then went for the horses. Bill, by this time, had everything packed up, so after going up the hill and loading the sheep on my saddle horse, we started down the range for a region where it was warmer and less strenuous and where the horse feed was better. That night we had mountain sheep ribs—the best meat that ever passed a human's mouth—and I had a head worth bringing home. A 16½-inch head is very rare in these days. I believe the record head measured about 19 inches. I remember distinctly, however, on another hunt in the Lillooet district of British Columbia, finding in the long grass of a valley the half-decayed head of an enormous ram. I measured the pith of the skull where the horn had been and it recorded 18 inches. The horn itself must have been at least 21 inches. The ram probably died of old age or was unable to get out of the high altitude when the snow came.

We journeyed on and on, having a glorious time in the freedom of the mountains. We were traveling in a circle, the diameter of which was about three hundred miles. One day we struck an enormous glacier and had to bend way off to the right to avoid it. For days as we travelled that glacier kept us company. It had its origin way up in a mass of peaks and perpetual snow, being fed from a dozen valleys. At least six moraines could be distinctly seen on its surface, and the air in its vicinity was decidedly cool. Where we first struck it it was probably six miles wide and I believe it was not a bit less than fifty miles long. We named it Chilco glacier, because it undoubtedly drained into a large lake of that name near the coast. At this point we were not over two hundred miles from the Pacific Ocean.

As the leaves on the aspen trees started to turn we gradually edged around and headed toward our starting point, going by another route, however, trusting to luck and the careful map we had been making to bring us out somewhere on the Scumscum river above the post. The days were getting short now and the nights very cold. We had to travel during almost all the daylight and our horses started to get poor. The shoes we had taken for them were used up by this time and we had to avoid as much as possible the rocky country. We travelled fast for a month until we struck the headwaters of the Scumscum; then knowing that we were practically safe from being snowed up in the mountain we made a permanent camp on a hillside where the horsefeed was good and started to hunt and tramp to our hearts' delight, while our horses filled up on the grass. We never killed any more game than we could use, which was about one animal every ten days. In this climate meat will keep for a month if protected from flies in the daytime and exposed to the night air after dark.

We were very proud of our permanent camp. The tent was pitched under a large pine tree in a thicket of willows and quaking aspen. All around it was built a windbreak of logs and pine boughs, leaving in front a yard, in the center of which was our camp fire. The windbreak went up six feet high and when a fire was going in front of the tent we were as warm as though in a cabin, no matter how hard the wind blew. Close beside the tent was a little spring, and a half a mile away was a lake full of trout from fifteen pounds down. We spent three days laying in a supply of firewood. Altogether it was the best camp I ever slept in. The hunting within tramping distance was splendid. We rarely hunted together, each preferring to go his own way. When we did not need meat we hunted varmints, and I brought in quite a number of prime coyote pelts and one wolf. One evening Bill staggered into camp with a big mountain lion over his shoulders. He just happened to run across it in a little pine thicket. That was the only one we saw on the whole trip, although their tracks were everywhere and we frequently heard their mutterings in the still evenings. The porcupines at this camp were unusually numerous. They would frequently get inside our wind break and had a great propensity for eating our soap. Lion, the hound, would not bother them; he had learned his lesson well. When they came around he would get an expression on his face as much as to say, "You give me a pain."

The nights were now very cold. It froze every night and we bedded ourselves down with lots of skins and used enormous logs on the fire so that it would keep going all night. We shot some marmots and made ourselves fur caps and gloves and patched up our outer garments with buckskin. And still the snow did not come.

One day while out hunting I saw a big goat on a bluff off to my right and determined to try to get him for his head, which appeared through my telescope to be an unusually good one. He was about half a mile off when I first spied him and the bluff extended several miles to the southwest like a great wall shutting off the view in that direction. I worked up to the foot of the bluffs and then along; climbing up several hundred feet I struck a shelf which appeared to run along the face at about the height I had seen the goat. It was ticklish work, for the shelf was covered with slide rock which I had to avoid disturbing, and then, too, in places it dwindled to a ledge barely three feet wide with about five hundred feet of nothing underneath. After about four hundred yards of this work I heard a rock fall above me and looking up saw the billy leaning over an outrageous corner looking at me. Aiming as nearly as I could straight up I let drive at the middle of the white mass. There was a grunt, a scramble and a lot of rocks, and then down came the goat, striking in between the cliff and a big boulder and not two feet from me. I fairly shivered for fear he would jump up and butt me off the ledge, but he only gave one quiver and lay still. The 330-grain bullet entering the stomach, had broken the spine and killed instantly. He was an old grandfather and had a splendid head, which I now treasure very highly. I took the head, skin, fat and some of the meat back to camp that night, having to pack it off the bluff in sections. The fat rendered out into three gold-pans full of lard. Goat-fat is excellent for frying and all through the trip it was a great saving on our bacon.

Then one night the snow came. We heard it gently tapping on the tent, and by morning there was three inches in our yard. The time had come only too soon to pull out, which we did about ten o'clock, bidding good-bye to our permanent camp with its comfortable windbreak, its fireplace, table and chairs. Below us the river ran through a canon and we had to cross quite a high mountain range to get through. As we ascended the snow got deeper and deeper. It was almost two feet deep on a level on top of the range. We had to go down a very steep hog-back, and here had trouble in plenty. The horses' feet balled up with snow and they were continually sliding. A pack horse slid down on top of my saddle horse and started him. I was on foot in front and they knocked me down and the three of us slid until stopped by a fallen tree. Such a mess I never saw. One horse was on top of another. The pack was loose and frozen ropes tangled up with everything. It took us half an hour to straighten up the mess and the frozen lash ropes cut our hands frightfully. My ankle had become slightly strained in the mix-up and for several days I suffered agonies with it. There was no stopping—we had to hit the trail hard or get snowed in. One day we stopped to hunt. Bill went out while I nursed my leg. He brought in a fine seven-point buck.

Speaking of the hunt he said: "I jumped the buck in a flat of down timber. He was going like mad about a hundred yards off when I first spied him. I threw up the old rifle and blazed away five times before he tumbled. Each time I pulled I was conscious that the sights looked just like that trademark of the Lyman sight showing the running deer and the sight. When I went over to look at the buck I had a nice little bunch of five shots right behind the shoulder. Those Lyman sights are surely the sights for a hunting rifle." Bill was one of the best shots on game I ever saw. One day I saw him cut the heads off of three grouse in trees while he sat in the saddle with his horse walking up hill. Both our rifles did mighty good work. The more I use a rifle the more I become convinced of the truth of the saying, "Beware of the man with one gun." Get a good rifle to suit you exactly. Fix the trigger pull and sights exactly as you wish them and then stick to that gun as long as it will shoot accurately and you will make few misses in the field.

Only too soon we drove our pack-train into the post. As we rode up two men were building a shack. One of them dropped a board and we nearly jumped out of our skins at the terrific noise. My! how loud everything sounded to our ears, accustomed only to the stillness of those grand mountains. We stayed at the post three days, disposing of our horses and boxing up our heads and skins, and then pulled out for civilization. Never again will such experiences come to us. The day of the wilderness hunter has gone for good. And so the hunt of our lives came to an end.

The Alaskan Grizzly

[HAROLD McCRACKEN]

The great Alaskan grizzly—the Kodiak brown bear (*Ursus middendorffi*) and its even larger Alaska Peninsula brother (*Ursus gyas*)—is probably as far famed as either the African lion or the Bengal tiger. And yet, probably less is known of its life history than of any of the other larger mammals. He is, nevertheless, a sort of fictitious by-word at the hearths of all those hunter-sportsmen who enjoy the savor of genuine hazard in their quest for sport and trophies. A beast whom most prefer to "talk" about hunting, rather than face in mortal combat. And his 1,000 to 2,000 pounds of brawn and power is unquestionably the embodiment of all that even the most adventurous care to seek. He is supreme in size, in brute power, as well as in physical dexterity, sagacity, and pernicious damnableness in the animal kingdom. And this, not in the mere belief of a casual observer, but weighed and tried on the scales of science. To go into details regarding the life history, the "whys" and "whens" and "hows" of his life career, would entail a goodly volume, which, though immensely interesting in every detail, would be far too cumbersome in such a place as this.

His home is that long, slightly curved arm that reaches out from the southwestern corner of Alaska, separating the North Pacific Ocean from the Bering Sea, and dabbling off in the spattered Aleutian Islands. The Alaska Peninsula is today one of the most wild, least visited and less known of all the districts on this continent.

But in reality, the Alaska Peninsula is, for the most part, a terribly wild Garden of Eden. Its waterways boast more fine fish than any other similar sized section of the globe; on its rounded undulating hills and tundra lands are great herds of caribou, the finest of edible flesh; it is carpeted with berry bushes; there are fine furred animals in abundance; millions of wildfowl, duck, geese, eiders, seals, sea lions; big bears—everything necessary for the welfare and happiness of primitive man. It is a truly primitive land.

While the great Alaska Peninsula bear is a carni-

vore, or flesh eater—and what applies to this bear
also applies in many respects to his brothers, the sub-
and sub-sub-species of other districts of Alaska—yet
he has frequently and correctly been called "the
great grass-eating bear" and also "the great fish-
eating bear." All animals subsist in the manner and
on the foods that demand the least efforts, hazard and
inconvenience to their life and comforts. Thus the
bears of the Alaska Peninsula have chosen fish and
grass and berries as their main diet of food, varied
with an occasional caribou, a seal, or meal from the
carcass of a dead whale or walrus washed up on
the beach. During most of the months of the year,
the streams are choked with salmon, affording him
an inexhaustible supply until well into the middle of
the winter. And as hibernation is for the most part
only an alternative for existing under winter conditions, when it is hard or sometimes impossible to get
food, and as the Alaska Peninsula is in winter moder-
ated by the warming Japan Current, making it a
quite mild and livable heath for old Gyas, he is forced
to spend but a relatively short period in the "long
sleep." This increased activity, together with the
abundance of fine food, accounts for the unusual size
to which the bears of that district grow.

And he is very much aware of his size and
strength; and the fact that he has had no outside nat-

ural enemy through the line of his ancestors has made him aggressive, haughty and overbearing, fearing nothing and crushing all that impedes his way.

Thus the Alaska Peninsula grizzly is to be found a most unscrupulous fighter, and his acquaintance with man and his high-powered rifles is as yet too short and limited to have impressed upon his brute mind that here is a most powerful mortal enemy. He usually charges when wounded, more than frequently when a female with very young cubs is suddenly surprised or attacked, and occasionally when watching a fresh "kill" or "cache," and surprised. And, if old Gyas decides to fight, woe betide our bold Nimrod unless he is a good shot and nonexcitable, or accompanied by someone who possesses these valuable faculties. For a wounded grizzly will not stop for one to reload his gun, nor pause to be shot at until the vital spot is struck. He means blood! Fifty bullets that are not placed in the proper spot will not stop him; and you can't back out once he accepts your challenge. Not that one is certain of being charged by every Alaskan grizzly that he fells; I have had even females retreat until knocked down. But these cases are really the exception, and the experiences of practically all the old bear hunters of that district—I have known most of them—will bear me out in the statement that these Alaskan griz-

zlies almost invariably charge under the three circumstances I have cited. The natives of Alaska do
not often go to look for these big bears. They have a
great deal of respect for them—as all others who
know them have.

We are at King Cove, a native village near the site
of the once famous village of Belkovski, center of
the sea otter hunting grounds of old. We are about
600 miles southwest of Kodiak, the nearest town of
over fifteen white inhabitants; and very near the
extreme western end of the Alaska Peninsula, and
almost due north of Honolulu by location. And
here, where the traveler is almost never seen, we will
start out to hunt for the biggest of carnivora—start it
by incidentally being shipwrecked, almost drowned
and getting a foot severely frozen.

It was on the morning of Wednesday, November
1, 1916, that I left King Cove in a 28-foot covered-
over powerboat with Captain Charlie Madsen. We
headed for the Isanotski Straits, at the end of the
peninsula, and the Bering Sea country, where I
intended hunting Grant's Barren Ground caribou
and the big grizzlies at several desirable localities
near the end of the peninsula.

It was cloudy; looked like another snowstorm; but
the wind being from the north, rave it might and the
low hills of the mainland would protect us until we

reached the end of the peninsula, where we could hunt bear and wait for more favorable winds. But the winds of the North are most fickle!

It was a most magnetic sight as we plied out towards the cape at the entrance of the bay, sending flock after flock of salt-water ducks flopping off over the swelling surface of the blue-green sea. An occasional seal could be seen plunging headlong into the water from the jut of a reef or an outcrop of the rocky shoreline. The hills were gray, dappled with the first settling snows of winter, and the clouds were heavy and leaden looking.

As we rounded the cape the swells became more pronounced, carrying a deep, rolling, green-sided trough. But our boat plied steadily on, plunging its nose fearlessly into the rising waves.

Breasting some five miles of rocky coastline, we rounded the second cape at the entrance to Cold (Morofski) Bay, which protrudes some twenty-five miles back into the peninsula, almost making what is to the west an island and what is to the east the end of the peninsula. As we had expected, the wind was raging out of the bay to seaward. But heading the boat's nose towards Thin Point, about ten miles distant, we started fighting our way to the protection of the opposite cape.

Madsen had been watching the sky with misgiv-

ing and shortly announced that the wind was changing to the southwest.

I naturally inquired what would be the best course
to pursue, knowing that it undoubtedly meant more
storm and that we would soon be in the thick of it.

"Cap" decided we would take a chance on reaching Thin Point before the wind had swung to the
southwest and thrown the storm in our faces. Once
behind the cape we would be safe.

But we were not halfway across when the wind,
swinging out past the protection of the peninsula
and clashing against the tide, was soon lashing the sea
into a stormy havoc. Diving into one great swell, the
wind toppled its crest over the boat, washing over-
board the hatch-cover and pouring a volume of
water into the hold upon our supplies and outfit. I
got on deck and endeavored to get a piece of canvas
nailed over the open hatchway before another big
one should pour its volume into the boat, at the same
time clinging as best I could to the pitching vessel.

In the midst of all this, and as if to impress more
forcibly upon us our insignificance in this big
affair, our engine stopped. Gas engines are hellish
things anyhow, and always buck in just the wrong
place. But one must act quickly in a case such as
this, and almost before I knew it the boat's sail was
up and we were racing back before the wind,

toward the entrance to the bay we had not long left.

I took the rope and wheel, while Madsen endeavored to get the engine running again, though vainly.

But the wind was now coming in such gusts that each one nigh turned our boat onto its nose. It was also snowing and sleeting, almost hiding the outline of the coast.

A gust hit our sail, turning the boat clear on its side, taking water over the rail, and we narrowly escaped finding ourselves in the arms of Neptune himself. Madsen left the engine and decided we would run before the wind and tack into King Cove Bay.

We crossed the entrance to the bay, driven at top speed towards the opposite cape and line of rocky reefs.

Going as close to as safe, the sail was drawn in with an endeavor to throw it to the opposite side, thus turning the boat. But the wind was too strong and the sea too rough, and try as we might, we would only be driven helplessly on towards the reef where the waves were dashing their foam and spray high in the air. Then a big wave took the flopping sail, pulling the boat over onto its side until the canvas was torn from end to end. As a last resort the anchor was thrown out; this failed to catch sufficiently to hold us and was regained at great difficulty when we saw that hitting the reef was inevitable.

The first rock of the reef that the boat hit, jammed its head through the bottom of the hull and we clambered out into the big dory we were towing and started for shore through the narrow, raging channels in the reef. But this being an open boat, it soon swamped in the breakers and we were forced to take to the water and make shore as best we could. Swimming was impossible, but keeping our heads above the water as best we could, and riding the waves, we were soon washed up on the rocky shore, like half-drowned rats.

To build a fire was impossible for lack of material; we must wait until the boat washed over the reef and was driven ashore. So, wet and cold, and facing a biting snow and sleet and rain-pelted wind, we walked back and forth over the rocks and waited.

Through all this, while we had been battling with the elements for our very lives, I had noticed with no small interest how very little the storming and havoc had inconvenienced the little creatures that made their homes in or on the sea. The ducks swam about, quacking, and apparently thoroughly enjoying their buoyant existence. So even storms at sea, it seemed, were a mere matter of relativity and part of the everyday life of those that made their home thereon.

Eventually the boat came ashore—it was fortunately high tide—and getting aboard we got out block and tackle, sunk our anchor as a deadman, and pulled the boat up as best we could. Supplies and everything were drenched and several planks in the hull were smashed.

When we had done all that we could we started for the village—a hard hike. It was well after dark when we reached the squatty barrabaras, or native dirt huts, of King Cove, and we were wet and tired and miserable—ready for a meal and the blankets.

As I began to thaw out, however, I found that part of my right foot had frozen—the leather boots I had been wearing having shrunk and stopped the circulation of blood, causing the freezing. I was laid up for over a week with my foot, though it took Madsen, with the assistance of several natives, somewhat longer to get the boat repaired and back to the village.

Such are but a bit of the "pleasures" that often come with hunting big bear at the western end of the Alaskan Peninsula.

I was especially fortunate in making a one-day bag of four of these Alaska Peninsula bears, a big female and her three yearling cubs, the latter being as large as quite mature Southern brown bears I have gotten.

Deciding to spend a day alone in the hills after caribou, I took the .30–40 Winchester—in consideration of the bear—and followed the beach of a lagoon or bay to its head about two and half miles from the village. From the head of the lagoon a valley rose at an easy pitch for about two miles to a low divide on the opposite side of which was a large valley extending out onto the Pacific. This was a very good place for caribou.

At the head of the lagoon I stopped to shoot some salt water ducks with a .22 Colt revolver, but had fired but a few shots when I was attracted by the bawling of a bear. Glancing in the direction of the sound, I saw a brown bear making a speedy, somewhat noisy, getaway up through the alders from where he had been no doubt eating salmon in the creek a few hundred yards up-valley from me. He was then a good five hundred yards distant and in the alders. I fired, hoping at least to turn him back down the hillside, but he made the top of the ridge and went over it out of sight. I started a speedy climb up through the alders towards the top, not far from where he went over. By the time I reached this, Mr. Ursus had gone down the other side and was making a "hiyu clattewa" along the opposite side of the valley. I started up the ridge toward an open space in the alders with the intent of hurrying down to the creek and descending it with hopes of heading the bear off or getting a shot at him while crossing a wide rock slide a few hundred yards below. But I had not gone a dozen steps when I saw three other bears coming along at a good pace on quite the same course that Number One had taken. This was somewhat more of a "bear party" than I had really antic-ipated inviting myself to!

I felt quite certain that they would cross a small saddle through which the previous one had passed, and I decided to wait until they had come out of this and were somewhat below me before chancing a shot. I was alone, I remembered.

Squatting down in the alders, I waited with gun ready and, I must say, nerves tense. The first one to come through the saddle was the old female, a big, high-shouldered brute that strode in a manner indi-cating it was looking for me every bit as much as I was waiting for it. She was followed by her other two yearlings—big fellows almost as tall and as broad as they were long. Being alone, and feeling that the female would undoubtedly fight, I deemed it most wise to play doubly safe. Conditions were fortu-nately in my favor. The wind was from seaward, and the alders were heavy enough to conceal me from her none too good eyesight, and it would be difficult for her to determine from just which direction the report of my rifle came. The dispatching of the old one was of course my first move. The rest would be comparatively easy. I did not have an opportunity of a good shot, however, until the three had reached the creek bed and crossed and started up along the other side. I slipped into a heavy clump of alders and waited. She was not then, I was quite sure, aware of my whereabouts at least. She lumbered slowly along, yet ever watchful, I could see. Coming out in a little open space she stopped and made an apparent survey of the surrounding vicinity. I took a coarse bead and let drive at her shoulder. I could fairly hear the bullet slap into her. With a nasal bellow she wheeled and made a vicious swipe at the nearest yearling. I fired again, at which she wheeled and charged madly along the hillside opposite me. She went into a small ravine and in a moment came up into sight on one side and stopped, snout swaying high in the air to catch a scent of the danger. I steadied my aim and at the report she went down in a heap and rolled out of sight. "A bull's-eye!" I thought, and breathed a sigh of relief.

The two cubs had made off in the opposite direction, stopping occasionally to look about. I knocked down one of these at the second shot, breaking his back, though he raised on his forelegs and bawled for all he was worth. I was about to let him have another, when out of the ravine came Mrs. Ursus, mad and apparently as much alive as ever, although dragging her right foreleg. She scrambled through the alders straight to the bawling cub. Greatly surprised, and a little uneasy, I again let drive at her. She threw her head to one side, at the same time letting forth another nasal cry. At my next shot she wheeled completely around and charged along the mountainside for a short distance with head held high and every nerve strained to its utmost to locate the cause of her molestation—snarling and bawling in a manner that made me perspire uncomfortably. She was desperate and no doubt calling upon the souls of all her past ancestors to assist her in locating the peculiar new enemy. Then she charged back to the cub. Finally she made a dash almost straight in my direction.

One does not fully appreciate the thrills of real bear hunting until he has experienced just such circumstances as this. To be alone in such a case is a quite different matter from being in company—poor though it may be.

She at last came to a standstill, standing half sidelong to me, and I clamped the gold bead square on her neck and let drive. She went down, got up, and tearing a few alders up by the roots, unwillingly sank in a heap. She had finished her career as a big brown bear on the Alaska Peninsula.

The rest was quite easy and uneventful.

With the assistance of three natives I skinned the four, took the necessary measurements for mounting, and brought the pelts in by boat. The natives, however, made a second trip, bringing in every bit of the meat of all four, salting it down for winter use. The pelts were in fine condition and beautiful specimens, the large one measuring a full ten feet. They are now in the Ohio State Museum.

It was on Sunday, November 19, 1916, that I bagged the original "bearcat"—one of the largest bears ever killed on the continent.

We were hunting around the eastern side of Frosty Peak, a high volcanic mountain towering between Morzhovi and Morofski Bays and about ten miles from the Pacific. This is about twenty miles from King Cove, near the end of the peninsula, and a very good place for big bears. It was a *big* one that I wanted now; and though numerous tracks and one medium-sized bear were seen, none were bothered until the original "bearcat" was found. That took two days under Old Frosty.

I had previously been hunting Grant's Barren Ground caribou on the Bering Sea side of the peninsula and before we landed at the foot of Frosty Peak on our return there was a good twelve inches of snow on the ground. In places it had already drifted to a depth of five feet. Bear hunting was quite an easy matter—though a little unpleasant on account of the snow and cold—as it was a small matter to track the animals. As the streams were still open and full of salmon, but a small percentage of the bruins had sought their winter quarters, the pads of their big clawed feet having beaten paths along

the iced shores of the stream where they came peri-
odically to gorge themselves.

It was late afternoon of the second day under
Frosty Peak that we found the fresh trail of our
longed-for quarry. We had been investigating the
broad alder-patched table of one of the valleys that
cut up toward the pinnacle of Old Frosty. There
were numerous tracks along the creek where the
brownies had been feasting on the silver salmon,
though no fresh ones of a really large bear. But as we
came well up to the head of the valley we saw the
well-distinguished trail of an unquestionably large
bear where it had made its way up through the snow
on the mountainside into a heavy growth of alders.
This was at the very foot of the peak and in the
highest growth of alders. Upon reaching the tracks
we were well satisfied that they could have been
made only by the paw and claw of just the bear that
we were seeking. Although it was evident that he
had been in no special hurry in making the climb,
yet it was all that a six-foot man could possibly do to
step from one track to the next.

To the left of the alder patch was a comparatively
open track of rocky ground with only a spare patch
of brush here and there. It was certain that he could
not, if still in the thicket, escape in that direction
without being noticed. But on the right there was a
low ridge, the opposite side of which dipped down

into a deep wide ravine. The alders extended to within a few yards of this ridge, and to see the other side it was necessary to mount to the top of it. Also, it was quite probable that the bear had already gone over this ridge and might then be high up in the canyon near to its hibernation quarters.

Being unable to locate the bear with my glasses, I decided to make a complete detour around the patch, to be assured whether or not he was still in there.

So leaving Charlie on the flat below, I took the two natives and started up through the alders on the trail of old Ursus. As soon as possible we mounted the ridge at the right and went along the extent of it to assure ourselves that the bear had not crossed. This he had not. But to make doubly sure that he was still in the alder patch, we went above and around it to complete the circle about the place. He was without question lying somewhere in that thicket.

Upon reaching the flat, and as a last resource, we fired several volleys up through the alders. Then one of the natives spotted him standing in a thick growth of the alders, where he had gotten up and was looking inquiringly down at us. We moved down opposite to him and I fired from the shoulder. He started off along the mountainside, like an animal that had just broken from its cage. Then I fired again. Mounting a little knoll in the open he peered dubiously down at us—in unmistakable defiance. I held on him full in the chest for my next shot, at which he let out a bellow and came for us. My shots had hit, though he had not so much as bit or clawed at the wound on either occasion—merely jumped slightly. He was then about 200 yards distant, though I was well aware of the short time that it would take him to cover that distance. And he was a big fellow—looked literally more like a load of hay than a bear, coming down the mountainside.

I had previously told the others not to shoot until I called for help, as I was anxious to fell this big brute single-handed. But on he came, and though try as I might, I could not stop him. My shots seemed to be taking no effect whatever. And then, when he had come about half the distance, I yelled "Shoot!" And I'd have liked to have done so long before. The four guns spoke simultaneously, but old Gyas still kept coming.

I squatted down in the snow, and resting my elbows on my knees, decided to take the long chance—a shot for the head. I was confident that Madsen could stop him before he reached us, and determined to take a chance shot of dropping him in a heap. The two natives, however, were not so confident and began to move backward, shooting as they went.

He turned an angle to cross a small ravine, and while he was mounting the opposite side at a decreased pace I held just forward of the snout. The first shot missed, as I saw a small flit of snow where it hit just in front of him. But at the second shot he dropped in a heap, falling on his belly with his nose run into the snow. After waiting for some moments to make certain he was beyond the trouble point, we climbed up through the alders to where he lay. The others stood by with guns ready while I went up and poked him with the end of my own gun. He was dead.

This had all taken but a few moments, though relatively it seemed a great deal longer.

He was indeed a big fellow—a genuine bearcat. We gutted him, and as it was then getting late, hit for camp. The next morning we went back to skin the animal—and no small task it was!

He had been hit twelve times, we found. Nine of the shots had entered the neck and shoulder and two in the head and one in the abdomen. One bullet had hit him squarely in the mouth, shattering the tops of his lower teeth on one side, piercing the tongue and lodging in the back of his throat. Four of the .30 caliber leads were retrieved from the shoulder, where they had not so much as reached the bone. The shot that stopped him struck well up on the brain box, but squarely enough to break the casing of the bone and penetrate the skull, though only a part of the lead entered the brain, the most of it spattering off in the fleshy part of the head. It was a lucky shot on an even more lucky day!

We estimated his live weight at from 1,600 to 1,800 pounds, and the skin at twelve feet in length. The actual measurements of the tanned skin, however, as made by Chas. A. Ziege, noted taxidermist of Spokane, Wash., are: eleven feet four inches maximum length, by ten feet six inches spread of fore legs. The skull, measured one year after killing, eighteen and one-quarter inches, or one-half inch under the world record, according to Washington, D. C., authorities.

The Plural of Moose Is Mise

[IRWIN S. COBB]

At the outset, when our expedition was still in the preparatory stages, we collectively knew a few sketchy details regarding the general architectural plan and outward aspect of the moose. One of us had once upon a time, years and years before, shot at or into—this point being debatable—a moose up in Maine. Another professed that in his youth he had seriously annoyed a moose with buckshot somewhere in Quebec. The rest of us had met the moose only in zoos with iron bars between us and him or in dining halls, where his head, projecting in a stuffed and mounted condition from the wall, gave one the feeling of dining with somebody out of the Old Testament. Speaking with regard to his family history, we understood he was closely allied to the European elk—the Unabridged told us that—and we gathered that, viewed at a distance, he rather suggested a large black mule with a pronounced Roman nose and a rustic hatrack sprouted out between his ears. Also, through our reading upon the subject, we knew that next to the buffalo he was the largest vegetarian in North America and, next to a man who believes in the forecast of a campaign manager on the eve of an election, the stupidest native mammal that we have. By hearsay we had been made aware that he possessed a magnificent sense of smell and a perfectly wonderful sense of hearing, but was woefully shy on the faculty of thought, the result being that while by the aid of his nose and his ear he might all day elude you, if then perchance you did succeed in getting within gunning range of him he was prone to remain right where he was, peering blandly at you and accommodatingly shifting his position so as to bring his shape broadside on, thereby offering a better target until you, mastering the tremors of eagerness, succeeded in implanting a leaden slug in one of his vital areas.

But, offhand, we couldn't decide what the plural of him was. Still if the plural of goose were geese and the plural of mouse were mice it seemed reasonable to assume that the plural of moose should be mise. Besides, we figured that when we had returned and met friends and told them about our trip it would sound more impressive, in fact more plural, to say that we had slain mise rather than that we had slaughtered moose. In the common acceptance of the term as now used, moose might mean one moose or a herd of them, but mise would mean at least a bag of two of these mighty creatures and from two on up to any imaginable number.

One mentally framed the conversation:

"Well, I hear you've been up in Canada moose hunting." This is the other fellow speaking. "Kill any moose?"

"Kill any moose? Huh, we did better than that—we killed mise."

So by agreement we arranged that mise it should be. This being settled we went ahead with plans for outfitting ourselves against our foray into the game country. We equipped ourselves with high-powered rifles, with patent bedding rolls, with fanciful conceits in high boots and blanket overcoats. We bought everything that the clerk in the shop, who probably had never ventured north of the Bronx in all the days of his sheltered life, thought we should buy, including wicked-looking sheath knives and hand axes to be carried in the belt, tomahawk fashion, and pocket compasses. Personally, I have never been able to figure out the exact value of a compass to a man adrift in a strange country. What is the use of knowing where north is if you don't know where *you* are? Nevertheless, I was prevailed upon to purchase a compass, along with upward of a great gross of other articles large and small which the clerk believed would be needful to one starting upon such an expedition as we contemplated.

On my account he did a deal of thinking. Not since the fall of 1917, when we were making the world safe for the sporting-goods dealers of America, could he have spent so busy and so happy an afternoon as the afternoon when I dropped in on him.

By past experience I should have known better than to permit myself to be swept off my feet by this tradesman's flood of suggestions and recommendations. Already I had an ample supply of khaki shirts that were endeared to me by associations of duck-hunting forays in North Carolina and chill evenings in an Adirondack camp and a memorable journey to Wyoming, where the sage hen abides. I treasured a pair of comfortable hunting boots that had gone twice to European battlefields and down into the Grand Canyon and up again and across the California desert, without ever breeding a blister or chafing a shin. Among my most valued possessions I counted an ancient shooting coat, wearing which I had missed quail in Kentucky, snipe on Long Island, grouse in Connecticut, doves in Georgia, and woodcock in New York State. Finally, had I but taken time for sober second consideration, I should have recalled that the guides I have from time to time known considered themselves properly accoutered for the chase when they put on the oldest suit of store clothes they owned and stuck an extra pair of wool socks in their pockets. But to the city-bred sportsman half the joy of going on a camping trip consists in getting ready for it. So eminent an authority as Emerson Hough is much given to warning the amateur sportsman against burdening himself with vain adornments, and yet I am reliably informed that the said Hough has a larger individual collection of pretty devices in canvas and leather than any person in this republic.

That clerk had a seductive way about him; he had a positive gift. Otherwise I suppose he would have been handling some line which practically sells itself, such as oil stocks or mining shares. Under the influence of his blandishments I invested in a sweater of a pattern which he assured me was being favored by the really prominent moose hunters in the current season, and a pair of corduroy hunting pants which, when walked in, gave off a pleasant swishing sound like a soft-shoe dancer starting to do a sand jig. I was particularly drawn to these latter garments as being the most vocal pants I had ever seen. As I said before, I bought ever and ever so many other things; I am merely mentioning some of the main items.

We assembled the most impassive group of guides in the whole Dominion—men who, filled with the spirit of the majestic wilds, had never been known publicly to laugh at the expense of a tender-footed stranger. They did not laugh at Harry Leon Wilson's conception of the proper equipment for a man starting upon such an excursion as this one. Wilson on being wired an invitation to go on a hunt for moose promptly telegraphed back that to the best of his recollection he had not lost any moose, but that if any of his friends had been so unfortunate or so careless as to mislay one he would gladly join in the quest for the missing. He brought along an electric flashlight, in case the search should be prolonged after nightfall, a trout rod and a camera. The guides did not laugh at Colonel Tillinghast Houston's unique notion of buying an expensive rifle and a hundred rounds of ammunition and then spending his days in camp sitting in a tent reading a history of the Maritime Provinces in two large volumes. They did not laugh at Colonel Bozeman Bulger's overseas puttees or at Damon Runyon's bowie knife, or at Major McGeehan's eight-pound cartridge belt—it weighed more than that when loaded; I am speaking of it, *net*—or at Frank Stevens' sleeping cap or at Bill MacBeth's going-away haircut—the handiwork of a barber who was a person looking with abhorrence upon the thought of leaving any hair upon the human neck when it is so easy to shave all exposed surfaces smooth and clean from a point drawn across the back of the head at the level of the tops of the ears on down as far as the rear collar button. He must have been a lover of the nude in necks, that barber.

The guides did not laugh even at my vociferous corduroys, which at every step I took, went *hist, hist*, as though entreating their wearer to be more quiet so they might the better be heard.

By a series of relay journeys we moved up across the line into Quebec, thence back again below the boundary and across the state of Maine, thence out of Maine into New Brunswick and to the thriving city of St. John, with its justly celebrated reversible falls which, by reason of the eccentricities of the tide, tumble upstream part of the time and downstream part of the time, thence by steamer across that temperamental body of water known as the Bay of Fundy, and so on into the interior of Nova Scotia. If anywhere on this continent there is a lovelier spot than the southern part of Nova Scotia in mid-fall I earnestly desire that, come next October, someone shall take me by the hand and lead me to it and let me rave. It used to be the land of Evangeline and the Acadians; now it is the land of the apple. You ran out of the finnan-haddie belt in and around Digby into the wonderful valley of the apples. On every hand are apples—on this side of the right-of-way, orchards stretching down to the blue waters of one of the most beautiful rivers in America, on that side, orchards climbing up the flanks of the rolling hills to where the combing of thick timber comes down and meets them; and everywhere, at roadside, on the verges of thickets, in pastures and old fields, are seedlings growing singly, in pairs and in clumps. They told us that the valley scenically considered is at its best in the spring after the bloom bursts out upon the trees and the whole countryside turns to one vast pink and white bridal bouquet, but hardly can one picture it revealing itself as a more delectable vision than when the first frosts have fallen and every bough of every tree is studded with red and green and yellow globes and the scent of the ripened fruit rises like an incense of spices and wine.

The transition from the pastoral to the wilderness is abrupt. You leave Annapolis Royal in a motor car—that is, you do if you follow in our footsteps—and almost immediately you strike into the big game country. Not that the big game does not lap over into the settlements and even into the larger towns on occasion, for it does. It is recorded that on a certain day a full-grown moose—and a full-grown moose is almost the largest full-grown thing you ever saw—strolled through one of the principal streets of St. John and sought to enter—this being in the old sinful times—a leading saloon. A prominent lawyer of the same city told me that some four weeks before our arrival a woman client of his, living some two miles from the corporate limits, called him on the telephone at his office to ask his professional advice as to how legally she might go about getting rid of a bull moose which insisted on frequenting her orchard and frightening her children when they went to gather pippins. She felt, she said, that a lawyer was the proper person to seek in the emergency that had arisen, seeing that the closed season for moose was still on and it would be unlawful to take a shot at the intruder, so what she particularly desired to know was whether she couldn't have him impounded for trespass or something of that nature.

But such things as these do not happen every day. Probably a man could spend months on end in St. John without seeing the first of the above-mentioned animals rambling down the sidewalk in the manner of a young moose-about-town and trying to drop into the place where the saloon used to be, only to back out again, with chagrin writ large upon his features, upon discovering that the establishment in question had been transformed into a hat store.

To meet the moose where frequently he is and not merely where occasionally he is, one must go beyond the outlying orchards and on into the vasty expanse of the real moose country—hundreds of hundreds of miles of virgin waste, trackless except for game trails and portages across the ridges between waterways. It is a country of tamaracks and hemlocks, of maples and beech and birch, of berries and flowering shrubs, of bogs and barrens and swampy swales, of great granite boulders left behind by the glaciers when the world was young and thawing, of countless lakes and brawling white rapids and deep blue pools where, in the spawning season, the speckled trout are so thick that the small trout have to travel on the backs of the larger ones to avoid being crushed in the jam. I did not see this last myself; my authority for the statement is my friend the veracious lawyer of St. John. But I saw all the rest of it—the woods wearing the flaunting war-paint colors of the wonderful Canadian Indian summer—crimson of huckleberry, tawny of tamarack, yellow of birch, scarlet of maple; the ruffed grouse strutting, unafraid as barnyard fowl and, thanks be to a three-year period of protection, almost as numerous as sparrows in a city street; the signs of hoofed and padded creatures crossing and crisscrossing wherever the earth was soft enough to register the foot tracks of wild things.

And if you want to know how interior New Brunswick looked after Nova Scotia, you are respectfully requested to reread the foregoing paragraph, merely leaving out some of the lakes and most of the boulders.

On a flawless morning, in a motorboat we crossed a certain lake, and I wish I knew the language that might serve to describe the glory of the colors that ringed that lake around and were reflected to the last flame-tipped leaf and the last smooth white column of birchen trunk in its still waters, but I don't. I'll go further and say I can't believe Noah Webster had the words to form the picture, and he had more words than anybody up to the time William J. Bryan went actively into politics. As for myself, I can only say that these colors fairly crackled. There were hues and combinations of hues, shadings and contrasts such as no artist ever has painted and no artist will care to paint, either, for fear of being called a nature faker.

The scene shifts to our main camp. We have met our guides and have marveled at their ability to trot over steep up-and-down-hill portages carrying, each one of them, upon his back a load which no humane man would put on a mule, and have marveled still more when these men, having deposited their mountainous burdens at the farther end of the carry, go hurrying back across the ridge presently to reappear bearing upon their shoulders upturned canoes, their heads hidden inside the inverted interiors and yet by some magic gift peculiar to their craft, managing somehow to dodge the overhanging boughs of trees and without losing speed or changing gait to skip along from one slick round-topped boulder top to another.

Now we are in the deep woods, fifty miles from a railroad and thirty miles from a farmhouse. We sleep at night in canvas leantos, with log fires at our feet; we wash our faces and hands in the lake and make high resolves—which we never carry out—to take dips in that same frosty water; we breakfast at sun-up and sup at dusk in a log shanty set behind the cluster of tents, and between breakfast and supper we seek, under guidance, for fresh meat and dining-room trophies.

We have come too late for the calling season, it seems. In the calling season Mr. Moose desires female society, and by all accounts desires it mightily. So the guide takes a mean advantage of his social cravings. Generally afoot, but sometimes in a canoe, he escorts the gunner to a likely feeding ground or a drinking place and through a scroll of birch bark rolled up in a megaphone shape, he delivers a creditable imitation of the call of the flirtatious cow moose. There are guides who can sound the love note through their cupped hands, but most of the fraternity favor the birchen cornucopia. The sound—part lonely bleat, part plaintive bellow—travels across the silent reaches for an incredible distance. Once when the wind was right there is record of a moose call having been heard six miles away

from where it was uttered, but in this case the instru-
mentalist was Louis Harlowe, a half-breed Micmac
Indian, the champion moose caller of Nova Scotia
and perhaps of the world.

In the bog where he is lying, or on the edge of the
barren where he is feeding, the bull hears the pleading entreaty and thereby is most grossly deceived.
Forgetting the caution which guides his course at
other times, he hurries to where the deceiver awaits
him, in his haste smashing down saplings, clattering
his great horns against the tree boles, splashing
through the brooks. And then when he bursts forth
into the open, snorting and puffing and grunting, the
hunter beholds before him a target which in that setting and with that background must loom up like a
grain elevator. Yet at a distance of twenty yards or
thirty, he has been known to miss the mark clean and
to keep on missing it, while the vast creature stands
there, its dull brain filled with wonder that the
expected cow should not be where he had had every
vocal assurance that she would be, and seemingly
only mildly disturbed by the crashing voice of the
repeater and by the unseen, mysterious things which
pass whistling over his back or under his belly as the
gun quivers in the uncertain grasp of the overanx-
ious or mayhap the buckague-stricken sportsman.

Once though he has made up his sluggish mind
that all is not well for him in that immediate vicinity,

he vanishes into deep cover as silently as smoke and as suddenly as a wink.

The mating time comes in mid-September and lasts about a month, more or less; and since the open season does not begin until October the first, it behooves the hunter who wishes to bag his moose with the least amount of physical exertion to be in camp during the first two weeks of October, for after that the bull moose is reverting to bachelorhood again. He may answer the call, but the chances are that he will not.

A little later on, after the snows have come, one may trail him with comparative ease. Besides, he is browsing more liberally then and consequently is moving pretty consistently. But between the time when the leaves begin to fall and the time when the snow begins to fly he is much given to staying in the densest coverts he can find and doing the bulk of his grazing by night.

So he must be still-hunted, as the saying goes, and it was still-hunting that we were called upon to do. The guide takes his birch-bark horn along each morning when he starts out, carrying it under one arm and an axe under the other, and upon his back a pouch containing the ingredients for a midday lunch and the inevitable fire-blackened teapot, which he calls by the affectionate name of "kittle." He never speaks of stopping for lunch. When the sun stands

overhead and your foreshortened shadow has snug-
gled up close beneath your feet like a friendly black
puppy, he suggests the advisability of "biling a kittle," by which he means building a fire and making
tea. So the pack between his shoulders is necessary
but the moose call is largely ornamental; it is habit
for him to tote it and tote it he does; but mainly he
depends upon his eyes and his ears and his uncanny
knowledge of the ways of the thing we aim to
destroy.

Yes, they call it still-hunting and still-hunting it
truly is so far as Louis Harlowe, the half-breed, or
Sam Glode, the full-blooded Micmac, or Charley
Charlton, the head guide, is concerned, as he goes
worming his way through the undergrowth in his
soft-soled moccasins, instinctively avoiding the rot-
ted twig, the loose bit of stone and the swishy
bough. But the pair of us, following in his footsteps,
in our hard-bottomed, hobnailed boots, our creaky
leather gear and our noisy waterproofed nether garments, cannot, by the wildest latitude in descriptive
terminology, be called still-hunters. Carrying small
avalanches with us, we slide down rocky slopes
which the guide on ahead of us negotiated in pussy-
footed style; and we blunder into undergrowth; and
we trip over logs and we flounder into bogs and out
of them again with loud, churning sounds. Going
into second on a hillside we pant like switch engines.

I was two weeks behind with my panting when I came out of Canada and at odd times now I still pant briskly, trying to catch up.

Reaching level ground we reverse gears and halt to blow. Toward mid-afternoon, on the homebound hike, our weary legs creak audibly at the joints and our tired feet blunder and fumble among the dried leaves. We create all the racket which, without recourse to bass drums or slide trombones, it is humanly possible for a brace of overdressed, city-softened sojourners to create in deep woods. And still our guide—that person so utterly lacking in a sense of humor—speaks of our endeavor as still-hunting. If an ethical Nova Scotian guide—and all professional guides everywhere, so far as I have observed, are most ethical—were hired to chaperon Sousa's band on a still-hunt through the wilderness and on the way Mr. Sousa should think up a new march full of oom-pahs and everything, and the band should practice it while cruising from bog to barren, the guide, returning to the settlements after the outing, would undoubtedly refer to it as a still-hunt.

In our own case, I trust that our eagerness in some measure compensated for our awkwardness. At least, we worked hard—worked until muscles that we never knew before we had achingly forced them-selves upon our attention. Yes, if for the first day or

two our exertion brought us no reward in the shape
of antlered frontlets or great black pelts drying on
the rocks at the canoe landing or savory moose
steaks in the frying pan; if it seemed that after all we
would have to content ourselves with taking home a
stuffed guide's head or so; if twilight found us
reuniting at the supper table each with tales of endless miles of tramping to our credit but no game,
nevertheless and notwithstanding, the labor we spent
was not without its plenteous compensations.

To begin with, there was ever the hope that
beyond the next thicket or across the next swale old
Mr. Sixty Inch Spread would be browsing about
waiting for us to come stealing upon him with all
the stealthy approach of a runaway moving van and
blow him over. There was the joy of watching our
guide trailing, he reading the woods as a scholar
reads a book and seeing there plain as print what we
never would have seen—the impress of a great
splayed hoof in the yellowed moss, the freshly
gnawed twigs of the moose wood, the scarred bark
high up on a maple to show that here a bull had
whetted his horns, the scuffed earth where a bear
had been digging for grubs, the wallow a buck deer
had made at a crossing. And when he told us that the
moose had passed this way, trotting, less than an hour
before, but that the deer's bed was at least two nights
old, while the bear's scratching dated back for days,

we knew that he knew. Real efficiency in any line carries its own credentials and needs no bolstering affidavits. There may be better eyes in some human head than the pair Louis Harlowe owns or than that equally keen pair belonging to Harry Allen, the dean of New Brunswick guides, but I have yet to see their owner, and I am quite sure that for woodcraft there are no better equipped men anywhere than the two I have named.

We couldn't decide which was the finer—the supper at night with a great log fire chasing back the dense shadows, and the baked beans and the talk and the crisp bacon and the innocent lies passing back and forth or the midday lunch out in the tangy, painted forest, miles and miles away from anywhere at all, with the chickadees and the snowbirds and the robins flittering about, waiting their chance to gather the crumbs they knew we would leave behind for them, and with the moose birds informally dropping in on us before ever the kettle had begun to sing.

Naturalists know the moose bird, I believe, as the Canada jay and over the line in the States they call him the venison hawk, but by any name he is a handsome, saucy chap, as smart as Satan and as impudent as they make 'em. The first thin wisp of your fire, rising above the undergrowth, is his signal. For some of the denizens of the wilderness it may be just twelve o'clock, but to him it's feeding time. Here he comes in his swooping flight, a graceful, slate-blue figure with his snowy bib and tucker like a trencher-man prepared. And there, following close behind him, are other members of his tribe. There always is one in the flock more daring than the rest. If you sit quietly, this fellow will flit closer and closer, his head cocked on one side, uttering half-doubtful, half-confident cheeps until he is snatching up provender right under your feet or even out of your hand. His preference is for meat—raw meat for choice, but his taste is catholic; he'll eat anything. Small morsels he swallows on the spot, larger tidbits he takes in his bill and flies away with to hide in a nearby tree crotch. His friends watch him, and by the time he has returned for another helping they have stolen his cache, so that chiefly what he gets out of the burden of his thrifty industry is the exercise. I do not know whether this should teach us that it is better to strive to lay something against a rainy day and take a chance on the honesty of the neighbors or to seize our pleasure when and where we find it and forget the morrow. Aesop might be able to figure it out, but, being no Aesop, I must continue to register uncertainty.

Campfire suppers and high noon barbecues and glorious sunrises and shooting the rapids in the rivers and paddling across the blue lake, scaring up the black duck and the loons from before us, and all the rest of it, was fine enough in its way, but it was not killing the bull moose. So we hunted and we hunted. We dragged our reluctant feet through moose bogs—beaver meadows these are in the Adirondacks—and we ranged the high ground and the low. Cow moose we encountered frequently and calves aplenty. But the adult male was what we sought.

We had several close calls, or perhaps I should say he did. One of our outfit—nameless here because I have no desire to heap shame upon an otherwise well-meaning and always dependable companion—had been cruising through thick timber all day without seeing anything to fire at. Emerging into an open glade on a ridge above Little Red Lake, he was moved to try his new and virgin automatic at a target. So he loosed off at one of the big black crows of the North that was perched, like a disconsolate undertaker, with bunched shoulders and drooping head, on a dead tamarack fifty yards away. He did not hit Brother Corbie but he tore the top out of the tamarack snag. And then when he and the guide had rounded the shoulder of the little hill and descended to a swamp below they read in certain telltale signs a story which came near to moving the marksman to tears.

Moving up the slope from the other side the guide had been calling, a bull moose—and a whaling big one, to judge by his hoof marks—had been stirred to inquire into the circumstances. He had quitted the swamp and had ambled up the hill to within a hundred yards of the crest when—as the guide deduced it—the sound of the shot just above caused him to halt and swing about and depart from that neighborhood at his very best gait. But for that unlucky rifle report he probably would have walked right into the enemy. My friend does not now feel toward crows as he formerly felt. He thinks they should be abolished.

An experience of mine was likewise fraught with the germs of a tragic disappointment. In a densely thicketed district, my guide, with a view to getting a view of the surrounding terrain above the tops of the saplings, scaled the steep side of a boulder that was as big as an icehouse and then beckoned to me to follow.

But as a scaler I am not a conspicuous success. By main strength and awkwardness I managed to clamber up. Just as I reached the top and put my rifle down so that I might fan breath into myself with both hands, my boot soles slipped off the uncertain surface and I slid off my perch into space. Wildly I threw out both arms in a general direction. My clutching fingers closed on a limb of a maple which overshadowed the rock and I swung out into the air twelve feet or so above the inhospitable earth, utterly unable to reach with my convulsively groping feet the nearermost juts of granite. For an agonized moment it seemed probable that the only thing that might break my fall would be myself. But I kept my presence of mind. I flatter myself that in emergencies I am a quick thinker. As I dangled there an expedient came to me. I let go gradually.

And then as I plumped with a dull sickening thud into the herbage below and lay there weaponless, windless and jarred I saw, vanishing into the scrub not a hundred feet away, the black shape of a big and startled moose. I caught one fleeting glimpse of an enormous head, of a profile which might have belonged to one of the major prophets, of a set of horns outspreading even as the fronded palm outspreads itself, of a switching tail and a slab-sided rump, and then the shielding bushes closed and the apparition was gone, and gone for keeps. For my part there was nothing to do but to sit there for a spell and cherish regrets. Under the circumstances, trailing a frightened bull moose would have been about as satisfactory as trailing a comet, and probably not a bit more successful as to results.

For the majority of the members of our troupe the duration of the hunt had a time limit. On the afternoon of the last day in camp two of the party strolled into the immediate presence of a fair-sized bull and, firing together, one of them put a slug of lead in a twitching ear which he turned toward them. It must have been his deaf ear, else he would have been aware of their approach long before. But one moose was singular and the achievement of the plural number was our ambition. So four of us crossed back into New Brunswick, where, according to all native New Brunswickers, the moose grow larger than they do in the sister province, Nova Scotians taking the opposing side and being willing to argue it at all times.

With unabated determination the gallant quartet of us hunted and hunted. Three big deer died to make holiday for us but the moose displayed a coyness and diffidence which might be accounted for only on the ground that they heard we were coming. Indeed they could not very well help hearing it.

Each morning under the influence of the frost the flaming frost colors showed a dimming hue. Day before yesterday they had been like burning brands, yesterday there were dulled embers, today smoldering coals; and tomorrow they would be as dead ashes. Each night the sun went down in a nimbus of cold gray clouds. There was a taste and a smell as of snow in the air. The last tardy robin packed up and went south; the swarms of juncos grew thicker; wedge-shaped flights of coot and black duck passed overhead, their bills all pointing toward the Gulf of Mexico. Then on the last day there fell a rain which turned to sleet and the sleet to snow—four inches of it—and in the snow on that last day the reward which comes—sometimes—to the persevering was ours.

To know the climactic sensation which filled the triumphant amateur you must first of all care for the outdoors and for big-game shooting, and in the second place you must have known the feeling of hope deferred, and in the third place you must have reached the eleventh hour, so to speak, of your stay in these parts with the anticipation you had been nurturing for all these weeks since the trip was first proposed still unrealized in your soul.

You and your camp mate and your guide were on the last lap of the journey back to camp; the sun was slipping down the western wall of the horizon; the shadows were deepening under the spruces; you rounded the shoulder of a ridge and stood for a moment at your guide's back looking across a fire-burned barren. He stiffened like a pointer on a warm scent and pointed straight ahead. Your eye followed where his finger aimed, and two hundred yards away you saw a dark blot against a background of faded tamarack—a bull standing head-on. You shot together, you and your companion. Apparently the animal swung himself about and started moving at the seemingly languid lope of the moose, which really is a faster gait than you would suppose until you measure the length of his stride. You kept on firing, both of you, as rapidly almost as you could pull the triggers of your automatics. Twice he shook himself and humped his hindquarters as though stung, but he did not check his speed. You emptied your magazine, five shots. Your mate's fifth shell jammed in the chamber, putting him out of the running for the moment. In desperate haste you fumbled one more shell into your rifle, and just as the fugitive topped a little rise before disappearing for good into the shrouding second growth you got your sight full on the mark and sent a farewell bullet whistling on its way. The black hulk vanished magically.

"That'll do," said your guide, grinning broadly. "You got 'im. But load up again before we go down there. He's down and down for keeps, I think, judgin' by the way he flopped, but he might get up again."

But he didn't get up again. You came on him where he lay, still feebly twitching, with two flesh wounds in his flanks and a third hole right through him behind the shoulders—a thousand pounds of meat, a head worth saving and mounting and bragging about in the years to come, a pelt as big as a double blanket and at last the accomplished plural of moose was mise.

So then you did what man generally does when language fails to express what he feels. You harked back sundry thousands of years and you did as your remote ancestors, the cave dweller, did when he slew the sabretoothed whatyoumaycallhim. About the carcass of your kill you executed a war dance; at least you did if you chambered the emotions which filled the present writer to the choking point.

And then the next day, back in the settlements, when you reunited with the two remaining members of the outfit who had been in camp eight miles away from the camp where you stayed, and when you learned that now there was a total tally of three deceased beasties, the war dance was repeated, only this time it was a four-handed movement instead of a solo number.

Brant Shooting on
Great South Bay

[EDWIN MAIN POST]

Thirty years ago this spring my wise father built a flat-bottomed sloop, forty-five feet long on the keel and seventeen feet wide, with an enclosed cabin that has square windows instead of portholes, and head room of six feet all over it. This cabin is twenty-one feet long, and consists of one large room with four wide berths, and a toilet room and a kitchen on either side of the centerboard at the forward end. Forward of the cabin beneath the deck there are three berths for the crew, an icebox and a large place for the storage of provisions.

Father named the boat *Macy* after an old friend, and has had her continuously in commission since she was launched; and Andrew Sammis, her first captain, is still in charge—a bit gray now, but still the same careful and trustworthy skipper as of yore.

With the opening of the ducking season in October she goes into what we call winter commission, and when the end of the season comes around she is hauled out, thoroughly overhauled and prepared for the summer work. A few years ago we built an over-hanging stern on her and installed a gasoline engine, so that we are no longer the slaves of the wind god. The *Macy's Baby*, as the stool-boat that carries the battery★ is called, is always at her stern, and this, with the addition of two skiffs and one or more dinkies for use in the ice, makes quite a formidable tow for the old boat. When we have more than a day or two to spend in quest of the wily duck, we send the *Macy* out early to get a good place, and have a catboat meet us at the dock to sail us over to her. Generally we catch a train that arrives at Babylon, Long Island, at half-past three o'clock, and we reach the dock ten minutes afterwards.

Lay aside for a few moments your troubles and worries and come with us to kill some brant. The *Macy* is awaiting us, anchored just off the dock, and we see our good George coming off in the little skiff to speedily set us on board.

As you board the skiff you will not have to ask

★Editor's Note: Now illegal in waterfowling, the battery was a flat, raft-like boat in which a shooter would lie on his back and be almost invisible in a spread of decoys.

George, "Are there any birds?" for he will say: "Brant? Why, there's five million of the cusses in Cedar Island Cove. We'll have some o' them critters and don't you forget it." Captain Andrew greets us with a cheery "Good day, gentlemen," as we reach the side, and you enter the cabin to find upon the table a pleasant welcome in the shape of a generous cocktail for each of us. My father's hearty toast, "Glad to see you on board, sir," makes you feel at home at once, and as you glance around at the comfortable quarters you see that my tales of luxury have not been exaggerated.

We promptly lay aside our "store clothes" and don our old shooting things, as the men get the anchor up and hoist the sail, and are soon in the cockpit enjoying the fresh air. Our progress is slow and stately, due to the flotilla behind us, but we have only about four miles to go. Notice now the third member of our crew, a big, tall, fair-haired man with a smile that never comes off. This is Ansel, a newcomer to the *Macy* in comparison with the skipper, for Ansel has been with us only twenty years. He is a very important personage, for he is the engineer, chef, mate, general utility man and fun-maker for us all. Hark! There is his voice now calling us to dinner.

You sit down before a smoking leg of lamb and dishes of vegetables, with an appetite to which you have been a stranger for a long time, and eat and eat of the good things before you until you are astonished at yourself. Topping off with some of the chef's famous pudding, and helping yourself to a good cigar from the box on the centerboard trunk, you are content. I take the wheel to let the men go below to eat their dinner, and by the time they have finished we arrive at the place where we will set out the battery in the morning. While Andrew and George are furling the sail and making all snug on deck for the night, Ansel is putting things to rights below, and we cover the table with a green cloth and sit down to pass the time at a card game.

At ten o'clock we begin a round of jackpots, and when that is over, we turn into our berths ready for an early call to breakfast. At four o'clock we are called, and by the time we are dressed the breakfast is piping hot on the table. We hurry through our meal to let the men eat theirs, and while they are fixing out the battery and stool, we take a bit of a nap.

The skipper calls us when he sees the men have the stool nearly all out, and you and I put on our sweaters and a dark coat, take our guns and shells, and get into the skiff, to be rowed to the battery. The battery, or "box," as it is more often termed, is set pretty well to the windward of the bulk of the decoys, with just enough of them around it to hide it from birds coming down on the head; and in getting in we pick our way carefully through the decoys and step from the skiff well over toward the center, so as not to get any water in the boxes. On the deck of the box we have twelve iron decoys that are cut off on the bottom, so as not to loom up higher than those on the water, and these we distribute around, heads to the wind, to make the box lay level. We each have a rubber cloth and an old sweater to lie on, and a cloth-covered rubber pillow for our heads. Adjusting these comfortably, we load our guns, cock them and place them against the side on our right hand, taking care to keep at least two inches of the barrels over the end of the box, so that in case of an accidental discharge there will be no hole blown in the box. Long experience in battery shooting has taught me that the longer the barrels of a gun are, the safer it is, and I heartily recommend thirty-two-inch barrels.

Being all ready, we lie down, with only our eyes above the level of the water, and await the coming of our quarry. Two men with sharp eyes can keep a pretty thorough watch, except just behind them, and birds coming from that quarter generally swing off to one side or the other of the stool so that they can set their wings and light among the decoys headed up to the wind. You, as the guest of honor, are in the left-hand box, and just as the sun is rising I see a bunch of brant coming in over the beach from the ocean where they have been roosting. I think they will pass near enough to see our stool, so we lie very close, and occasionally I call them. But the moment they see the stool—and you can always tell this, because they give a sort of dart up in the air and, if they are coming in, settle down again headed toward us—I make no further calls, but say to you: "They are coming in on your side. Lie perfectly still until I say 'Now!' and then give it to them."

It is one of the most inspiriting sights in the world to see a bunch of these lordly birds headed for the stool, and a great many people are deceived as to the distance they are off, on account of their great size—often losing a good chance by rising too quickly. I watch them with one eye above the edge of the box as they set their wings and come gracefully to the stool, and when they are in good range, I say "Now! Let's try 'em!" and we sit up with our guns in our hands and fire. As they are on your side and headed up to windward, you will get the best show, because I must shoot at the tail of the bunch and will not have as good a chance to catch a double as you. You can count on my killing right and left, however, and as my second bird starts to fall, I see you have three down.

"Well done, my friend. We are not going to be skunked today. There are five of them, anyhow."

We both reload our guns, and I take my cap in my hand and swing it until I see an answering signal from the *Macy*. This means that they are to come down in the skiff and pick up our game.

There are three things of great importance in battery shooting: the first to be able to kill when the bird is in range, the second to be able to call, and the third to know how to use the "flopper." It is a bundle of worn-out mittens, tied together with a bit of string, that I keep in my hand as we lie in wait for the game, and it is used to attract the attention of birds that are passing too far away to see the stool. As I am about to explain the use of this queer contrivance, I see a bunch of brant leading through the bay to the north of us, about a mile away. If they keep their present course they will pass us without seeing our stool. Something must be done to attract their attention. Quickly I flop the flopper up above the level of the box two or three times, carefully watching for any sign that the birds have noticed something. If there is no such sign, I flop again.

Ah, this time they have seen it, for they rise in the air and head toward us. Now we lie close, and they come straight for our stool. If I were to flop even once after they have seen the stool, they would be off like a shot—and it is just here that the science of using the flopper means so much. This time they head up on my side, and, when I give the word, we fire, you to kill two, while I am lucky enough to double with each barrel. When George arrives with the skiff and we tell him eleven brant are down, he smiles all over.

I call to George to bring father down when he comes out to pick up again, for your day would not be complete without an hour or two in the box with that peerless sportsman, who is today, at the age of seventy-seven, one of the best shots I have ever seen. We kill again, and George comes down with father. As I get into the boat, father steps into the box with agility equal to mine, and I leave you to an enjoyment that has been the dearest privilege in my life. We have scarcely reached the *Macy* when you swing again, and I take up the glasses to watch with interest your good work.

As noontide comes we get the *Macy* under way and drop down to the box, to reward you with a cocktail when you come aboard, and have all ready a smoking lunch of Ansel's best. After lunch we take turns in the battery, and, when the time comes to take up, we count a row of brant along the washer and find thirty-five. We return to Babylon in ample time for you to catch your train, and we do not let you go until you promise to come again.

FOR SHAME, MINNESOTA!

It is time that sportsmen awoke to the fact that they have interests to be considered and protected as well as any other class of citizens. Now Minnesota proposes to follow the selfish and mistaken policy pursued by other states and impose a tax upon nonresident sportsmen. It is hoped that such a measure will meet with serious opposition.—*Field & Stream, January, 1899.*

Some Tiger Stories

[SIR RICHARD DANE]

I shot my first tiger in the Kanker State in the Central Provinces in January, 1900, under the wing of a gentleman who had shot many tigers and had had much experience of the sport. The lesson, which I had taken most to heart, was that a long shot taken in the direction of the beat might drive the tiger back into the beat and lead to a casualty among the beaters. There were three tigers in the beat, a tigress and two three-quarter grown cubs. My machan had been tied in front so as to give me the first chance of a shot, and my mentor sat in a machan behind me, so as to shoot any animal which might escape me. My machan was badly tied, especially for a man shooting, as I do, from the left shoulder. The string bed, which formed it, was tied with one end facing the beat, and along the left of the machan there were tree trunks. On this side, there-fore, I could fire only straight in front of me, but I was too inexperienced to recognise fully the unsatis-factory nature of the position, and settled myself in the machan without making any objection. As the beat proceeded the tigress appeared and stood on my left front, looking up apparently at one of the stops. She gave me as good a shot as I have ever had in a beat, as she was broadside on and quite motionless; but the distance was over 100 yards, and, being very anxious not to be the cause of any mishap, I decided to allow her to approach. Suddenly, with a "Wouf," she started off at a gallop to the left, passed instantly out of my fire zone, and I was compelled to look on helplessly as she passed the machan. She was fired at but missed by my mentor, and got clean away. One of the cubs followed, and I got in a shot at it, as it passed, but missed. The other cub gave me an easy shot, and I killed it. If I had shot the tigress we should probably have bagged all three, but I had cor-rectly carried out instructions, and the instructions were absolutely sound. The line between success and failure, in big-game shooting, is a very narrow one.

I then shot a fine tiger in a beat in the Bustar State, killing him with a single shot as he walked fast through the bushes. I also killed a fine panther by moonlight, when sitting up over a kill, though the body was unfortunately not found until the skin was spoiled. On the whole, therefore, I did pretty well for a beginner in this expedition . . .

I then took part in a tiger-shoot with elephants in the Terai on the border of the Bahraich district of Oudh, in April, 1900, and my companions were Mr. Harrison, the Collector of the district, and Mr. A. Wood, the Manager of the Kapurthala Estates in Oudh. I had the elephant Chainchal on this occasion, and did pretty well. It was, I think, established that I put the first bullet into a tigress, which was subsequently killed by Harrison; but I made no claim for the skin, as the tigress was unquestionably knocked over and killed by him.

We then had a beat for a tiger which was fired at by both Harrison and myself, and badly wounded, and was eventually finished off by Wood. Both Harrison and myself were using black powder .500 Express rifles, but fortunately he had only wax in his bullets, and I had copper-tubes in mine. We both claimed the shot; and, as the result of a friendly discussion, it appeared probable that the successful shot was Harrison's. I therefore resigned the tiger with the best grace possible, and we were all round the carcass during the skinning operation, when Harrison's servant, who was groping in the inside of the tiger, held up something, saying, "What is this?" Examination showed that it was the copper tube of my bullet, making it clear that mine had been the successful shot, and the ownership of the tiger was accordingly transferred.

This tiger broke out of the beat and might have gone clear away before he was fired at; but the Maila nullah which we were beating, with its cool, shady trees and dense cane brake and a stream of water in the centre, was a favourite place for tigers in the hot weather, and the animal, sooner than face the burning heat of the sun at midday, returned to the nullah further on, and met with his death in consequence.

It is sometimes very difficult to decide who has fired the first successful shot, but, if the contending sportsmen are required to describe accurately the position of the tiger when they fired, a carefully conducted post-mortem examination, after removal of the skin, will generally disclose the truth. The excitement of a tiger-shoot is not, however, conducive to the frame of mind which is required for a judicial investigation, and heated arguments and disputes often result.

I shot a fine panther in the same beat as the tiger, and Harrison also shot a female panther. Two or three days afterwards Wood shot a good tigress. The bag, therefore, was very evenly distributed on this occasion.

My next tiger-hunt was in January, 1901, in the Patna State, which was, at the time, in the Central

Provinces, but has now been transferred to Bengal. I had a female elephant to ride and a good native shikari with me, but no European companion, and the country we were hunting contained buffaloes as well as tigers. The first tiger we heard of was said to have eaten a certain number of bullocks and buffaloes and two men, and the Uriya villagers, who had suffered from his depredations, were naturally very anxious to have him killed. The first bullock we tied out was completely devoured, and the tiger was not in the beat. He killed again the following night, however, and dragged the carcass of the bullock from the road on which it was tied to a place within a few yards of the edge of the jungle in the direction of the village, and there lay up with it. A machan was tied for me, and the beat was lined up in the rice-fields, within a few yards—as appeared from a subsequent examination—of the tiger's resting-place. The first yell given by the beaters evidently startled the tiger, and before the beat had well started I saw him emerging from the jungle on my right at a fast trot. The stop either did not see him or was seized with panic, as he made no attempt to check him. I turned quickly on the machan and fired, and the tiger broke into a gallop and disappeared. Examination showed that the shot had passed under the tiger and struck the ground well beyond the place where he had broken into a gallop. It missed him, therefore, by a few inches only. The direction was good, and the elevation only was wrong.

This was a serious disappointment, but in the night the tiger, who was evidently a very ravenous brute, returned to the kill and dragged the remains to another hiding-place in the same jungle. The shikari wanted me to sit up for him, but I decided to have another beat. On this occasion the tiger emerged at a fast walk and gave me an easy shot, but on my wrong side. I hit him with the first barrel low down in the stomach. He gave a tremendous "Wouf," and went off at a gallop. I swung round on the machan and, as he was galloping off, made a good shot with the second barrel, and put a bullet into the centre of his back. When the beaters came up I descended and we began to look for blood. I knew that I had hit him with the first barrel, and the stop on my left said that he had answered to the second shot also. There was no blood, however, and a small piece of fat about the size of my little finger-nail was the only trace of the tiger which could be found near the machan. The ground was most unfavourable, with clumps of bamboos at intervals and scrub jungle, as high as a man's waist, in between. There were, however, some trees. I sent for the riding elephant, and we advanced together, the elephant being a few paces in front, and I following on foot and keeping, as far as possible, a tree between me and the elephant, as I was doubtful of her staunchness. Before we had gone far the mahout declared that he heard the tiger growling, but I urged him to proceed, and we advanced a few paces farther. Then there was a roar, and the elephant swung round and bolted. I have never seen an elephant travel as she did on that occasion, and the mahout said afterwards that she had actually twisted his neck by the rapidity with which she swung round. It was, however, a case of "eyes front," and I stood waiting for the attack. Fortunately for me, the tiger did not charge, but retreated, attempting to escape.

The demonstration caused a general stampede, but after some time my attendants were reassured and returned. Mihtab Khan had, as he explained, laid hold of the shikari as he was retreating, but the shikari said that he had recently married a wife and was therefore obliged to take care of himself.

A protracted reconnaissance made from trees disclosed the fact that the tiger had gone, and in the bamboo clump, in which he was lying, there was a great pool of blood. The wounds had not bled until he lay down on the ground. This encouraged us all, and we started in pursuit, tracking the tiger by the blood which was now flowing. We followed him for a considerable distance into the open country, and there in a clump of bushes at the foot of a tree he lay up again. The Uriyas, as Indians often do, passed

from panic to over-confidence, and I had the greatest difficulty in keeping them behind me. I had
placed Mihtab Khan on the elephant, which followed along behind us, to give confidence to the
mahout; and from the elephant Mihtab Khan and
the mahout saw the tiger's ear move, as he lay in the
clump of bushes. The shikari and I had passed
within a few yards of him. We drew back and held a
council of war. I had the black powder .500 Express,
with which I had shot the other four tigers, and the
shikari had a Lee-Metford. My idea was to give the
Lee-Metford to Mihtab Khan and allow him to fire
from the back of the elephant, and to shoot the tiger,
as he rose, with the .500; but the mahout urged me
to mount the elephant and shoot, and, as she was
then standing very quietly, I decided to try this. The
elephant, as I afterwards heard, would not stand a
shotgun; but, when drawn back from the proximity
of the tiger, she allowed me to mount without difficulty and then, under pressure from the mahout, she
advanced and stood within 30 yards of the bushes.
After some time I made out the outline of the tiger
crouching in the bushes, and the elephant allowed
me to take a steady aim. As soon as I fired, however,
she swung round with amazing quickness; and, seeing that I must be thrown off, as I was merely sitting
on the pad and my hands were engaged with the
rifle, I jumped and landed on my feet, but fell back,

cracking the stock of my rifle. I sprang to my feet with very creditable rapidity, but fortunately for me the tiger was done for. He staggered to his feet but did not leave the bushes, and a shot by the shikari finally laid him low. My shot from the elephant merely passed through the forearm and did him no appreciable injury, but the shot in the back, as he galloped off, had inflicted a mortal wound. The shot in the lower part of the belly also caused serious internal injury.

He was a young tiger, with a very good coat. The shikari thought he was too young to have commenced man-eating, but there did not appear to be any other tiger in the neighbourhood, and he was a very voracious animal. The view that only old or crippled tigers become man-eaters is only partly correct. Cubs, which have been brought up on human flesh, and which have repeatedly seen their mother attacking and killing human beings, must frequently take to the business when they begin hunting on their own account, especially if game is scarce in the place in which they reside, as was the case in the Patna State. Altogether, this tiger provided three successive days' entertainment. The rifle, though damaged, was not completely unserviceable, and I was able to go on shooting.

For some days after this excitement the elephant was decidedly mischievous. On the day following the death of the tiger she tried to catch hold of a native with her trunk as he ran past her; and on another occasion, after the mahout's wife had given her some bananas, she seized the woman round the waist with her trunk and lifted her up, but did not actually injure her. I was in the tent when this occurred, but, hearing a row, I came out and found the mahout abusing the elephant as only an Indian can.

She was, I think, the fastest and most comfortable elephant I have ever ridden, but she had a temper and was said to have killed several people. The mahout managed her well, but he told me that she had been the favourite riding elephant of the Raja of Bustar, and that, on one occasion, when the Raja had gone down to the river to bathe and had dismounted from the elephant, she suddenly seized a man and tore him in two. The Raja, as was said, fell off his chair with fright, and after this, not unnaturally, parted with the elephant. The mahout said that she had killed five or six people at different times after this, but that he had succeeded in reducing her to submission. On one occasion, as he said, he had tied her up for the night and lain down to sleep at a safe distance, but had omitted to remove out of her reach the lance, which is used to subdue a refractory elephant. In the night he felt something in his hair, and, after brushing at it ineffectually, awoke to find that the elephant had got hold of the lance, broken it in two, and was trying to twist one of the broken pieces into his hair so that she might be able to pull him over to her. I am not prepared to vouch for the truth of this story; but, if it were a lie, it was exceedingly well told, and I saw no reason at the time to doubt the man. He became quite excited at the reminiscence. He was certainly a good mahout, and behaved well on the day when the tiger was shot.

On any occasion on which I was left alone on the back of the elephant, after hearing these stories, I was always glad to see the mahout return; but my personal relations with the elephant were very satisfactory.

We then started to hunt a man-eating family, which were said to have eaten over twenty people between August and the time of my visit in January. There were a tigress and two well-grown cubs, and a tiger was said to join the party occasionally. These tigers had created a scare, and we had to tie out our own buffaloes. It was rather creepy work, but the shikari did this bravely enough. The last kill had occurred about eight days before we arrived on the scene, and the villagers had been too frightened to visit the place. I went there with the old man, who had been with the victim when he was killed, and saw the two bundles of wood which they were tying up at the time. Death appeared to have been instantaneous, as his companion said that the man, when seized, did not utter a cry. The drag was clearly visible in the grass, and, after following it for a few yards, we found the man's loin-cloth, and, farther on, the place where he had been eaten. We hunted for some days and tied out baits, but saw nothing of the tigers, which had for some reason or other left the neighbourhood . . .

In April, 1901, I had another tiger-hunt in the Terai, on the border of the Bahraich district, with Mr. Faunthorpe, I.C.S., who was then the Collector, and Mr. A. Wood. We got no tigers in Nepal, and the expedition was in danger of being a complete failure, when we received news of a tigress which had killed in one day three head of cattle in a village in the Bahraich district, near the border. We moved camp to this place, and we found that the cover in which the tigress was lying, consisted of a triangular patch of high reeds on the border of a small lagoon. The line of elephants was formed at the base of the triangle, and the beat was a pretty and exciting one. Wood was with the line; I had the next position in front of the beat, and Faunthorpe was beyond me. The tigress was soon on the move, and we could hear her splashing in the reeds as she moved along the edge of the lagoon. When the line was half-way through the patch of reeds she charged the elephants with a roar and threw the line into confusion. With a little more courage she could have broken through and escaped, but her heart failed her and she retreated until she was pushed up into the very apex of the triangle. She might have escaped across the water, as this side of the beat was unprotected; but she would not face the open. At last, when driven into the extreme corner of the reeds, she rushed out on the side where we were all standing. Wood had a shot at her but missed, and she came straight for my elephant. Seeing the elephant, she declined the encounter, and swung round, and as she swung round I fired. A second later Faunthorpe's shot rang out. Our shots were so nearly simultaneous that he did not hear my shot, but I heard his. Two more shots were fired by Wood and myself at the tigress, as she was struggling in the grass; but these were misses. My shot struck the tigress in the heart, and Faunthorpe's shot struck her in the back near the shoulder as she was end on to him. I was using an Express and firing shell, and the others fired solid bullets; there was, therefore, no difficulty in identifying the different shots on this occasion. Our two shots were fired almost simultaneously, but Faunthorpe, seeing that my shot had killed the tigress, did not make any claim. I rode an elephant belonging to the Maharajah of Balrampur on this occasion, and she stood staunchly when the shots were fired though she was not highly tried.

In 1903–4, I had a run of ill-luck, taking part in

three expeditions to the Terai, in the course of which no less than nine tigers and tigresses and two cubs were shot, and the only animal which fell to my lot was a large panther, which I shot over a kill.

On the first occasion, in April, 1903, the party consisted of Mr. A. Wood, the late Major Lumsden, I.M.S., Mr. Channer, the Divisional Forest Officer, and myself, and we hunted a portion of the Terai at some distance from the ground which we hunted during my first two expeditions. Major Lumsden rode the elephant Chainchal, and I was riding an elephant which was lent me by the Maharajah of Balrampur. Shortly after our arrival on the ground a good tiger was marked down in a very small patch of thick jungle on the bank of a small deep nullah, or stream, which was overhung with trees. The tiger had killed a chital, and dragged the carcass into the cover, and it was therefore a sure find. Lumsden was with the beat; Wood had the best place on the bank of the nullah at the end of the patch of cover; and Channer and I were among the trees on the opposite side of the nullah. The guns were, therefore, roughly speaking, at the four corners of a square with the corner, at which Wood was posted, projecting. The patch of jungle was very thick, and Lumsden was not thought to have any chance. Chainchal's mahout, however (Karim by name), was a very plucky, intelligent fellow, with very good vision, and while the elephants were trying to force their way into the patch of jungle, he saw the tiger standing in thick cover. Lumsden failed to see him until he moved. He then fired both barrels, but he had missed his chance, and the tiger rushed from the thicket and plunged into the water with a tremendous splash, swimming straight across to where I was posted among the trees on the other bank. An overhanging branch obscured my vision at the particular point at which the tiger was crossing; and, though I could see the water moving as he swam, I could not actually see his head. He was, however, making for the bank very near the place where my elephant was standing; and the shikari in the howdah behind me, who perhaps saw the animal, was adjuring me to shoot. Very unwisely, therefore, I fired. The tiger answered to the shot with a roar, and the bullet evidently struck the water very near him. My elephant then swung round so that I could not fire again, and, looking backwards, I could just see the tiger climb the bank behind me. Wood had a shot at him as he ascended the bank, but missed. The tiger then made off along the bank and ran right into Channer. Thinking he was trapped, he turned with a roar and plunged with another splash into the water, and swam back to the thicket in which he was lying at the outset. Owing to the overhanging trees, he was not visible after he sprang into the water until he reached cover. After some time he was beaten out again, and this time took the line he was expected to take, giving Wood a good chance. A shot near the head stopped him, and a second bullet finished him off. My shot was thought to have been a hit, but examination showed that it was Wood's tiger. This is the only occasion I can remember in which every member of a party had a fair chance in turn at a tiger. The beat also was one of the prettiest and most exciting in which I have ever taken part.

After this the shikaris reported that there were no other tigers in the vicinity of the camp, and went to some place at a considerable distance to look for tracks. We were reconciling ourselves to some hot days of waiting, but very soon after the shikaris had gone some herdsmen came in and said that a tiger had killed one of their buffaloes. We went to the place and found a recently killed buffalo; but the only patch of forest which was near the place had been fired, and, although it had apparently been too damp to burn well, some fallen trees were actually on fire. We tried a beat, and the tiger was there right enough. In shooting with elephants, there is very little danger to the beaters, and, as everyone is anxious to put the first bullet into the tiger, there is often some rather wild shooting. As the line advanced both Wood and I had shots. I fired without success at a movement in the high grass; and

then the tiger, which was fairly cornered, broke with
a roar into the open, a little to my left front. It was a
grand spectacle, as the tiger showed up magnifi-
cently on the short green grass. With Chainchal, I
should probably have got that tiger; but my elephant
was not a good one, and I tried her rather severely.
Leaning well out of the howdah, I waited until the
tiger was close up so as to make sure of the shot;
but, just as I was pulling the trigger, the elephant
funked and swung round with a jerk, and the rifle
went off in the air. By the time the elephant had
been turned round the tiger had galloped some distance; shots fired at his tail by Wood and myself
were unsuccessful, and he got clean away. It was
very disappointing; but it was partly my fault, as I
ought to have made allowance for the possibility of
the elephant funking, and fired as soon as the tiger
appeared.

The Terai, or moist alluvial land, lying between
the branches of the mighty Gagra River, provides
grazing in the hot weather for large herds of cattle
and buffaloes. The grass is burnt in the spring, and at
the end of April, the land is covered with short green
grass. Tigers still abound in this part of India, and
toll is taken of the herds. These grazing buffaloes
will, as one of the herdsmen informed me, respond
to a particular call announcing the advent of a tiger,
and will charge *en masse* and drive the animal away;

but young buffaloes, when detached from the herd, are not infrequently attacked and killed.

A tigress with three small cubs was then marked down in a dry ravine near a village. The tigress was in poor condition, and evidently found a difficulty in feeding her numerous progeny; and apparently she had taken up her quarters in the ravine on the chance of killing one of the village cattle, as there was no game in the vicinity. Wood was with the line of elephants on this occasion; Lumsden was on the left bank, and Channer and I were on the right bank of the ravine. The beat was up the ravine. Shortly after the beat started Wood, whose elephant was moving along the bed of the ravine, saw the tigress crouching on the sand, facing him at a short distance. He fired at her with a shotgun loaded with ball, and the shot passed through one of her ears, which was evidently cocked forward. Subsequent examination showed that the bullet drilled a small round hole, the edges of which were not even reddened with blood. It was a close shave, but the animal was quite uninjured and blood was not drawn. The tigress then appeared near Lumsden, who fired, and, as he subsequently said, knocked her over into the ravine. Very shortly after this she appeared on my side of the ravine. She walked quietly and quickly round a bush, and did not appear to be wounded, and I fired, hitting her with my Express on the near side, but rather far back. She disappeared into the ravine and wandered about there for a little time. Then Channer, who was shooting with a small-bore, high-velocity rifle, saw her and fired, and shortly after, she was seen to be dead. Two bullet-holes were visible in the skin, one a small one in the back near the neck, and the other a large one in the near side. Lumsden was quite confident that he had hit the tigress and knocked her over, and suggested that the large hole in the side was the hole of exit of his bullet. Both the other sportsmen thought that the tiger was Lumsden's, and Channer did not claim a hit. There was much blood in the ravine, but it was impossible to say from which wound it proceeded, and I therefore contented myself with pointing out that the hole in the side was the hole of my bullet, and did not claim the tigress and was not present at the post-mortem. The natives who skinned and cut up the tigress were told to produce the bullets, and mine was duly produced, and was admitted by Major Lumsden to be not his. His bullet, which was also an expanding one, was not found. On the following morning, when we were looking at the skin, Lumsden himself noticed a small round hole in the skin of the belly, but he was so convinced that he had shot the tigress that he did not give the matter much attention. I said nothing, but thought a good deal. It was clear to me that Lumsden had missed the tigress, and that I had put the first bullet into her, and that she had then been killed by Channer, whose bullet had entered the back and come out through the belly. I kept my conclusions, however, to myself, merely resolving that I would always be present at a post-mortem in the future. Poor Lumsden was a good sportsman, and was perfectly convinced that he had shot the tigress; but, as already said, a painstaking investigation is often necessary before it can be determined who has scored the first hit.

A forest officer of my acquaintance told me that on one occasion he had arranged a tiger-shoot for two military officers. One had, if I remember right, shot a tiger before, and the other had not. The tiger went first to the more experienced sportsman of the two, who fired at it. The tiger then went to the other man, who fired at it and killed it. Overjoyed at his good fortune, he chaffed his friend about his bad shot, and the other accepted the chaff. The forest officer, from curiosity, went along the route by which the tiger had approached the second machan, and found blood all along the track. But, where ignorance is bliss, it is folly to be wise; both the sportsmen were satisfied, and he left them in blissful ignorance of his discovery.

Major Lumsden shot two of the small cubs. The third must also have died, as they were much too young to hunt for themselves.

Our next hunt was an exciting one. A tiger was

marked down in a thick bed of reeds in a swampy clearing in the middle of sal forest. We posted ourselves round the reeds, and the tiger broke out near the place where Channer was posted; but, as well as I remember, he did not, owing to some difficulty with his elephant, get a shot. As the tiger was disappearing into the forest Lumsden fired and put a bullet into him. There was very little blood, and it was uncertain how far the tiger had gone; but we formed a long line in the forest, with the elephants about 50 yards apart, and drove forward in the hope of rounding him up. I was on the extreme right of the line, and before we had gone far the mahout said that he heard the tiger growling. I heard him also and ought, perhaps, to have called a halt and sent for the others. I was afraid, however, that the tiger might escape, as he did not appear to be badly wounded, and was also, it must be admitted, very anxious to see a fine charge. The prospect of an encounter, therefore, was not unwelcome. I accordingly encouraged the mahout to proceed; and, as soon as we advanced, the tiger burst from some bushes at the foot of a tree in which he was lying and charged.

I have heard it said that a tiger always charges at a fast run. This one charged at a gallop. He was in the middle of a spring, with his forelegs stretched out in front and the hind-legs stretched out straight behind him, when I fired. Directly I fired, the elephant swung round so that I could not fire the second barrel, and the tiger pushed home the charge and seized her by the middle of the thigh. In the struggle that ensued I received a severe bruise on the forearm, but was not otherwise injured, though I was in great danger of being crushed, as the howdah was in constant collision with a tree or trees. The howdah, which was very strongly built, was much damaged. I was quite unable to shoot, and got down into the howdah and trusted for safety to the elephant. Presently she flopped down, and I thought the tiger had pulled her over, but apparently she sat down so as to pinch the tiger's head and make him let go. The manœuvre succeeded, as she shook him off, and then got up and bolted. She did not, however, go far, and the mahout recovered control and stopped her. Mihtab Khan, who was behind me in the howdah, seized a bough in the struggle, and, being a powerful man, swung himself up into a tree. He had a Lee-Metford rifle in one hand, and it was a fine acrobatic performance; but he made no attempt to fire at the tiger.

I then sent for the others, and Wood and Lumsden joined me. The tiger had retreated to the bushes from which he had charged, and lay there growling. We all advanced upon him together, but my elephant was badly shaken and would not keep in line with the other two. Wood saw, or thought he saw, the tiger, and fired the first shot, but the tiger made no response and continued his low growling. Lumsden then pushed forward on Chainchal, and saw the tiger lying on the ground, and put a bullet into his brain. There were two bullet-holes in his side, and his hind-leg was broken to pieces below the hock. My bullet had struck him in the flank and run down his hind-leg, as it was stretched out behind him in the gallop. But for this he would probably have sprung on top of the elephant, and might have pulled one of us out of the howdah, as he was in no way crippled and made a most determined charge. The elephant was badly mauled, but recovered under treatment. If she had not turned round, I might have finished off the tiger without difficulty with the second barrel.

This was the best tiger-shoot in which I ever took part, though in the matter of the bag I personally came off badly. My elephant did not serve me well, but in the first beat I made a bad error of judgment. I think, however, that I put the first bullet into one of the three full-grown tigers which were killed, and contributed materially to the death of another. I may possibly have transposed the order of one or two of the hunts, but the different events and scenes are still fresh in my memory.

On the next expedition the party consisted of Mr. Wood, Major Lumsden, and myself. Wood shot a tigress and a young tiger in a beat in which we were seated in machans, but I think these were the only two shots which were fired at tigers in the course of the expedition, which was comparatively unsuccessful and uneventful. . . .

On the next occasion on which I visited the Terai, the party consisted of Major Lumsden, Mrs. Lumsden, and myself; and Mrs. Lumsden, who was a very good shot, killed a tiger in fine style. The tiger had killed in a sandy nullah, and lain up with the kill in a small patch of thick cover under the high bank of the nullah. We were all posted in the forest facing the high bank in question, Lumsden on the right, Mrs. Lumsden, who was on Chainchal, in the centre, and I on the left. We took up our positions just in time, as the tiger, scenting trouble, tried to slink away before the beat commenced. He came towards Mrs. Lumsden, who hit him with her first shot with the Rigby-Mauser she was using, but missed him with the second, as he turned and dashed back into the beat. He soon appeared again on the same line, and Mrs. Lumsden fired, hitting him in the mouth. The bullet, however, merely broke one of the canine teeth, and was diverted. A shot in the head is often a very unsatisfactory one. The tiger then tried to slink out on the right, and Lumsden had two shots at him, hitting him with one and turning him back into the beat, but missing him with the other. He then broke out at a gallop between Major and Mrs. Lumsden; and the latter, with a well-placed shot, rolled him over. I was on lower ground, and, although I was not more than 100 yards distant from Mrs. Lumsden, I could not see what was going on.

The tiger had rather a small head, and was certainly wanting in spirit, as he made no attempt to take the offensive; but he was the largest tiger that I have ever seen shot, measuring between pegs fixed in the ground, at the head and tail, 9 feet 8 inches.

A day or two after this we had a beat for two young tigers in the very place in which Wood had shot the two tigers on the previous expedition; and, as before, we were posted in machans. Mrs. Lumsden had shots at the tigers, as they broke, but failed to stop them. We then formed a long line, and hunted them through the sal forest for some hours. Lumsden had a shot at one of them, a young tigress, which then passed me at a gallop. The distance, when I fired, was considerable, but the tigress passed me apparently unwounded. One of the two shots, however, was evidently a hit, as the tigress was seen shortly afterwards lying up behind a tree. I had a staunch but very slow elephant, and Lumsden reached the place before me and put a bullet into the tiger. One or two more shots were then fired to finish her off. I made no claim, as the tigress may possibly have been wounded by Lumsden's first shot, and he certainly gave her the *coup de grâce;* but the idea among the men was that I had put a bullet into her.

After the death of the tigress we sat unsuccessfully over two kills which had occurred in the forest until a late hour, and then had a long elephant-ride back to camp, arriving there long after dark. It was hot weather, and, for a lady, it was a wonderful exhibition of endurance. We got no more tigers; but I shot the panther already referred to in the course of this expedition.

I had also an interesting but most exasperating experience, when sitting up over a kill for a tiger. One of our buffaloes had been killed, and we had beaten the ground, but the beat was blank. It was decided, therefore, that I should sit up for the tiger on the chance of his returning to the kill. A machan was constructed, and a local shikari, who was with us, climbed into it. I ordered him out, but he pleaded very hard to be allowed to remain; and, as the kill was lying among bushes, I unfortunately thought that his hearing might be of use, and allowed him to sit with me. Before it was dark the tiger came, and the shikari, suddenly seeing him standing on some rising ground above the level of the machan, completely lost his nerve. He stammered out that the tiger had come, and threw his arms round me to turn me around to have a shot at it. The tiger of course saw the movement, or heard the noise and was off. I have always regarded it as creditable to my forbearance that I did not lay a hand on the shikari . . .

In April, 1905, I made my last expedition to the Terai. The party on this occasion consisted of Mr. W. B. M. Bird, Mr. A. Wood, and myself. Major Fullerton, who had succeeded Major Lumsden as Civil Surgeon of Bahraich, was also with us during part of the time. On this occasion I rode the elephant Chainchal, and had better fortune. Our shooting-camp was on the bank of the Rapti River; and we reached the camp on the 20th of April. In the afternoon of that day and on the 21st, we hunted without any definite information and without success, but on the 22nd, a tigress was marked down in some very thick cover. The first beat we had for her was unsuccessful, but she did not leave the place, and we beat the cover again on the following day from a different direction. I was on one side of the cover a little in advance of the line of elephants, and when the line had advanced for some distance the tigress came along the edge of the cover, quite near the elephant. She was not properly visible, and I was doubtful about firing; but the mahout, Karim, pointed in the direction in which the bushes were moving and urged me to shoot. I decided, therefore, to chance a shot and fired. The shot, by good fortune, struck the tigress near the root of the tail, and she turned and rushed in the direction of the beaters outside the edge of the jungle. Chainchal stood staunchly, and with the second barrel I broke the tigress's left shoulder as she charged past me. She then lay up under a bush in the cover, and with some difficulty I made her out from the howdah and finished her off. This tigress had a very beautifully marked skin, which makes a very handsome trophy.

On the next day a good tiger was marked down, and, having shot the tigress, I was put in what was supposed to be the worst place, at the end of the beat, Wood having the position on the side of the beat, while Bird was covering him. But fortune favoured me, and, as the line of elephants advanced, I saw the tiger's head in the jungle about 80 yards away. He was standing broadside on the Wood, and at no great distance, but was hidden from him by the bushes. Momentarily I expected to hear his rifle, but he did not fire, and the tiger remained standing with his head slightly turned, listening to the advancing elephants. I accordingly fired from a standing position in the howdah, aiming between the eyes. I made a good shot, the bullet striking the tiger between the nose and the left eye. Subsequent examination showed that the bullet, which was a shell from a .500 black powder Express, broke the palate, nearly severed the tongue, and tore off two big molar teeth, one in the upper and one in the lower jaw. The tiger probably would have died, but for the time being he was in no way crippled. For some seconds, however, he was knocked out of time; and, as nothing was visible, I hoped that I had killed him. He then got up and dashed out of the jungle at a gallop, mad with pain and rage. I failed to stop him; but, after galloping aimlessly about for some seconds, he passed near Bird, who knocked him over and then finished him, with two well-directed shots. As already said, a shot in the head or face often gives very unsatisfactory results.

On the 26th of April, Bird got his chance and shot a fine tiger, killing it with a single shot. He was using a double-barrelled .360 bore high-velocity rifle, and the tiger, with a bullet through his heart, galloped, apparently uninjured, for at least one hundred yards. Thinking he had missed, Karim urged Chainchal to speed to cut him off, and, just as an encounter was imminent, the tiger collapsed in his gallop, and fell stone dead in a small ditch. He lay in this ditch all limp and crumpled up, like a well-shot rabbit.

On the 28th, Bird shot a bear, which was marked down by the shikaris in a clump of bushes; and on the 30th of April, he shot a second tiger.

This tiger had apparently had a fight with another tiger, or with a bear, and had come off second best. He had lost one eye and was badly clawed about the body. When beaten out of the cover, in which he was lying, he broke at a gallop; but his blind eye prevented him from seeing Bird, whose elephant was standing in a fairly open place. The tiger therefore passed close to him, and was killed by a single well-placed shot.

On the 1st of May, Bird and I had a very interesting but unsuccessful sit for another tiger. The tiger had killed and eaten two or three of our buffaloes, but could not be located for the purposes of a beat. He was, evidently, a very cunning brute. One day the shikaris returned full of confidence, having marked him down in a very favourable locality, but he cleared out before we arrived and the beat was blank. We decided, therefore, to sit up over a live buffalo, which was tied upon the road upon which the other buffaloes had been killed. Our machan was well screened, having been tied in a thick leafy tree, but we could see only to our front, and could neither shoot nor see anything up the road behind us. The buffalo was tied about 20 paces from us down the road. There was no moon, but the night was clear, and the tiger came at about ten o'clock. I was dozing at the time, but Bird was watchful and heard him, and, at a touch from him, I took in the situation. The tiger stood for some time on the road to the rear of the machan, watching the buffalo, and then, as could be seen in the morning, lay down in the grass to our right, nearly parallel to the machan. Then he got up and walked round the buffalo, without showing himself; but apparently he was suspicious of a trap, and made no attack. The buffalo did not appear to be particularly alarmed, but kept head on to the tiger, and, as the tiger moved, the buffalo's head followed it round. After an hour or so, the tiger departed, and we sat there until the dawn without any further excitement. We heard spotted deer calling in the distance, and the tiger was apparently in pursuit of them.

I have heard it said, more than once, that a tiger will not kill readily a buffalo with a white blaze on his forehead. The one tied out had a white blaze, and this may have been the reason why the tiger would not attack. There certainly was no other cause apparent. I do not think the tiger could possibly have detected our presence, as we both sat very still and quiet, and the machan was well hidden.

Some days of waiting and unsuccessful hunting followed, but on the 6th of May, a tigress was marked down in the same cover in which I had shot the tiger on the 24th. Fullerton was given the best place, and had a good shot at the tigress, but unfortunately missed. I had two shots at her as she galloped away, but she broke out of the cover to my right and at some distance from me, and I failed to stop her.

This ended the hunt, and on the 7th of May, we struck our tents and started for Nipal Ganj on our return journey to Bahraich.

Bear Hunting in the Smokies

[**HORACE KEPHART**]

G it up, pup! You've scrounged right in hyur in front of the far [fire]. You Dred! Whut makes you so blamed contentious?"

Little John shoved both dogs into a corner, and strove to scrape some coals from under a beech forestick that glowed almost hot enough to melt brass.

"This is the wust coggled-up far I ever seen, to fry by. Bill, hand me some Old Ned from that suggin' o' mine."

A bearded hunchback reached his long arm to a sack that hung under our rifles, drew out a chunk of salt pork, and began slicing it with his jackknife. On inquiry I learned that "Old Ned" is merely slang for fat pork, but that "suggin" or "sujjit" (the *u* pronounced like *oo* in look) is true mountain dialect for

a bag, valise or carryall, its etymology being something to puzzle over.

Four dogs growled at each other under a long
bunk of poles and hay that spanned one side of our
cabin. The fire glared out upon the middle of an
unfloored and windowless room. Deep shadows
clung to the walls and benches, charitably concealing
much dirt and disorder left by previous occupants,
much litter of our own contributing.

We were on a saddle of the divide, a mile above
sea level, in a hut built years ago for temporary lodg-
ment of cattlemen herding on the grassy "balds" of
the Smokies. A sagging "shake" roof covered its two
rooms and the open space between them that we
called our "entry." The state line between North
Carolina and Tennessee ran through this unenclosed
hallway. The Carolina room had a puncheon floor
and a clapboard table, also better bunks than its mate;
but there had risen a stiff southerly gale that made
the chimney smoke so abominably that we were
forced to take quarters in the neighbor state.

Granville lifted the lid from a big Dutch oven and
reported "Bread's done."

There was a flash in the frying-pan, a curse and a
puff from Little John. The coffee-pot boiled over.
We gathered about the hewn benches that served for
tables, and sat *à la Turc* upon the ground. For some

time there was no sound but the gale without and the munching of ravenous men.

"If this wind'll only cease afore mornin', we'll git us a bear tomorrow."

A powerful gust struck the cabin, by way of answer; a great roaring surged up from the gulf of Defeat, from Desolation, and from the other forks of Bone Valley—clamor of ten thousand trees struggling with the blast.

"Hit's gittin' wusser."

"Any danger of this roost being blown off the mountain?" I inquired.

"Hit's stood hyur twenty year through all the storms; I reckon it can stand one more night of it."

"A man couldn't walk upright outside the cabin," I asserted, thinking of the St. Louis tornado, in which I had lain flat on my belly, clinging to an iron post.

The hunchback turned to me with a grave face. "I've seed hit blow, here on top o' Smoky, till a hoss couldn't stand up agin it. You'll spy, tomorrow, that several trees has been wind-throwed and busted to kindlin'."

I recalled that "several," in the South, means many—"a good many," as our own tongues phrase it.

"Oh shucks, Bill Cope," put in "Doc" Jones, "whut do you-uns know about windstorms? Now,

I've hed some experiencin' up hyur that'll do to tell about. You remember the big storm three year ago, come grass, when the cattle all huddled up atop o' each other and friz in one pile, solid."

Bill grunted an affirmative.

"Wal, sir, I was a-herdin', over at the Spencer Place, and was out on Thunderhead when the wind sprung up. There come one turrible vyg'rous blow that jest nacherally lifted the ground. I went up in the sky, my coat ripped off, and I went a-sailin' end-over-end."

"Yes?"

"Yes. About half an hour later, I lit spang in the mud way down yander in Tuckaleechee Cove—yes, sir; ten mile as the crow flies, and a mile deeper'n trout-fish swim."

There was silence for a moment. Then Little John spoke up: "I mind about that time, Doc, but I disremember which buryin'-ground they-all planted ye in."

"Planted! *Me?* Huh! But I had one tormentin' time findin' my hat!"

The cabin shook under a heavier blast.

"Old Wind-maker's blowin' liars out o' North Car'lina. Hang on to yer hat, Doc! Whoop! Hear 'em a-comin'"

"Durn this blow, anyhow! No bear'll cross the mountain sich a night as this."

"Can't we hunt down on the Carolina side?" I asked.

"That's whar we're goin' to drive; but hit's no use if the bear don't come over."

"How is that? Do they sleep in one state and eat in the other?"

"Yes. You see, the Tennessee side of the mountain is powerful steep and laurely, so man nor dog cain't git over it in lots o' places: that's whar the bears den. But the mast, sich as acorns and beech and hickory nuts, is mostly on the Car'lina side; that's whar they hafter come to feed. So, when its blows like this, they stay at home and suck their paws."

"So we'll have to do, at this rate."

"I'll go see whut the el-e-ments looks like."

We arose from our squatting postures. John opened the little shake door, which swung violently backward as another gust of wind boomed against the cabin. Dust and hot ashes scattered in every direction. The dogs sprang up, one encroached upon another, and they flew at each other's throats. They were powerful beasts, dangerous to man as well as to the brutes they were trained to fight; but John was their master, and he soon booted them into surly subjection.

"The older dog don't ginerally raise no ruction;

hit's the younger one that's ill," by which he meant vicious. "You Coaly, you'll git some o' that meanness shuck outen you if you tackle an old she-bear tomorrow!"

"Has the young dog ever fought a bear?"

"No, he don't know nothin'. But I reckon he'll pick up some larnin' in the next two, three days."

"Have those dogs got the Plott strain? I've been told that the Plott hounds are the best bear dogs in the country."

" 'Tain't so," snorted John. "The Plott curs are the best; that is, half hound, half cur—though what weuns call the cur, in this case, raelly comes from a big furrin dog that I don't rightly know the breed of. Fellers, you can talk as you please about a streak o' the cur spilin' a dog; but I know hit ain't so—not for bear fightin' in these mountains, whar you cain't foller up on hossback, but hafter do your own runnin'."

"What is the reason, John?"

"Wal, hit's like this: a plumb cur, of course, cain't foller a cold track—he jest runs by sight; and he won't hang—he quits. But, t'other way, no hound'll raelly fight a bear—hit takes a big severe dog to do that. Hounds has the best noses, and they'll run a bear all day and night, and the next day, too; but they won't never tree-they're afeared to close in. Now look at them dogs o' mine. A cur ain't got no dewclaws—them dogs has. My dogs can foller ary trail, same's hound; but they'll run right in on the varmint, snappin' and chawin' and worryin' him till he gits so mad you can hear his tuches pop half a mile. He cain't run away—he haster stop every bit and fight. Finally he gits so tarred [tired] and het up that he trees to rest hisself. Then we-uns ketches up and finishes him."

"Mebbe you-uns don't know that a dew-clawed dog is snakeproof—"

But somebody, thinking that dog talk had gone far enough, produced a bottle of soothing-syrup that was too new to have paid tax. Then we discovered that there was musical talent, of a sort, in Little John. He cut a pigeon-wing, twirled around with an imaginary banjo, and sang in a quaint minor:

"Did you *ever* see the devil,
With his *pitchfork* and ladle,
And his *old* iron shovel,
And his old gourd head?

O, I *will* go to meetin',
And I *will* go to meetin',
Yes, I *will* go to meetin',
In an old tin pan."

Other songs followed, with utter irrelevance— mere snatches from "ballets" composed, mainly, by the mountaineers themselves, though some dated back to a long-forgotten age when the British ancestors of these Carolina woodsmen were battling with lance and long bow. It was one of modern and local origin that John was singing when there came a diversion from without—

La-a-ay down, boys,
   Le's take a nap:
Thar's goin' to be trouble
   In the Cumberland Gap—

Our ears were stunned by one sudden thundering crash. The roof rose visibly, as though pushed upward from within. In an instant we were blinded by moss and dried mud—the chinking blown from between the logs of our shabby cabin. Dred and Coaly cowered as though whipped, while "Doc's" little hound slunk away in the keen misery of fear. We men looked at each other with lowered eyelids and the grim smile that denotes readiness, though no special eagerness, for dissolution. Beyond the "gant-lot"* we could hear trees and limbs popping like pistol shots.

Gant-lot: a fenced enclosure into which cattle are driven after cutting them out from those of other owners. So called because the mountain cattle run wild, feeding only on grass and browse, and "they couldn't travel well to market when they were filled up on green stuff; so they're penned up to git *gant* and nimble."

Then that tidal wave of air swept by. The roof settled again with only a few shingles missing. We went
to "redding up." Squalls broke against the mountainside, hither and yon, like the hammer of Thor
testing the foundations of the earth. But they were
below us. Here, on top, there was only the steady
drive of a great surge of wind; and speech was possible once more.

"Fellers, you want to mark whut you dream
about, tonight: hit'll shore come true tomorrow."

"Yes: but you mustn't tell whut yer dream was till
the hunt's over, or it'll spile the charm."

There ensued a grave discussion of dream lore, in
which the illiterates of our party declared solemn
faith. If one dreamt of blood, he would surely see
blood the next day. Another lucky sign for a hunter
was to dream of quarreling with a woman, for that
meant a she-bear. It was favorable to dream of clear
water, but muddy water meant trouble.

The wind died away. When we went out for a
last observation of the weather we found the air so
clear that the lights of Knoxville were plainly visible, in the north-northwest, thirty-two miles in an
air line. Not another light was to be seen on earth,
although in some directions we could scan for
nearly a hundred miles. The moon shone brightly.
Things looked rather favorable for the morrow,
after all.

• • •

"Brek-k-k-*fust*!"

I awoke to a knowledge that somebody had built a roaring fire and was stirring about. Between the cabin logs one looked out upon a starry sky and an almost pitch-dark world. What did that pottering vagabond mean by arousing us in the middle of the night? But I was hungry. Everybody half arose on elbows and blinked about. Then we got up, each after his fashion, except one scamp who resumed snoring.

"Whar's that brekfust you're yellin' about?"

"Hit's for you-uns to help *git!* I knowed I couldn't roust ye no other way. Here, you, go down to the spring and fetch water. Rustle out, boys; we've got to git a soon start if you want bear brains an' liver for supper."

The "soon start" tickled me into good humor.

Our dogs were curled together under the long bunk, having popped indoors as soon as the way was opened. Somebody trod on Coaly's tail. Coaly snapped Dred. Instantly there was action between the four. It is interesting to observe what two or three hundred pounds of dog can do to a ramshackle berth with a man on top of it. Poles and hay and ragged quilts flew in every direction. Sleepy Matt went down in the midst of the melee, swearing valiantly. I went out and hammered ice out of the washbasin while Granville and John quelled the riot.

Presently our frying-pans sputtered and the huge coffeepot began to get up steam.

"Wal, who dreamt him a good dream?"

"I did," affirmed the writer. "I dreamt that I had an old colored woman by the throat and was choking dollars out of her mouth—"

"Good la!" exclaimed four men in chorus. "You hadn't orter a-told."

"Why? Wasn't that a lovely dream?"

"Hit means a she-bear, shore as a cap-shootin' gun, but you've spiled it all by tellin'. Mebbe somebody'll git her today, but *you* won't—your chanct is ruined."

So the reader will understand why, in this veracious narrative, I cannot relate any heroic exploits of my own in battling with Ursus Major.

There was still no sign of rose color in the eastern sky when we sallied forth. The ground, to use a mountaineer's expression, was "all spewed up with frost." Rime crackled underfoot and our mustaches soon stiffened in the icy wind.

It was settled that Little John Cable and the hunchback Cope should take the dogs far down into Bone Valley and start the drive, leaving Granville, Doc, Matt, and myself to picket the mountain. I was given a stand about half a mile east of the cabin, and had but a vague notion of where the others went.

By jinks, it was cold! I built a fire between the buttressing roots of a big mountain oak, but still my toes and fingers were numb. This was the 25th of November, and we were at an altitude where sometimes frost forms in July. The other men were more thinly clad than I, and with not a stitch of wool beyond their stocking; yet they seemed to revel in the keen air. I wasted some pity on Cope, who had no underwear worthy of the name; but afterwards I learned that he would not have worn more clothes if they had been given to him. This fellow never owned a coat until after his marriage. It is literal fact that some of these mountaineers (women and children, as well as men) think nothing of running around barefooted for hours in snow that is ankle-deep. One of my neighbor's children went barefooted all one winter, when the thermometer several times went below zero Fahrenheit. Many a night my companions had slept out on the mountain without blanket or shelter, when the ground froze and every twig in the forest was coated with rime from the winter fog.

Away out yonder beyond the mighty bulk of Clingmans Dome, which, black with spruce and balsam, looked like a vast bear rising to contemplate the northern world, there streaked the first faint, nebulous hint of dawn. Presently the big bear's head was tipped with a golden crown flashing against the scarlet fires of the firmament, and the earth awoke.

A rustling some hundred yards below me gave signal that the gray squirrels were on their way to water. Out of a tree overhead popped a mountain "boomer" (red squirrel), and down he came, eyed me, and stopped.

Somewhere from the sky came a strange, half-human note, as of someone chiding: "*Wal*-lace, *Wal*-lace, *Wat*!" I could get no view for the trees. Then the thing sailed into sight—a raven—flexibly changing its voice to a deep-toned "Co-*logne*, Co-*logne*, Co-*logne*."

As the morning drew on, I let the fire die to ashes and basked lazily in the sun. Not a sound had I heard from the dogs. My hoodoo was working malignly. Well, let it work. I was comfortable now, and that old bear could go to any other doom she preferred. It was pleasant enough to lie here alone in the forest and be free! Aye, it was good to be alive, and to be far, far away from the broken bottles and old tin cans of civilization.

For many a league to the southward clouds covered all the valleys in billows of white, from which rose a hundred mountain tops, like islands in a tropic ocean. My fancy sailed among and beyond them, beyond the horizon's rim, even unto those far seas that I had sailed in my youth, to the old times and the old friends that I should never see again.

But a forenoon is long-drawn-out when one has breakfasted before dawn, and has nothing to do but sit motionless in the woods and watch and listen. I got to fingering my rifle trigger impatiently and wishing that a wild Thanksgiving gobbler might blunder into view. Squirrels made ceaseless chatter all around my stand. Large hawks shrilled by me within tempting range, whistling like spent bullets. A groundhog sat up on a log and whistled, too, after a manner of his own. He was so near that I could see his nose wiggle. A skunk waddled around for twenty minutes, and once came so close that I thought he would nibble my boot. I was among old mossy beeches, scaled with polyphori, and twisted into postures of torture by their battles with the storms. Below, among chestnuts and birches, I could hear the *t-wee, t-wee* of "joree-birds" (towhees), which winter in the valleys. Incessantly came the *chip-chip-chip* of ground squirrels, the saucy bark of the grays, and great chirruping among the "boomers."

Far off on my left a rifle cracked. I pricked up and listened intently, but there was never a yelp from a dog. Since it is a law of the chase to fire at nothing smaller than turkeys, lest big game be scared away, this shot might mean a gobbler. I knew that Matt Hyde, to save his soul, could not sit ten minutes on a stand without calling turkeys (and he *could* call them with his unassisted mouth better than anyone I ever heard perform with leaf or wing bone or any other contrivance).

Thus the slow hours dragged along. I yearned mightily to stretch my legs. Finally, being certain that no drive would approach my stand that day, I ambled back to the hut and did a turn at dinner-getting. Things were smoking, and smelt good, by the time four of our men turned up, all of them dog-tired and disappointed, but stoical.

"That pup Coaly chased off atter a wildcat," blurted John. "We held the old dogs together and let him rip. Then Dred started a deer. It was that old buck that everybody's shot at, and missed, this three year back. I'd believe he's a hant if 't wasn't for his tracks—they're the biggest I ever seen. He must weigh two hundred and fifty. But he's a foxy cuss. Tuk right down the bed o' Desolation, up the left prong of Roaring Fork, right through the Devil's Race-path (how a deer can git through thar *I* don't see!), crossed at the Meadow Gap, went down Eagle Creek, and by now he's in the Little Tennessee. That buck, shorely to God, has wings!"

We were at table in the Carolina room when Matt Hyde appeared. He was the worst tatterdemalion I had seen outside of a hobo camp, his lower extremities being almost naked. Sure enough, he bore a turkey hen.

"I was callin' a gobbler when this fool thing showed up. I fired a shoot as she riz in the air, but only bruk her wing. She made off on her legs like the devil whoppin' out fire. I run, an' she run. Guess I run her half a mile through all-fired thickets. She piped '*Quit—quit*,' but I said 'I'll see you in hell afore I quit!' and the chase resumed. Finally I knocked her over with a birch stob, and here we are."

Matt ruefully surveyed his legs. "Boys," said he, "I'm nigh breachless."

None but native-born mountaineers could have stood the strain of another drive that day, for the country that Cope and Cable had been through was fearful, especially the laurel up Roaring Fork and Killpeter Ridge. But the stamina of these withey little men was even more remarkable than their endurance of cold. After a slice of meat (about half what a Northern office man would eat), a chunk of half-baked johnny-cake, and a pint or so of coffee, they were as fresh as ever.

I had made the coffee strong, and it was good stuff that I had brought from home. After his first deep draught, Little John exclaimed: "Hah! boys, that coffee hits whar ye hold it!"

I thought that a neat compliment from a sharp-shooter.

We took new stands; but the afternoon passed without incident to those of us on the mountain tops. I returned to camp about five o'clock, and was surprised to see three of our men lugging across the gant-lot a small female bear.

"Hyar's yer old black woman," shouted John.

"How's this? I didn't hear any drive."

"Thar wa'n't none."

"Then where did you get your bear?"

"In one of Steve Howard's traps, dum him! Boys, I wish we *hed* roasted the temper outen them trap springs, like we talked o' doin'."

"The bear was alive, wasn't it?"

"As live as a hot coal. See the pup's head!"

I examined Coaly, who looked sick. The flesh was torn from his lower jaw and hung down a couple of inches. Two holes in the top of his head showed where the bear's tusks had done their best to crack his skull.

"When the other dogs found her, he rushed right in. She hadn't been trapped more'n a few hours, and she larned Coaly somethin' about the bear business."

"Won't this spoil him for hunting hereafter?"

"Not if he has his daddy's and mammy's grit. We'll know by tomorrow whether he's a shore-enough bear dog; for I've larned now whar they're crossin'—seed sign a-plenty."

All of us were indignant at the setter of the trap. It had been hidden in a trail, with no sign to warn a man from stepping into it. In Tennessee, I was told, it is a penitentiary offense to set out a bear trap. We agreed that a similar law ought to be passed in North Carolina.

"It's only two years ago," said Granville, "that Jasper Millington, an old man living on the Tennessee side, started acrost the mountain to get work at the Everett mine. Not fur from where we are now he stepped into a bear trap that was hid in the leaves, like this one. It broke his leg, and he starved to death in it."

Despite our indignation meeting, it was decided to carry the trapped bear's hide to Howard, and for us to use only the meat as recompense for trouble, to say nothing of risk to life and limb. Such is the mountaineers' regard for property rights!

The animal we had ingloriously won was undersized, weighing a scant 175 pounds. The average weight of Smoky Mountain bears is not great, but occasionally a very large beast is killed. Matt Hyde told us that he killed one on the Welch Divide in 1901, the meat of which, dressed, without the hide, weighed 434 pounds, and the hide "squared eight feet" when stretched for drying.

We spent the evening in debate as to where the next drive should be made. Some favored moving six miles eastward to the old mining shack at Siler's Meadow and trying the head waters of Forney's

Creek, around Rip Shin Thicket and the Gunstick Laurel, driving towards Clingmans Dome and over into the bleak gulf, southwest of the Sugarland Mountains, that I had named Godforsaken—a title that stuck. We knew there were bears in that region, though it was a desperately rough country to hunt in.

But John and the hunchback had found "sign" in the opposite direction. Bears were crossing from Little River in the neighborhood of Thunderhead and Briar Knob, coming up just west of the Devil's Court House and "using" around Block House, Woolly Ridge, Bear Pen, and thereabouts. The motion carried, and we adjourned to bed.

We breakfasted on bear meat, the remains of our Thanksgiving turkey and wheat bread shortened with bear's grease until it was light as a feather, and I made tea. It was the first time that Little John ever saw "store tea." He swallowed some of it as if it had been boneset, under the impression that it was some sort of "yerb" that would be good for his insides.

"Wal, people," exclaimed Matt, "I 'low I've done growed a bit, after that mess of meat. Le's be movin'."

It was a hard trip for me, climbing up the rock approach to Briar Knob. You may laugh as you please about a lowlander's lungs feeling rarefaction at

5,000 or 5,500 feet, but in the very moist air of the Southern mountains, with fog (cloud) in the bargain, most newcomers do feel it for a few days.

The boys were anxious for me to get a shot. I was paying them nothing; it was share-and-share alike; but their neighborly kindness moved them to do their best for the "furriner."

So they put on me what was probably the best stand for the day. It was above the Fire Scald, a *brûlé* or burnt-over space on the steep southern side of the ridge between Briar Knob and Laurel Top, overlooking the grisly slope of Killpeter. Here I could both see and hear an uncommonly long distance, and if the bear went either east or west I would have timely warning.

I had shivered on the mountain top for a couple of hours, hearing only an occasional bark from the dogs, which had been working in the thickets a mile or so below me, when suddenly there burst forth the devil of a racket. On came the chase, right in my direction. Presently I could even distinguish the different notes—the deep bellow of old Dred, the houndlike baying of Rock and Coaly, and Little Towse's yelp. I thought that the bear might chance the comparatively open space of the Fire Scald, because there were still some ashes on the ground which would dust the dogs' nostrils and tend to throw them off the scent. And such, I do believe, was

his intention. But the dogs caught up with him.
They nipped him fore and aft. Time after time he
shook them off; but they were true bear dogs, and
knew no such word as quit.

I took a last squint at my rifle sights, made sure
there was a cartridge in the chamber, and then felt
my ears grow as I listened. Suddenly the chase
swerved at a right angle and took straight up the side
of Saddle-back. Either the bear would tree, or he
would try to smash on through to the low rhodo-
dendron of the Devil's Court House, where dogs
who followed might break their legs. I girded myself
and ran, "wiggling and wingling" along the main
divide, and then came the steep pull up Briar Knob.
As I was grading around the summit with all the
lope that was left in me, I heard a rifle crack, half a
mile down Saddle-back. Old Doc was somewhere in
that vicinity. I halted to listen. Creation, what a
rumpus! Then another shot. Then the war whoop of
the South that we read about.

By and by, up they came, John and Cope and Doc,
carrying the bear on a trimmed sapling. Presently
Hyde joined us, then came Granville, and we filed
back to camp, where Doc told his story:

"Boys, them dogs' eyes shined like new money.
Coaly fit again, all right, and got his tail bit. The
bear div down into a sink-hole with the dogs atop
o' him. Soon's I could shoot without hittin' a dog, I

let him have it. Thought I'd shot him through the head, but he fit on. Then I jumped down into the sink an' kicked him loose from the dogs, or he'd a-killed Coaly. Wal, sir, he wa'n't hurt a bit—the ball just glanced off his head. He riz and knocked me down with his left paw, an' walked right over me, an' lit up the ridge. The dogs treed him in a minute. I went to shoot up at him, but my new hulls fit loose in this old chamber and the one drap out, so the gun stuck. Had to git my knife out and fit hit. Then the dad-burned gun wouldn't stand roostered (cocked); the feather-spring had jumped out o' place. But I held back with my thumb, and killed him anyhow."

"Bears," said John, "is all left-handed. Ever note that? Hit's the left paw you want to look out fer. He'd a-knocked somethin' out o' yer head if thar'd been much in it, Doc."

And so, laughing and chaffing, we finished dinner.

The mountaineers have a curious way of sharing the spoils of the chase. A bear's hide is sold and the proceeds divided equally among the hunters, but the meat is cut up into as many pieces as there are partners in the chase; then one man goes indoors or behind a tree, and somebody at the carcass, laying his hand on a portion, calls out: "Whose piece is this?"

"Granville Calhoun's," cries the hidden man, who cannot see it.

"Whose is this?"

"Bill Cope's."

And so on down the line. Everybody gets what chance determines for him, and there can be no charge of unfairness.

The next morning John announced that we were going to get another bear.

"Night afore last," he said, "Bill dremp that he saw a lot o' fat meat lyin' on the table; an' it done come true. Last night I dremp one that never was known to fail. Now you'll see it!"

It did not look like it by evening. We all worked hard and endured much—standers as well as drivers—but not a rifle had spoken up to the time when, from my far-off stand, I yearned for a hot supper.

Away down in the rear I heard the snort of a locomotive, one of those cog-wheel affairs that are specially built for mountain climbing. With a steam-loader and three camps of a hundred men each, it was despoiling the Tennessee forest. Slowly, but inexorably, a leviathan was crawling into the wilderness to consume it.

Wearily I plodded back to camp. No one had arrived but Doc. The old man had been thumped rather severely in yesterday's scrimmage, but complained only of "a touch o' rheumatiz." Just how the latter had left his clothes in tatters he did not explain.

It was late when Matt and Granville came in. The crimson and yellow of sunset had turned to a faultless turquoise, and this to a violet afterglow; then suddenly night rose from the valleys and enveloped us.

About nine o'clock I went out on the Little Chestnut Bald and fired signals, but there was no answer. The last we had known of the drivers was that they had been beyond Thunderhead, six miles of hard travel to the westward. There was fog on the mountain. Then Granville and Matt took the lantern and set out for Briar Knob. Doc was too stiff for travel, and I, being at that time a stranger in the Smokies, would be of no use hunting amid clouds and darkness. Doc and I passed a dreary three hours. Finally, at midnight, my shots were answered, and soon the dogs came limping in. Dred had been severely bitten in the shoulders and Rock in the head. Coaly was bloody about the mouth, where his first day's wound had reopened. Then came the four men, empty-handed, it seemed, until John slapped a bear's "melt" (spleen) upon the table. He limped from a bruised hip.

"That bear went 'way around all o' you-uns. We follered him clar over to the Spencer Place, and then he doubled and come back on the fur side o' the ridge. He crossed through the laurel on the Devil's Court House and tuk down an almighty steep place.

It was plumb night by that time. I fell over a rock clift twenty feet down, and if't hadn't been for the laurel I'd a-bruk some bones. I landed right in the middle of them, bear and dogs, fightin' like game-cocks. The bear clim a tree. Bill sung out 'Is it fur down that?' and I said 'Pretty fur.' 'Wal, I'm a-comin',' says he; and with that he grabbed a laurel to swing hisself down by, but the stem bruk, and down he came suddent, to jine the music. Hit was so dark I couldn't see my gun barrel, and we wuz all tangled up in green briars as thick as plough-lines. I had to fire twicet afore he tumbled. Then Matt an' Granville come. The four of us tuk turn-about crawlin' up out o' thar with the bear on our back. Only one man could handle him at a time—and he'll go a good two hundred, that bear. We gutted him, and left him near the top, to fotch in the mornin'. Boys, this is the time I'd give nigh all I'm worth for half a gallon o' liquor—and I'd promise the rest!"

"You'd orter see what Coaly did to that varmint," said Bill. "He bit a hole under the fore leg, through hide and ha'r, clar into the holler, so that you can stick your hand in and seize the bear's heart."

"John, what was that dream?"

"I dremp I stole a feller's overcoat. Now d'ye see? That means a bear's hide."

Coaly, three days ago, had been an inconsequential pup; but now he looked up into my eyes with the calm dignity that no fool or braggart can assume. He had been knighted. As he licked his wounds he was proud of them. "Scars of battle, sir. You may have your swagger ribbons and prize collars in the New York dog show, but *this* for me!"

The Forest and the Steppe

[IVAN TURGENEV]

And slowly something began to draw him
Back to the country, to the garden dark,
Where lime-trees are so huge, so full of shade,
And lilies of the valley, sweet as maids,
Where rounded willows o'er the water's edge
Lean from the dyke in rows, and where the oak
Sturdily grows above the sturdy field,
Amid the smell of hemp and nettles rank. . . .
There, there, in meadows stretching wide,
Where rich and black as velvet is the earth,
Where the sweet rye, far as the eye can see,
Moves noiselessly in tender, billowing waves,
And where the heavy golden light is shed
From out of rounded, white, transparent clouds:
There it is good. . . .
(From a poem consigned to the flames)

The reader is, very likely, already weary of my sketches; I hasten to reassure him by promising to confine myself to the fragments already printed; but I cannot refrain from saying a few words at parting about a hunter's life.

Hunting with a dog and a gun is delightful in itself, *für sich*, as they used to say in old days; but let us suppose you were not born a hunter, but are fond of nature and freedom all the same; you cannot then help envying us hunters. . . . Listen.

Do you know, for instance, the delight of settling off before daybreak in spring? You come out on to the steps. . . . In the dark-grey sky stars are twinkling here and there; a damp breeze in faint gusts flies to meet you now and then; there is heard the secret, vague whispering of the night; the trees faintly rustle, wrapt in darkness. And now they put a rug in the cart, and lay a box with the samovar at your feet. The trace-horses move restlessly, snort, and daintily paw the ground; a couple of white geese, only just awake, waddle slowly and silently across the road. On the other side of the hedge, in the garden, the watchman is snoring peacefully; every sound seems to stand still in the frozen air—suspended, not moving. You take your seat; the horses start at once; the cart rolls off with a loud rumble. You ride—ride past the church, downhill to the right, across the dyke. . . . The pond is just beginning to be covered with mist. You are rather chilly; you cover your face with the collar of your fur cloak; you doze. The horses' hoofs splash sonorously through the puddles; the coachman begins to whistle. But by now you have driven over four versts . . . the rim of the sky flushes crimson; the jackdaws are heard, fluttering clumsily in the birch-trees; sparrows are twittering about the dark hayricks. The air is clearer, the road more distinct, the sky brightens, the clouds look whiter, and the fields look greener. In the huts there is the red light of flaming chips; from behind gates comes the sound of sleepy voices. And meanwhile the glow of dawn is beginning; already streaks of gold are stretching across the sky; mists are gathering in clouds over the ravines; the larks are singing musically; the breeze that ushers in the dawn is blowing; and slowly the purple sun floats upward. There is a perfect flood of light; your heart is fluttering like a bird. Everything is fresh, gay, delightful! One can see a long way all round. That way, beyond the copse, a village; there, further, another, with a white church, and there a birch-wood on the hill; behind it the marsh, for which you are bound . . . Quicker, horses, quicker! Forward at a good trot! . . . There are three versts to go—not more. The sun mounts swiftly higher; the sky is clear. It will be a glorious day. A herd of cattle comes straggling from the village to meet you. You go up the hill. . . . What a view! the river winds for ten versts, dimly blue through the mist; beyond it meadows of watery green; beyond the meadows sloping hills; in the distance the plovers are wheeling with loud cries above the marsh; through the moist brilliance suffused in the air the distance stands out clearly . . . not as in the summer. How freely one drinks in the air, how quickly the limbs move, how strong is the whole man, clasped in the fresh breath of spring! . . .

And a summer morning—a morning in July! Who but the hunter knows how soothing it is to wander at daybreak among the underwoods? The print of your feet lies in a green line on the grass, white with dew. You part the drenched bushes; you are met by a rush of the warm fragrance stored up in the night; the air is saturated with the fresh bitterness of wormwood, the honey sweetness of buckwheat and clover; in the distance an oak wood stands like a wall, and glows and glistens in the sun; it is still fresh, but already the approach of heat is felt. The head is faint and dizzy from the excess of sweet scents. The copse stretches on endlessly. Only in places there are yellow glimpses in the distance of ripening rye, and narrow streaks of red buckwheat. Then there is the creak of cart wheels; a peasant makes his way among the bushes at a walking pace, and sets his horse in the shade before the heat of the day. You greet him, and turn away; the musical swish of the scythe is heard behind you. The sun rises higher and higher. The grass is speedily dry. And now it is quite sultry. One hour passes, another. . . . The sky grows dark over the horizon; the still air is baked with prickly heat. "Where can one get a drink here, brother?" you inquire of the mower. "Yonder, in the ravine's a well." Through the thick hazel bushes, tangled by the clinging grass, you drop down to the bottom of the ravine. Right under the cliff a little spring is hidden; an oak bush greedily spreads out its twigs like great fingers over the water; great silvery bubbles rise trembling from the bottom, covered with fine velvety moss. You fling yourself on the ground, you drink, but you are too lazy to stir. You are in the shade, you drink in the damp fragrance, you take your ease, while the bushes face you, glowing and, as it were, turning yellow in the sun. But what is that? There is a sudden flying gust of wind; the air is astir all about you: was not that thunder? Is it the heat thickening? Is a storm coming on? . . . And now there is a faint flash of lightning. Yes, there will be a storm! The sun is still blazing; you can still go on hunting. But the storm-cloud grows; its front edge, drawn out like a long sleeve, bends over into an arch. Make haste! over there you think you catch sight of a hay-barn . . . make haste! . . . You run there, go in. . . . What rain! What flashes of lightning! The water drips in through some hole in the thatch-roof on to the sweet-smelling hay. But now the sun is shining bright again. The storm is over; you come out. My God, the joyous sparkle of everything! the fresh, limpid air, the scent of raspberries and mush-rooms! And then the evening comes on. There is the blaze of fire glowing and covering half the sky. The sun sets; the air near you has a peculiar transparency as of crystal; over the distance lies a soft, warm-looking haze; with the dew a crimson light is shed on the fields, lately plunged in floods of limpid gold; from trees and bushes and high stacks of hay run long shadows. The sun has set; a star gleams and quivers in the fiery sea of the sunset; and now it pales; the sky grows blue; the separate shadows van-ish; the air is plunged in darkness. It is time to turn homewards to the village, to the hut, where you will stay the night. Shouldering your gun, you move briskly, in spite of fatigue. Meanwhile, the night comes on: now you cannot see twenty paces from you; the dogs show faintly white in the dark. Over there, above the black bushes, there is a vague bright-ness on the horizon. What is it?—a fire? . . . No, it is the moon rising. And away below, to the right, the village lights are twinkling already. And here at last is your hut. Through the tiny window you see a table, with a white cloth, a candle burning, supper. . . .

Another time you order the racing droshky to be got out, and set off to the forest to shoot woodcock.

It is pleasant making your way along the narrow path between two high walls of rye. The ears softly strike you in the face; the corn-flowers cling round your legs; the quails call around; the horse moves along at a lazy trot. And here is the forest, all shade and silence. Graceful aspens rustle high above you; the long hanging branches of the birches scarcely stir; a mighty oak stands like a champion beside a lovely lime-tree. You go along the green path, streaked with shade; great yellow flies stay suspended, motionless, in the sunny air, and suddenly dart away; midges hover in a cloud, bright in the shade, dark in the sun; the birds are singing peacefully; the golden little voice of the warbler sings of innocent, babbling joyousness, in sweet accord with the scent of the lilies of the valley. Further, further, deeper into the forest . . . the forest grows more dense. . . . An unutterable stillness falls upon the soul within; without, too, all is still and dreamy. But now a wind has sprung up, and the tree-tops are booming like falling waves. Here and there, through last year's brown leaves, grow tall grasses; mushrooms stand apart under their wide-brimmed hats. All at once a hare skips out; the dog scurries after it with a resounding bark. . . .

And how fair is this same forest in late autumn, when the snipe are on the wing! They do not keep in the heart of the forest; one must look for them along the outskirts. There is no wind, and no sun, no light, no shade, no movement, no sound; the autumn perfume, like the perfume of wine, is diffused in the soft air; a delicate haze hangs over the yellow fields in the distance. The still sky is a peacefully untroubled white through the bare brown branches; in parts, on the limes, hang the last golden leaves. The damp earth is elastic under your feet; the high dry blades of grass do not stir; long threads lie shining on the blanched turf, white with dew. You breathe tranquilly; but there is a strange tremor in the soul. You walk along the forest's edge, look after your dog, and meanwhile loved forms, loved faces, dead and living, come to your mind; long, long slumbering impressions unexpectedly awaken; the fancy darts off and soars like a bird; and all moves so clearly and stands out before your eyes. The heart at one time throbs and beats, plunging passionately forward; at another it is drowned beyond recall in memories. Your whole life, as it were, unrolls lightly and rapidly before you; a man at such times possesses all his past, all his feelings and his powers—all his soul; and there is nothing around to hinder him—no sun, no wind, no sound. . . .

And a clear, rather cold autumn day, with a frost in the morning, when the birch, all golden like some tree in a fairy-tale, stands out picturesquely against the pale-blue sky; when the sun, standing low in the sky, does not warm, but shines more brightly than in summer; the small aspen copse is all a-sparkle through and through, as though it were glad and at ease in its nakedness; the hoar-frost is still white at the bottom of the hollows; while a fresh wind softly stirs up and drives before it the falling, crumpled leaves; when blue ripples whisk gladly along the river, lifting rhythmically the scattered geese and ducks; in the distance the mill creaks, half hidden by the willows; and with changing colours in the clear air the pigeons wheel in swift circles above it.

Sweet, too, are dull days in summer, though the hunters do not like them. On such days one can't shoot the bird that flutters up from under your very feet and vanishes at once in the whitish dark of the hanging fog. But how peaceful, how unutterably peaceful it is everywhere! Everything is awake, and everything is hushed. You pass by a tree: it does not stir a leaf; it is musing in repose. Through the thin steamy mist, evenly diffused in the air, there is a long streak of black before you. You take it for a neigh-bouring copse close at hand; you go up—the copse is transformed into a high row of wormwood in the boundary-ditch. Above you, around you, on all sides—mist. . . . But now a breeze is faintly astir; a patch of pale-blue sky peeps dimly out; through the thinning, as it were, steaming mist, a ray of golden-yellow sunshine breaks out suddenly, flows in a long stream, strikes on the fields and in the copse—and now everything is overcast again. For long this struggle is drawn out, but how unutterably brilliant and magnificent the day becomes when at last light triumphs and the last waves of the warmed mist here unroll and are drawn out over the plains, there wind away and vanish into the deep, softly shining heights.

Again you set off into outlying country, to the steppe. For some ten versts you make your way over cross-roads, and here at last is the highroad. Past endless trains of waggons, past wayside taverns, with the hissing samovar under a shed, wide-open gates and a well, from one hamlet to another; across endless fields, alongside green hempfields, a long, long time you drive. The magpies flutter from willow to willow; peasant women with long rakes in their hands wander in the fields; a man in a threadbare nankin overcoat, with a wicker pannier over his shoulder, trudges along with weary step; a heavy country coach, harnessed with six tall, broken-winded horses, rolls to meet you. The corner of a cushion is sticking out of a window, and on a sack up behind, hanging on to a string, perches a groom in a fur cloak, splashed with mud to his very eyebrows. And here is the little district town with its crooked little wooden houses, its endless fences, its empty stone shops, its old-fashioned bridge over a deep ravine. On, on! . . . The steppe country is reached at last.

You look from a hill-top; what a view! Round low hills, tilled and sown to their very tops, are seen in broad undulations; ravines, overgrown with bushes, wind coiling among them; small copses are scattered like oblong islands; from village to village run narrow paths; churches stand out white; between willow bushes glimmers a little river, in four places dammed up by dykes; far off, in a field, in a line, an old manor house, with its outhouses, orchard, and threshing-floor, huddles close up to a small pond. But on, on you go. The hills are smaller and ever smaller; there is scarcely a tree to be seen. Here it is at last—the boundless, untrodden steppe!

And on a winter day to walk over the high snow-drifts after hares; to breathe the keen frosty air, while half-closing the eyes involuntarily at the fine blinding sparkle of the soft snow; to admire the emerald sky above the reddish forest! . . . And the first spring day when everything is shining, and breaking up, when across the heavy streams, from the melting snow, there is already the scent of the thawing earth; when on the bare thawed places, under the slanting sunshine, the larks are singing confidingly, and, with glad splash and roar, the torrents roll from ravine to ravine.

But it is time to end. By the way, I have spoken of spring: in spring it is easy to part; in spring even the happy are drawn away to the distance. . . . Farewell, reader! I wish you unbroken prosperity.

Bob White,
Down 't Aberdeen

⌯

[NASH BUCKINGHAM]

ndrew's letter was characteristic. "Entirely
all right and welcome to include the Gentleman from Boston. Never mind the Yan-
kee strain in his breeding. If he proves a good shot
and able to negotiate a few of Colonel Lauderdale's
75–90 h.p. toddies, the Rebels will stand for his
pedigree, and even though it leaks out that he's a
Republican, why our game laws will protect him. I
know a place where the birds are holding a conven-
tion. Down across the river, about eight miles from
here, in a sandy-loam and pine-hill country full of
sedge, pea patches and sorghum. I have a fine old
friend there. He runs a water mill, but the last man
he killed was a Prohibitionist. Grinds his own flour
and believe me, boy, he is *a* biscuit maker. If you

don't choose goggle-eyed hen eggs (from contented hens) about twice the size of fifty-dollar gold pieces, and can't choke down real all-pork sausage and baked hams, why bring along your own sum'p'n t'eat. The plug gets in so late that you all may have to go to the hotel for the night but Johnny'll move your outfit out to the house next day. Couldn't do much with Johnny after dark anyhow. There's a ghost scare on down here. A phantom called Mother Hubbard is working around the streets and Johnny claims that she 'done run sev-ul uv his frens' right on to degradation.' Fat chance to get him to hang around till midnight!"

How pleasant the recollection that drifted back a twelvemonth in prospective enjoyment of another visit! We were sitting again in comfortable cane-bottomed rockers on the wide veranda of the High Private's ancestral home. From crevices of the lofty, iron-capped columns clung villages of nests, in and out of which twittered the sparrows, bent either upon warlike sally against shrill encroaching jays or engaged in piercing squabbles relating to matters of domestic retention. It was Sunday afternoon on the Old Home Place, in the sweet purpling of a brave autumnal day. From down Matubba road the *puffity-pant* of the cotton gin was hushed. No crop wagons creaked past in swirls of Indian summer dust with their sputtering crackle of long blacksnake whips, uncoiling over the sodgerin' back and along sleek ribs of "jug-haids." There was no jocose lingo of the mule curse; no bare-fanged country dogs, entrenched beneath the wagons. It was the time of year when flashing dawns melted away the tinge of frost scrolls from russet woodland; when gaud and arrogance of capricious color gave riotous defiance to the approach of sombrous winter. Black fingers twinkled among the hoary yield of cotton bolls; 'possum and coon throve in the bottoms; darky chants rose to exultant pitch with divers harbingers of peace and plenty. Doomed by ripe fatness and assaults with stick and stone, luscious persimmons plumped to earth and schoolboy stomachs. "Egg-bustin'" puppies raced abroad, causing Brer Rabbit to hoist subject-to-change-without-notice signs. Canvas-coated hunters rode afield; lithe pointers and setters searched hill and dale for Bob Whites that leaped roaring from embrowning covert. And then—

I glanced mournfully through an office window into the forbidding bleakness of our latest cold snap. Surely, I reflected, it was a fine day for a murder or to set a hen. But, to the Gentleman from Boston, languishing at his hotel, I broke the glad tidings of our invitation, and grouchily set about waiting a squarer deal from the elements. Next day dawned clear as a bell. I had just spread the sporting section when

Andrew called over Long Distance. At five that afternoon we cast off, aboard the "Plug," an abused little red-in-the-face train with a seven-hour-or-more-trip staring us straight in the stomach. Fast trains chased us into sidings and burly freights hooted us into submission, leaving the poor Plug to scramble home out of breath, practically discouraged and ready to give up. It was past midnight when we finally boomed across the Tombigbee, did a "gran' right an' left" in the switching line and bumped into the silent and aristocratic town of Aberdeen, Mississippi.

Two night-owl porters for rival hotels quarreled bitterly over our bags, one darky threatening to "part yo' hair, niggah, ef yo' doan turn loose dat grip-sack; don' yo' see dat fine-lookin' white man from Memphis don' want to stop at nobody's house 'cep mine?" This sable and subtle flattery had an effect of quelling the incipient riot, so we hastened uptown, registered at the comfortable Clopton House and dug far into our warm beds.

Morning came with reverse English on the fair weather. Leaden, blowy skies, an icy wind that promised chilly creeps and deeply gashed gumbo roads frozen into treacherous depths. Andrew was on hand early and regretted that it would be practically impossible to reach his selected territory. "But," said he, "we'll take in some ground I shot over last week and find all the birds we're lookin' for."

Breakfast over, the steeds were led up; Andrew whistled for Flash and Jim and we were off. The horse allotted the Gentleman from Boston was of dignified personality and winning ways, but the brute I drew was a "low-life" pure and simple. Scarcely had I a leg up, when, for the edification of a morbidly curious public, the wretch came undone right there on Main street. The idea of a regular, everyday Southern horse trying to sunfish and timberline rather surprised me, to say the least, and for a moment, just a moment, I had a good notion to hang my spurs in him and accompany the scratching with a tremendous beating over the head with my hat and a lot of yelling thrown in or off. But I had no spurs, so kept my hat out of the ring, clung to my weapon and pulled leather until Seldom-Fed quit hogging.

Our trek led through the stately old burg past the huge courthouse, crumbly with its struggle against the years, reminiscent of impassioned oratory and bitter but courtly legal battles. At intervals we glimpsed through spacious boundaries of wintered cedar hedge, oak, and locust, old-fashioned homes of singular and comforting beauty. Some, with their broad porches and superb lines of colonial paneling drooping into an almost sagging dilapidation of wartime impoverishment; others bespeaking an eloquent survival and defiance of time.

Leaving town we struck off into a bottom land of

down corn and thicket. Out of the north a freezing, stinging wind wrung tears from our eyes with its biting whip. At the first ditch Andrew broke ice, wet our dogs' feet and applied a coating of tannic acid. A moment later, when cast off, they headed up through a corn field. Almost in the same breath it seemed, they froze on a point at an impenetrable thicket bordering a wide pond. We were more than glad to dismount and hurry toward the find. Approaching, we saw the birds flush wild and sweep across the pond into some briar tangles. We skirted the marsh, and, shooting in turn, managed to start the ball rolling with five singles. Leading our mounts, for walking proved far more preferable than facing the wind, we plugged through a creek bottom. We were joined here by a strange pointer belonging, Andrew said, to a gentleman in Aberdeen. "Flight" had evidently observed the departure of our safari, and being of congenial trend, had taken up the trail. Rounding a thicket clump we discovered Jimmy holding staunchly, with Flash backing as though his very life depended upon it. The new dog celebrated his arrival by pausing a second, as though to contemplate the picture, then dashed in, sending birds in every direction. The Gentleman from Boston accomplished a neat double, Andrew singled, but I was too far away to do much of anything save cuss and watch down a single or two. Andrew had Flash and Jim retrieve, then turned and eyed the guilt-stricken Flight with narrowed lids. Placing his gun against a convenient bush, he ripped a substantial switch from a sapling and grittingly invited the hapless one approach. This he did, in fawning, contrite hesitation, while the other dogs loafed in to enjoy the circus and give him the laugh. A moment later his cries rent the air, but the whaling had its effect—he flushed no more that day and attended strictly to business. At the horses we found Joe Howard, Andrew's cousin, who brought with him his good pointer, Ticket. Joe had ridden from his home two miles beyond town and reported tough sledding.

Fording a slushy bayou, we rode a short distance before seeing Flash, rigid as a poker, pointing in a ravine. Tick and Jim flattened on sight and Flight, with vivid memory of his recent dressing down, sprawled when Andrew's sharp warning reached him. A huge bevy buzzed from the sedge. "Blam-blam and blooie-blooie" ensued, with the result that each man tucked away a pair of birds in his coat. The singles went "home-free" by winging it across an ice-gorged back water. Farther on, Flight re-established himself somewhat in our good graces by a ripping find. It was ludicrous to see the fellow roll his protruding eyes and warn off the covetous Ticket who wormed a bit too near in an effort to assist. But best of all a glorious sun burned a blazing way through the clouds and cheered up everything.

In higher country, following the direction taken by some split-covey singles we saw Flight and Flash standing perhaps forty feet apart at the edge of a dense timber bottom. Thinking they had spotted some truants we separated; the Boston Boy and I going to Flash while Joe and Andrew pinned their faith to Flight's fancy. To our amazement two clustrous bevies roared from the clover almost simultaneously. Ed and I dropped four from our rise, while Joe and Andrew drew equal toll from theirs. For the next half hour we enjoyed the most magnificent of all shooting—single birds scattered in hedge boundaries and along the leaf-strewn files of the timber. We kicked about here and there, joking, laughing, betting on shots, taking turns as the dogs ranged stealthily ahead, pointing, it seemed, almost every moment. Occasionally, when a bird lay low or flushed wild some smooth chap, made a getaway, but we begrudged not one of these his escape. Finally, with bulging pockets we returned to the horses.

At a free-flowing artesian well Joe and Andrew produced capacious saddle pockets and unwound savory bundles. Their contents would have made the weariest Fletcherite drool at the mouth and forget his number of chews. There was cold quail and crisp "beat" biscuit. Then came "hog-haid" sandwiches and meaty spareribs, home-made pickles and hard-boiled eggs. And to top off came a jam cake and a chocolate one, the latter inlaid with marshmallow sauce and studded with walnut and pecan hearts.

Nothing disturbed the noon stillness save grunts of purest satisfaction serene and an occasional yell of "Aw, git away f'um here, dawg." After lunch came a pipe for the others and a "touch" by an old colored mammy who came like Rebekah to the Well, with her pitcher and a hard-luck story of the burned cabin. We each shelled out "two bits," and in addition to this purse a fat cane-cutter rabbit that Joe had bowled over surreptitiously sent her on her way rejoicing.

Climbing into our saddles we rode down through the spongy accretions of the bottoms, across a wide slough and out into a vast section of waste or "ole po' land" as Andrew termed it. A short way on Jim was discovered gazing rapturously into a plum thicket. We saw the birds go up and wing past, settling across a drainage ditch. One of the dogs had evidently come along down wind and frisked Jim out of a point, for he was very much embarrased. Then in rapid succession the dogs found birds seemingly right and left. Three big gangs were turned up within a radius of ten acres. It was glorious sport and the afternoon wore away almost without our knowledge. What with a puffy kill here, a miss there and the ever-recurring thrill when some tireless dog whirled into discovery, we were almost glad to gather up our reins and hit off toward the line of greening hills that marked the direction of our circle home.

In a short while we splashed across an expanse of meadow and began climbing through sedge-strewn valleys and steep ridges of pine forest. Shadows were lengthening among the trees and our horses' steps were muffled in the needle bedding underfoot. In an opening we halted and look away across the low-lands of our morning to where Aberdeen lay brooding in the peace and quiet of tranquil, fading sunshine. The piercing blast had softened with the chill of falling night. It seemed a thousand miles to the warmth of indoors and the delight of complete well-fed weariness. The faithful dogs had as yet evinced no signs of fatigue, in fact they were splitting the grass at top speed. Just as we reached the Gillespie place boundary fence Jimmy paused at a dry ditch along the road, sniffed, and then with head in air, walked forward as though treading on eggs.

"He's got his Sunday clothes on ag'in, ain't he?" asked Andrew, his face lighting with pardonable pride and a lean expansive grin. "But I believe we've all got pretty durn near the limit."

"Les'try 'em jus' one mo' fair fall," replied Joe, "it would be a shame to put one over on Jim dog after all his trouble."

"Satisfactory to me," pronounced Andrew. "Light

down, gents, and bust a few night caps"—shoving two shells into his stubby Parker. Here Jimmy broke his point and tiptoed gingerly after the running birds. Then, out over the brink boiled a veritable beehive of quail. Ensued a miniature sham battle, followed by shouts of "I got two" and counter claims of "I killed that one" and "Fetch daid, suh." Discipline was forgotten for the nonce, but matters were adjusted when the dogs brought in enough birds to credit each man with a clean, undisputed double. "Better count up here," said Joe, "I've gotta leave you lads at the nex' gate." So the tally began, with low murmurings as each chap pulled bird after bird from his multipocketed coat.

"The limit here," announced Andrew, finishing first.

"For the first time in my young life a limit," chortled the Boston Boy.

"Another victory for the untrammeled Democracy," said Joe.

"Sufficiency here," I confessed.

At a padlocked gate, down the road, Joe took leave of us with a parting shout of "See you in the morning, boys, at the Houston place gate." The sun was glowing faintly behind its borderland of western ridge spires. Our dogs, seeming to realize that their day's work was done, leaped gladly along to keep our pace. Through field and brake we trotted, and at length, swinging into a black buckshot road, straightened out for the home stretch down Life Boat Chapel lane. It was to me a familiar way, past homely daubed shacks and cabins, ashine with the gleam of lowly lamplight, redolent of wood fires, frying bacon and contentment.

And how the dogs did bark when we swung into the grounds of our host! What is there better in life than an evening spent within the domain of Sweet Hospitality? What is more delightful than when, clothed in the refreshened garb of citizenry, one lies at ease in a deep armchair or sits down to such a dinner as only an "Auntie" can dish up and send in to her "white folks"? And surely out upon the sea of night there rides no fairer craft than a towering four-poster.

It was past seven o'clock when we found ourselves at family breakfast. You have, no doubt, often begun the morning meal with a luscious orange. But listen! Have you ever seen a "yard boy" stagger in under a huge platter, wide as the bottom of a boat, piled high with quail, smothered as only Aunt Hannah can turn the trick, with a whole bucket of bird gravy for the hominy and grits? You may suit yourself about the spiced aromatic spirits of little pigs, or slices of float-away omelette, but personally I prefer to rather economize on space until the waffles start flocking in in droves. Did you ever tenderly smear a pair of round, crisp, eat-me-quick-for-the-love-of-Mike members of the waffle family; watching the molten country butter search out the receptive crevices and overflow each hollow? Then slathered the twain with a ruddy coating of home-kettled, right-from-the-heart, ribbon cane molasses? But at length Pud sounded retreat by announcing the horses. Scabbards and saddle pockets were tied on and we were off in the bright sunshine of a perfect day.

At the Houston place gate we found Joe waiting with the ever ready Ticket and Lady, the latter a Marse Ben-Bragg-Gladstone pup. Within two hours we had raised six bevies. Ticket was the first to make birds, stiffening in a clover patch along a railroad cut. Then little Lady raced away across a hill and made a neat find on the cast. Flash and Jim were old stagers on these grounds. Jim nailed a gang for Andrew near a blackjack stretch and Flash, after handling some of the singles, delved far into the interior and fastened upon a covey. For some time we had royal sport trying to make respectable averages in the dense tangle and the dogs tried hard to overlook the messy work their masters were doing when brown bullets would whir from the dead leaves and top the blackjacks in whizzing farewell.

After lunch we rode the hill crests, letting the dogs cut up the sides and valleys. On an opposite ridge we saw Andrew approach the top with Lady and Jim flagging ahead. Down went the pair on a clean-cut point.

"It's a shame to take the money," shouted Andrew, and, sure enough, he whirled two of the crowd into bird paradise. Midafternoon is the ideal time for bird finding and it was a treat to see the Boston Boy's eyes widen in wonderment when the dogs picked up bunch after bunch.

"By the gills of the sacred codfish," he exclaimed, feverishly ripping open a fresh box of shells, "I never knew there were this many birds in existence." But at length it again neared knocking-off time, so we spurred through the fields hoping for just one more find to make the day complete.

"There they are," called Joe, rising in his stirrups, pointing to Flash and Jim. And, sure enough, they were at it again, and such a whopper the covey proved! We were actually too amazed to shoot on the rise, but watched the fugitives settle in a marshy strip of iron weed bordering a willow "dreen." Suffice to say that we gave them our personal attention and when the war was over the result proved a fitting climax to another red-letter day. Twenty or twenty-five birds doesn't sound so many to a game hog, perhaps, but shooting four in a party, turn about or shooting alone, when a man has spent the hours afield with nature and taken from her cherished stores the satisfaction of twenty clean kills and the vagrant clinging pangs of many misses, he has done pretty much all that an unselfish heart could ever crave.

"Well," questioned Andrew, when our horses' heads were set toward home, "how does the Minute Man from ye Boston Towne like an everyday, Down-in-Dixie bird hunt, with a little Rebel Yell stuff on the side?"

The Gentleman from Boston sighed a sigh of rich content and stretched wearily in his saddle.

"You are now speaking," said he, with that methodical diction characteristic of the ultra-grammatical Bostonian, "of the very best thing in the universe."

"D'm'f'taint," I echoed softly.

And Andrew triple-plated this confirmation in the tongue of our Fatherland.

"Sho' is!"

Hunting on the Oregon Trail

[FRANCIS PARKMAN]

The country before us was now thronged with buffalo, and a sketch of the manner of hunting them will not be out of place. There are two methods commonly practised, "running" and "approaching." The chase on horseback, which goes by the name of "running," is the more violent and dashing mode of the two, that is to say, when the buffalo are in one of their wild moods; for otherwise it is tame enough. A practised and skilful hunter, well mounted, will sometimes kill five or six cows in a single chase, loading his gun again and again as his horse rushes through the tumult. In attacking a small band of buffalo, or in separating a single animal from the herd and assailing it apart from the rest, there is less excitement and less danger. In fact, the animals are at times so stupid and lethargic that there is little sport in killing them. With a bold and well-trained horse the hunter may ride so close to the buffalo that as they gallop side by side he may touch him with his hand; nor is there much danger in this as long as the buffalo's strength and breath continue unabated; but when he becomes tired and can no longer run with ease, with his tongue lolls out and the foam flies from his jaws, then the hunter had better keep a more respectful distance; the distressed brute may turn upon him at any instant; and especially at the moment when he fires his gun. The horse then leaps aside, and the hunter has need of a tenacious seat in the saddle, for if he is thrown to the ground there is no hope for him. When he sees his attack defeated, the buffalo resumes his flight, but if the shot is well directed he soon stops; for a few moments he stands still, then totters and falls heavily upon the prairie.

The chief difficulty in running buffalo, as it seems to me, is that of loading the gun or pistol at full gallop. Many hunters for convenience's sake carry three or four bullets in the mouth; the powder is poured down the muzzle of the piece, the bullet dropped in after it, the stock struck hard upon the pommel of the saddle, and the work is done. The danger of this is obvious. Should the blow on the pommel fail to send the bullet home, or should the bullet, in the act of aiming, start from its place and roll towards the muzzle, the gun would probably burst in discharging. Many a shattered hand and worse casualties besides have been the result of such an accident. To obviate it, some hunters make use of a ramrod, usually hung by a string from the neck, but this materially increases the difficulty of loading. The bows and arrows which the Indians use in running buffalo have many advantages over firearms, and even white men occasionally employ them.

The danger of the chase arises not so much from the onset of the wounded animal as from the nature of the ground which the hunter must ride over. The prairie does not always present a smooth, level, and uniform surface; very often it is broken with hills and hollows, intersected by ravines, and in the remoter parts studded by the stiff wild-sage bushes. The most formidable obstructions, however, are the burrows of wild animals, wolves, badgers, and particularly prairie-dogs, with whose holes the ground for a very great extent is frequently honeycombed. In the blindness of the chase the hunter rushes over it unconscious of danger; his horse, at full career, thrusts his leg deep into one of the burrows; the bone snaps, the rider is hurled forward to the ground and probably killed. Yet accidents in buffalo running happen less frequently than one would suppose; in the recklessness of the chase, the hunter enjoys all the impunity of a drunken man, and may ride in safety over gullies and declivities, where, should he attempt to pass in his sober senses, he would infallibly break his neck.

The method of "approaching," being practised on foot, has many advantages over that of "running"; in the former, one neither breaks down his horse nor endangers his own life; he must be cool, collected, and watchful; must understand the buffalo, observe the features of the country and the course of the wind, and be well skilled in using the rifle. The buffalo are strange animals; sometimes they are so stupid and infatuated that a man may walk up to them in full sight on the open prairie, and even shoot several of their number before the rest will think it necessary to retreat. At another moment they will be so shy and wary that in order to approach them the utmost skill, experience, and judgment are necessary. Kit Carson, I believe, stands preeminent in running buffalo; in approaching, no man living can bear away the palm from Henry Chatillon.

After Tête Rouge had alarmed the camp, no further disturbance occurred during the night. The Arapahoes did not attempt mischief, or if they did the wakefulness of the party deterred them from effecting their purpose. The next day was one of activity and excitement, for about ten o'clock the man in advance shouted the gladdening cry of *buffalo, buffalo!* and in the hollow of the prairie just below us, a band of bulls was grazing. The temptation was irresistible, and Shaw and I rode down upon them. We were badly mounted on our travelling horses, but by hard lashing we overtook them, and Shaw, running alongside a bull, shot into him both balls of his double-barreled gun. Looking round as I galloped by, I saw the bull in his mortal fury rushing again and again upon his antagonist, whose horse constantly leaped aside, and avoided the onset. My chase was more protracted, but at length I ran close to the bull and killed him with my pistols. Cutting off the tails of our victims by way of trophy, we rejoined the party in about a quarter of an hour after we had left it. Again and again that morning rang out the same welcome cry of *buffalo, buffalo!* Every few moments, in the broad meadows along the river, we saw bands of bulls, who, raising their shaggy heads, would gaze in stupid amazement at the approaching horsemen, and then breaking into a clumsy gallop, file off in a long line across the trail in front, towards the rising prairie on the left. At noon, the plain before us was alive with thousands of buffalo,—bulls, cows, and calves,—all moving rapidly as we drew near; and far off beyond the river the swelling prairie was darkened with them to the very horizon. The party was in gayer spirits than ever. We stopped for a nooning near a grove of trees by the river.

"Tongues and hump-ribs tomorrow," said Shaw, looking with contempt at the venison steaks which Deslauriers placed before us. Our meal finished, we lay down to sleep. A shout from Henry Chatillon aroused us, and we saw him standing on the cart-wheel, stretching his tall figure to its full height, while he looked towards the prairie beyond the river. Following the direction of his eyes, we could clearly distinguish a large, dark object, like the black shadow of a cloud, passing rapidly over swell after swell of the distant plain; behind it followed another of similar appearance, though smaller, moving more rapidly, and drawing closer and closer to the first. It was the hunters of the Arapahoe camp chasing a band of buffalo. Shaw and I caught and saddled our best horses, and went plunging through sand and water to the farther bank. We were too late. The hunters had already mingled with the herd, and the work of slaughter was nearly over. When we reached the ground we found it strewn far and near with numberless carcasses, while the remnants of the herd, scattered in all directions, were flying away in terror, and the Indians still rushing in pursuit. Many of the hunters, however, remained upon the spot, and among the rest was our yesterday's acquaintance, the chief of the village. He had alighted by the side of a cow, into which he had shot five or six arrows, and his squaw, who had followed him on horseback to the hunt, was giving him a draught of water from a canteen, purchased or plundered from some volunteer soldier. Recrossing the river, we overtook the party, who were already on their way.

We had gone scarcely a mile when we saw an imposing spectacle. From the river-bank on the right, away over the swelling prairie on the left, and in front as far as the eye could reach, was one vast host of buffalo. The outskirts of the herd were within a quarter of a mile. In many parts they were crowded so densely together that in the distance their rounded backs presented a surface of uniform blackness; but elsewhere they were more scattered, and from amid the multitude rose little columns of dust where some of them were rolling on the ground. Here and there a battle was going forward among the bulls. We could distinctly see them rushing against each other, and hear the clattering of their horns and their hoarse bellowing. Shaw was riding at some distance in advance, with Henry Chatillon; I saw him stop and draw the leather covering from his gun. With such a sight before us, but one thing could be thought of. That morning I had used pistols in the chase. I had now a mind to try the virtue of a gun. Deslauriers had one, and I rode up to the side of the cart; there he sat under the white covering, biting his pipe between his teeth and grinning with excitement.

"Lend me your gun, Deslauriers."

"Oui, Monsieur, oui," said Deslauriers, tugging with might and main to stop the mule, which seemed obstinately bent on going forward. Then everything but his moccasons disappeared as he crawled into the cart and pulled at the gun to extricate it.

"Is it loaded?" I asked.

"Oui, bien chargé; you'll kill, *mon bourgeois;* yes, you'll kill—*c'est um bon fusil."*

I handed him my rifle and rode forward to Shaw.

"Are you ready?" he asked.

"Come on," said I.

"Keep down that hollow," said Henry, "and then they won't see you till you get close to them."

The hollow was a kind of wide ravine; it ran obliquely towards the buffalo, and we rode at a canter along the bottom until it became too shallow; then we bent close to our horses' necks, and, at last, finding that it could no longer conceal us, came out of it and rode directly towards the herd. It was within gunshot; before its outskirts, numerous grizzly old bulls were scattered, holding guard over their females. They glared at us in anger and astonishment, walked towards us a few yards, and then turning slowly round, retreated at a trot which afterwards broke into a clumsy gallop. In an instant the main body caught the alarm. The buffalo began to crowd away from the point towards which we were approaching, and a gap was opened in the side of the herd. We entered it, still restraining our excited horses. Every instant the tumult was thickening. The buffalo, pressing together in large bodies, crowded away from us on every hand. In front and on either side we could see dark columns and masses, half hidden by clouds of dust, rushing along in terror and confusion, and hear the tramp and clattering of ten thousand hoofs. That countless multitude of powerful brutes, ignorant of their own strength, were flying in a panic from the approach of two feeble horsemen. To remain quiet longer was impossible.

"Take that band on the left," said Shaw; "I'll take these in front."

He sprang off, and I saw no more of him. A heavy Indian whip was fastened by a band to my wrist; I swung it into the air and lashed my horse's flank with all the strength of my arm. Away she darted, stretching close to the ground. I could see nothing but a cloud of dust before me, but I knew that it concealed a band of many hundreds of buffalo. In a moment I was in the midst of the cloud, half suffocated by the dust and stunned by the trampling of the flying herd; but I was drunk with the chase and cared for nothing but the buffalo. Very soon a long dark mass became visible, looming through the dust; then I could distinguish each bulky carcass, the hoofs flying out beneath, the short tails held rigidly erect. In a moment I was so close that I could have touched them with my gun. Suddenly, to my amazement, the hoofs were jerked upwards, the tails flourished in the air, and amid a cloud of dust the buffalo seemed to sink into the earth before me. One vivid impression of that instant remains upon my mind. I remember looking down upon the backs of several buffalo dimly visible through the dust. We had run unawares upon a ravine. At that moment I was not the most accurate judge of depth and width, but when I passed it on my return, I found it about twelve feet deep and not quite twice as wide at the bottom. It was impossible to stop; I would have done so gladly if I could; so, half sliding, half plunging, down went the little mare. She came down on her knees in the loose sand at the bottom; I was pitched forward against her neck and nearly thrown over her head among the buffalo, who amid dust and confusion came tumbling in all around. The mare was on her feet in an instant and scrambling like a cat up the opposite side. I thought for a moment that she would have fallen back and crushed me, but with a violent effort she clambered out and gained the hard prairie above. Glancing back, I saw the huge head of a bull clinging as it were by the forefeet at the edge of the dusty gulf. At length I was fairly among the buffalo. They were less densely crowded than before, and I could see nothing but bulls, who always run at the rear of a herd to protect their females. As I passed among them they would lower their heads, and turning as they ran, try to gore my horse; but as they were already at full speed there was no force in their onset, and as Pauline ran faster than they, they were always thrown behind her in the effort. I soon began to distinguish cows amid the throng. One just in front of me seemed to my liking, and I pushed close to her side. Dropping the reins, I fired, holding the muzzle of the gun within a foot of her shoulder. Quick as lightning she sprang at Pauline; the little mare dodged the attack, and I lost sight of the wounded animal amid the tumult. Immediately after, I selected another, and urging forward Pauline, shot into her both pistols in succession. For a while I kept her in view, but in attempting to load my gun, lost sight of her also in the confusion. Believing her to be mortally wounded and unable to keep up with the herd, I checked my horse. The crowd rushed onwards. The dust and tumult passed away, and on the prairie, far behind the rest, I saw a solitary buffalo galloping heavily. In a moment I and my victim were running side by side. My firearms were all empty, and I had in my pouch nothing but rifle bullets, too large for the pistols and too small for the gun. I loaded the gun, however, but as often as I levelled it to fire, the bullets would roll out of the muzzle and the gun returned only a report like a squib, as the powder harmlessly exploded. I rode in front of the buffalo and tried to turn her back; but her eyes glared, her mane bristled, and lowering her head, she rushed at me with the utmost fierceness and activity. Again and again I rode before her, and again and again she repeated her furious charge. But little Pauline was in her element. She dodged her enemy at every rush, until at length the buffalo stood still, exhausted with her own efforts, her tongue lolling from her jaws.

Riding to a little distance, I dismounted, thinking to gather a handful of dry grass to serve the purpose of wadding, and load the gun at my leisure. No sooner were my feet on the ground than the buffalo came bounding in such a rage towards me that I jumped back again into the saddle and with all possible despatch. After waiting a few minutes more, I made an attempt to ride up and stab her with my knife; but Pauline was near being gored in the attempt. At length, bethinking me of the fringes at the seams of my buckskin trousers, I jerked off a few of them, and, reloading the gun, forced them down the barrel to keep the bullet in its place; then approaching, I shot the wounded buffalo through the heart. Sinking to her knees, she rolled over lifeless on the prairie. To my astonishment, I found that, instead of a cow, I had been slaughtering a stout yearling bull. No longer wondering at his fierceness, I opened his throat, and cutting out his tongue, tied it at the back of my saddle. My mistake was one which a more experienced eye than mine might easily make in the dust and confusion of such a chase.

Then for the first time I had leisure to look at the scene around me. The prairie in front was darkened with the retreating multitude, and on either hand the buffalo came filing up in endless columns from the low plains upon the river. The Arkansas was three or four miles distant. I turned and moved slowly towards it. A long time passed before, far in the distance, I distinguished the white covering of the cart and the little black specks of horsemen before and behind it. Drawing near, I recognized Shaw's elegant tunic, the red flannel shirt, conspicuous far off. I overtook the party, and asked him what success he had had. He had assailed a fat cow, shot her with two bullets, and mortally wounded her. But neither of us was prepared for the chase that afternoon, and Shaw, like myself, had no spare bullets in his pouch; so he abandoned the disabled animal to Henry Chatillon, who followed, despatched her with his rifle, and loaded his horse with the meat.

We encamped close to the river. The night was dark, and as we lay down we could hear, mingled with the howling of wolves, the hoarse bellowing of the buffalo, like the ocean beating upon a distant coast.

No one in the camp was more active than Jim Gurney, and no one half so lazy as Ellis. Between these two there was a great antipathy. Ellis never stirred in the morning until he was compelled, but Jim was always on his feet before daybreak; and this morning as usual the sound of his voice awakened the party.

"Get up, you booby! up with you now, you're fit for nothing but eating and sleeping. Stop your grumbling and come out of that buffalo-robe, or I'll pull it off for you."

Jim's words were interspersed with numerous expletives, which gave them great additional effect. Ellis drawled out something in a nasal tone from among the folds of his buffalo-robe; then slowly disengaged himself, rose into a sitting posture, stretched his long arms, yawned hideously, and, finally raising his tall person erect, stood staring about him to all the four quarters of the horizon. Deslauriers' fire was soon blazing, and the horses and mules, loosened from their pickets, were feeding on the neighboring meadow. When we sat down to breakfast the prairie was still in the dusky light of morning; and as the sun rose we were mounted and on our way again.

"A white buffalo!" exclaimed Munroe.

"I'll have that fellow," said Shaw, "if I run my horse to death after him."

He threw the cover of his gun to Deslauriers and galloped out upon the prairie.

"Stop, Mr. Shaw, stop!" called out Henry Chatillon, "you'll run down your horse for nothing; it's only a white ox."

But Shaw was already out of hearing. The ox, which had no doubt strayed away from some of the government wagon trains, was standing beneath some low hills which bounded the plain in the distance. Not far from him a band of veritable buffalo bulls were grazing; and startled at Shaw's approach, they all broke into a run, and went scrambling up the hillsides to gain the high prairie above. One of them in his haste and terror involved himself in a fatal catastrophe. Along the foot of the hills was a narrow strip of deep marshy soil, into which the bull plunged and hopelessly entangled himself. We all rode to the spot. The huge carcass was half sunk in the mud, which flowed to his very chin, and his shaggy mane was outspread upon the surface. As we came near, the bull began to struggle with convulsive strength; he writhed to and fro, and in the energy of his fright and desperation would lift himself for a moment half out of the slough, while the reluctant mire returned a sucking sound as he strained to drag his limbs from its tenacious depths. We stimulated his exertions by getting behind him and twisting his tail; nothing would do. There was clearly no hope for him. After every effort his heaving sides were more deeply embedded, and the mire almost over-flowed his nostrils; he lay still at length, and looking round at us with a furious eye, seemed to resign himself to fate. Ellis slowly dismounted, and, level-ling his boasted yager, shot the old bull through the heart; then lazily climbed back again to his seat, pluming himself no doubt on having actually killed a buffalo. That day the invincible yager drew blood for the first and last time during the whole journey.

The morning was a bright and gay one, and the air so clear that on the farthest horizon the outline of the pale blue prairie was sharply drawn against the sky. Shaw was in the mood for hunting; he rode in advance of the party, and before long we saw a file of bulls galloping at full speed upon a green swell of the prairie at some distance in front. Shaw came scouring along behind them, arrayed in his red shirt, which looked very well in the distance; he gained fast on the fugitives, and as the foremost bull was dis-appearing behind the summit of the swell, we saw him in the act of assailing the hindmost; a smoke sprang from the muzzle of his gun and floated away before the wind like a little white cloud; the bull turned upon him, and just then the rising ground concealed them both from view.

We were moving forward until about noon, when we stopped by the side of the Arkansas. At that moment Shaw appeared riding slowly down the side of a distant hill; his horse was tired and jaded, and when he threw his saddle upon the ground, I observed that the tails of two bulls were dangling behind it. No sooner were the horses turned loose to feed than Henry, asking Munroe to go with him, took his rifle and walked quietly away. Shaw, Tête Rouge, and I sat down by the side of the cart to discuss the dinner which Deslauriers placed before us, and we had scarcely finished when we saw Munroe walking towards us along the river-bank. Henry, he said, had killed four fat cows, and had sent him back for horses to bring in the meat. Shaw took a horse for himself and another for Henry, and he and Munroe left the camp together. After a short absence all three of them came back, their horses loaded with the choicest parts of the meat. We kept two of the cows for ourselves, and gave the others to Munroe and his companions. Deslauriers seated himself on the grass before the pile of meat, and worked industriously for some time to cut it into thin broad sheets for drying, an art in which he had all the skill of an Indian squaw. Long before night, cords of raw hide were stretched around the camp, and the meat was hung upon them to dry in the sunshine and pure air of the prairie. Our California companions were less successful at the work; but they accomplished it after their own fashion, and their side of the camp was soon garnished in the same manner as our own.

We meant to remain at this place long enough to prepare provisions for our journey to the frontier, which, as we supposed, might occupy about a month. Had the distance been twice as great and the party ten times as large, the rifle of Henry Chatillon would have supplied meat enough for the whole within two days; we were obliged to remain, however, until it should be dry enough for transportation; so we pitched our tent and made other arrangements for a permanent camp. The California men, who had no such shelter, contented themselves with arranging their packs on the grass around their fire. In the mean time we had nothing to do but amuse ourselves. Our tent was within a rod of the river, if the broad sand-beds, with a scanty stream of water coursing here and there along their surface, deserve to be dignified with the name of river. The vast flat plains on either side were almost on a level with the sand-beds, and they were bounded in the distance by low, monotonous hills, parallel to the course of the stream. All was one expanse of grass; there was no wood in view, except some trees and stunted bushes upon two islands which rose from the wet sands of the river. Yet far from being dull and tame, the scene was often a wild and animated one; for twice a day, at sunrise and at noon, the buffalo came issuing from the hills, slowly advancing in their grave processions to drink at the river. All our amusements were to be at their expense. An old buffalo bull is a brute of unparalleled ugliness. At first sight of him every feeling of pity vanishes. The cows are much smaller and of a gentler appearance, as becomes their sex. While in this camp we forbore to attack them, leaving to Henry Chatillon, who could better judge their quality, the task of killing such as we wanted for use; but against the bulls we waged an unrelenting war. Thousands of them might be slaughtered without causing any detriment to the species, for their numbers greatly exceed those of the cows; it is the hides of the latter alone which are used for the purposes of commerce and for making the lodges of the Indians; and the destruction among them is therefore greatly disproportionate.

Our horses were tired, and we now usually hunted on foot. While we were lying on the grass after dinner, smoking, talking, or laughing at Tête Rouge, one of us would look up and observe, far out on the plains beyond the river, certain black objects slowly approaching. He would inhale a parting whiff from the pipe, then rising lazily, take his rifle, which leaned against the cart, throw over his shoulder the strap of his pouch and powder-horn, and with his moccasons in his hand, walk across the sand towards the opposite side of the river. This was very easy; for though the sands were about a quarter of a mile wide, the water was nowhere more than two feet deep. The farther bank was about four or five feet high, and quite perpendicular, being cut away by the water in spring. Tall grass grew along its edge. Putting it aside with his hand, and cautiously looking through it, the hunter can discern the huge shaggy back of the bull slowly swaying to and fro, as, with his clumsy, swinging gait, he advances towards the river. The buffalo have regular paths by which they come down to drink. Seeing at a glance along which of these his intended victim is moving, the hunter crouches under the bank within fifteen or twenty yards, it may be, of the point where the path enters the river. Here he sits down quietly on the sand. Listening intently, he hears the heavy, monotonous tread of the approaching bull. The moment after, he sees a motion among the long weeds and grass just at the spot where the path is channelled through the bank. An enormous black head is thrust out, the horns just visible amid the mass of tangled mane. Half sliding, half plunging, down comes the buffalo upon the river-bed below. He steps out in full sight upon the sands. Just before him a runnel of water is gliding, and he bends his head to drink. You may hear the water as it gurgles down his capacious throat. He raises his head, and the drops trickle from his wet beard. He stands with an air of stupid abstraction, unconscious of the lurking danger. Noiselessly the hunter cocks his rifle. As he sits upon the sand, his knee is raised, and his elbow rests upon it, that he may level his heavy weapon with a steadier aim. The stock is at his shoulder; his eye ranges along the barrel. Still he is in no haste to fire. The bull, with slow deliberation, begins his march over the sands to the other side. He advances his foreleg, and exposes to view a small spot, denuded of hair, just behind the point of his shoulder; upon this the hunter brings the sight of his rifle to bear; lightly and delicately his finger presses the hair-trigger. The spiteful crack of the rifle responds to his touch, and instantly in the middle of the bare spot appears a small red dot. The buffalo shivers; death has overtaken him, he cannot tell from whence; still he does not fall, but walks heavily forward, as if nothing had happened. Yet before he has gone far out upon the sand, you see him stop; he totters; his knees bend under him, and his head sinks forward to the ground. Then his whole vast bulk sways to one side; he rolls over on the sand, and dies with a scarcely perceptible struggle.

Waylaying the buffalo in this manner, and shooting them as they come to water, is the easiest method of hunting them. They may also be approached by crawling up ravines or behind hills, or even over the open prairie. This is often surprisingly easy; but at other times it requires the utmost skill of the most experienced hunter. Henry Chatillon was a man of extraordinary strength and hardihood; but I have seen him return to camp quite exhausted with his efforts, his limbs scratched and wounded, and his buckskin dress stuck full of the thorns of the prickly-pear, among which he had been crawling. Sometimes he would lie flat upon his face, and drag himself along in this position for many rods together.

On the second day of our stay at this place, Henry went out for an afternoon hunt. Shaw and I remained in camp, until, observing some bulls approaching the water upon the other side of the river, we crossed over to attack them. They were so near, however, that before we could get under cover of the bank our appearance as we walked over the sands alarmed them. Turning round before coming within gun-shot, they began to move off to the right in a direction parallel to the river. I climbed up the bank and ran after them. They were walking swiftly, and before I could come within gun-shot distance they slowly wheeled about and faced me. Before they had turned far enough to see me I had fallen flat on my face. For a moment they stood and stared at the strange object upon the grass; then turning away, again they walked on as before; and I, rising immediately, ran once more in pursuit. Again they wheeled about, and again I fell prostrate. Repeating this three or four times, I came at length within a hundred yards of the fugitives, and as I saw them turning again, I sat down and levelled my rifle. The one in the centre was the largest I had ever seen. I shot him behind the shoulder. His two companions ran off. He attempted to follow, but soon came to a stand, and at length lay down as quietly as an ox chewing the cud. Cautiously approaching him, I saw by his dull and jelly-like eye that he was dead.

When I began the chase, the prairie was almost tenantless; but a great multitude of buffalo had suddenly thronged upon it, and looking up I saw within fifty rods a heavy, dark column stretching to the right and left as far as I could see. I walked towards them. My approach did not alarm them in the least. The column itself consisted almost entirely of cows and calves, but a great many old bulls were ranging about the prairie on its flank, and as I drew near they faced towards me with such a grim and ferocious look that I thought it best to proceed no farther. Indeed, I was already within close rifle-shot of the column, and I sat down on the ground to watch their movements. Sometimes the whole would stand still, their heads all one way; then they would trot forward, as if by a common impulse, their hoofs and horns clattering together as they moved. I soon began to hear at a distance on the left the sharp reports of a rifle, again and again repeated; and not long after, dull and heavy sounds succeeded, which I recognized as the familiar voice of Shaw's double-barreled gun. When Henry's rifle was at work there was always meat to be brought in. I went back across the river for a horse, and, returning, reached the spot where the hunters were standing. The buffalo were visible on the distant prairie. The living had retreated from the ground, but ten or twelve carcasses were scattered in various directions. Henry, knife in hand, was stooping over a dead cow, cutting away the best and fattest of the meat.

When Shaw left me he had walked down for some distance under the river-bank to find another bull. At length he saw the plains covered with the host of buffalo, and soon after heard the crack of Henry's rifle. Ascending the bank, he crawled through the grass, which for a rod or two from the river was very high and rank. He had not crawled far before to his astonishment he saw Henry standing erect upon the prairie, almost surrounded by the buffalo. Henry was in his element. Quite unconscious that any one was looking at him, he stood at the full height of his tall figure, one hand resting upon his side, and the other arm leaning carelessly on the muzzle of his rifle. His eye was ranging over the singular assemblage around him. Now and then he would select such a cow as suited him, level his rifle, and shoot her dead; then quietly reloading, he would resume his former position. The buffalo seemed no more to regard his presence than if he were one of themselves; the bulls were bellowing and butting at each other, or rolling about in the dust. A group of buffalo would gather about the carcass of a dead cow, snuffing at her wounds; and sometimes they would come behind those that had not yet fallen, and endeavor to push them from the spot. Now and then some old bull would face towards Henry with an air of stupid amazement, but none seemed inclined to attack or fly from him. For some time Shaw lay among the grass, looking in surprise at this extraordinary sight; at length he crawled cautiously forward, and spoke in a low voice to Henry, who told him to rise and come on. Still the buffalo showed no sign of fear; they remained gathered about their dead companions. Henry had already killed as many cows as he wanted for use, and Shaw, kneeling behind one of the carcasses, shot five bulls before the rest thought it necessary to disperse.

The frequent stupidity and infatuation of the buffalo seems the more remarkable from the contrast it offers to their wildness and wariness at other times. Henry knew all their peculiarities; he had studied them as a scholar studies his books, and derived quite as much pleasure from the occupation. The buffalo were in a sense companions to him, and, as he said, he never felt alone when they were about him. He took great pride in his skill in hunting. He was one of the most modest of men; yet in the simplicity and frankness of his character, it was clear that he looked upon his pre-eminence in this respect as a thing too palpable and well established to be disputed. But whatever may have been his estimate of his own skill, it was rather below than above that which others placed upon it. The only time that I ever saw a shade of scorn darken his face was when two volunteer soldiers, who had just killed a buffalo for the first time, undertook to instruct him as to the best method of "approaching." Henry always seemed to think that he had a sort of prescriptive right to the buffalo, and to look upon them as something belonging to himself. Nothing excited his indignation so much as any wanton destruction committed among the cows, and in his view shooting a calf was a cardinal sin.

Henry Chatillon and Tête Rouge were of the same age; that is, about thirty. Henry was twice as large, and about six times as strong as Tête Rouge. Henry's face was roughened by winds and storms; Tête Rouge's was bloated by sherry-cobblers and brandy-toddy. Henry talked of Indians and buffalo;

Tête Rouge of theatres and oyster-cellars. Henry had led a life of hardship and privation; Tête Rouge never had a whim which he would not gratify at the first moment he was able. Henry moreover was the most disinterested man I ever saw; while Tête Rouge, though equally good natured in his way, cared for nobody but himself. Yet we would not have lost him on any account; he served the purpose of a jester in a feudal castle; our camp would have been lifeless without him. For the past week he had fattened in a most amazing manner; and, indeed, this was not at all surprising, since his appetite was inordinate. He was eating from morning till night; half the time he would be at work cooking some private repast for himself, and he paid a visit to the coffee-pot eight or ten times a day. His rueful and disconsolate face became jovial and rubicund, his eyes stood out like a lobster's, and his spirits, which before were sunk to the depths of despondency, were now elated in proportion; all day he was singing, whistling, laughing, and telling stories. Being mortally afraid of Jim Gurney, he kept close in the neighborhood of our tent. As he had seen an abundance of low fast life, and had a considerable fund of humor, his anecdotes were extremely amusing, especially since he never hesitated to place himself in a ludicrous point of view, provided he could raise a laugh by doing so. Tête Rouge, however, was sometimes rather troublesome; he had an inveterate habit of pilfering provisions at all times of the day. He set ridicule at defiance, and would never have given over his tricks, even if they had drawn upon him the scorn of the whole party. Now and then, indeed, something worse than laughter fell to his share; on these occasions he would exhibit much contrition, but half an hour after we would generally observe him stealing round to the box at the back of the cart, and slyly making off with the provisions which Deslauriers had laid by for supper. He was fond of smoking; but having no tobacco of his own, we used to provide him with as much as he wanted, a small piece at a time. At first we gave him half a pound together; but this experiment proved an entire failure, for he invariably lost not only the tobacco, but the knife intrusted to him for cutting it, and a few minutes after he would come to us with many apologies and beg for more.

We had been two days at this camp, and some of the meat was nearly fit for transportation, when a storm came suddenly upon us. About sunset the whole sky grew as black as ink, and the long grass at the edge of the river bent and rose mournfully with the first gusts of the approaching hurricane. Munroe and his two companions brought their guns and placed them under cover of our tent. Having no shelter for themselves, they built a fire of driftwood

that might have defied a cataract, and, wrapped in
their buffalo-robes, sat on the ground around it to
bide the fury of the storm. Deslauriers esconced
himself under the cover of the cart. Shaw and I,
together with Henry and Tête Rouge, crowded into
the little tent; but first of all the dried meat was piled
together, and well protected by buffalo-robes pinned
firmly to the ground. About nine o'clock the storm
broke amid absolute darkness; it blew a gale, and torrents of rain roared over the boundless expanse of
open prairie. Our tent was filled with mist and spray
beating through the canvas, and saturating everything within. We could only distinguish each other
at short intervals by the dazzling flashes of lightning,
which displayed the whole waste around us with its
momentary glare. We had our fears for the tent; but
for an hour or two it stood fast, until at length the
cap gave way before a furious blast; the pole tore
through the top, and in an instant we were half suffocated by the cold and dripping folds of the canvas,
which fell down upon us. Seizing upon our guns, we
placed them erect, in order to lift the saturated cloth
above our heads. In this agreeable situation, involved
among wet blankets and buffalo-robes, we spent several hours of the night, during which the storm
would not abate for a moment, but pelted down
with merciless fury. Before long the water gathered
beneath us in a pool two or three inches deep; so that

for a considerable part of the night we were partially immersed in a cold bath. In spite of all this, Tête Rouge's flow of spirits did not fail him; he laughed, whistled, and sang in defiance of the storm, and that night paid off the long arrears of ridicule which he owed us. While we lay in silence, enduring the infliction with what philosophy we could muster, Tête Rouge, who was intoxicated with animal spirits, cracked jokes at our expense by the hour together. At about three o'clock in the morning, preferring "the tyranny of the open night" to such a wretched shelter, we crawled out from beneath the fallen canvas. The wind had abated, but the rain fell steadily. The fire of the California men still blazed amid the darkness, and we joined them as they sat around it. We made ready some hot coffee by way of refreshment; but when some of the party sought to replenish their cups, it was found that Tête Rouge, having disposed of his own share, had privately abstracted the coffee-pot and drunk the rest of the contents out of the spout.

In the morning, to our great joy, an unclouded sun rose upon the prairie. We presented a rather laughable appearance, for the cold and clammy buck-skin, saturated with water, clung fast to our limbs. The light wind and warm sunshine soon dried it again, and then we were all encased in armor of intolerable stiffness. Roaming all day over the prairie and shooting two or three bulls, were scarcely enough to restore the stiffened leather to its usual pliancy.

Besides Henry Chatillon, Shaw and I were the only hunters in the party. Munroe this morning made an attempt to run a buffalo, but his horse could not come up to the game. Shaw went out with him, and being better mounted, soon found himself in the midst of the herd. Seeing nothing but cows and calves around him, he checked his horse. An old bull came galloping on the open prairie at some distance behind, and turning, Shaw rode across his path, levelling his gun as he passed, and shooting him through the shoulder into the heart.

A great flock of buzzards was usually soaring about a few trees that stood on the island just below our camp. Throughout the whole of yesterday we had noticed an eagle among them; today he was still there; and Tête Rouge, declaring that he would kill the bird of America, borrowed Deslauriers's gun and set out on his unpatriotic mission. As might have been expected, the eagle suffered no harm at his hands. He soon returned, saying that he could not find him, but had shot a buzzard instead. Being required to produce the bird in proof of his assertion, he said he believed that he was not quite dead, but he must be hurt, from the swiftness with which he flew off.

"If you want," said Tête Rouge, "I'll go and get one of his feathers; I knocked off plenty of them when I shot him."

Just opposite our camp, was another island covered with bushes, and behind it was a deep pool of water, while two or three considerable streams coursed over the sand not far off. I was bathing at this place in the afternoon when a white wolf, larger than the largest Newfoundland dog, ran out from behind the point of the island, and galloped leisurely over the sand not half a stone's-throw distant. I could plainly see his red eyes and the bristles about his snout; he was an ugly scoundrel, with a bushy tail, a large head, and a most repulsive countenance. Having neither rifle to shoot nor stone to pelt him with, I was looking after some missile for his benefit, when the report of a gun came from the camp, and the ball threw up the sand just beyond him; at this he gave a slight jump, and stretched away so swiftly that he soon dwindled into a mere speck on the distant sand-beds. The number of carcasses that by this time were lying about the neighboring prairie summoned the wolves from every quarter; the spot where Shaw and Henry had hunted together soon became their favorite resort, for here about a dozen dead buffalo were fermenting under the hot sun. I used often to go over the river and watch them at their meal. By lying under the bank it was easy to get a full view of them. There were three different kinds: the white wolves and the gray wolves, both very large, and besides these the small prairie wolves, not much bigger than spaniels. They would howl and fight in a crowd around a single carcass, yet they were so watchful, and their senses so acute, that I never was able to crawl within a fair shooting distance; whenever I attempted it, they would all scatter at once and glide silently away through the tall grass. The air above this spot was always full of turkey-buzzards or black vultures; whenever the wolves left a carcass they would descend upon it, and cover it so densely that a rifle bullet shot at random among the gormandizing crowd would generally strike down two or three of them. These birds would often sail by scores just above our camp, their broad black wings seeming half transparent as they expanded them against the bright sky. The wolves and the buzzards thickened about us every hour, and two or three eagles also came to the feast. I killed a bull within rifleshot of the camp; that night the wolves made a fearful howling close at hand, and in the morning the carcass was completely hollowed out by these voracious feeders.

After remaining four days at this camp we prepared to leave it. We had for our own part about five hundred pounds of dried meat, and the California men had prepared some three hundred more; this consisted of the fattest and choicest parts of eight or nine cows, a small quantity only being taken from each, and the rest abandoned to the wolves. The pack animals were laden, the horses saddled, and the mules harnessed to the cart. Even Tête Rouge was ready at last, and slowly moving from the ground, we resumed our journey eastward. When we had advanced about a mile, Shaw missed a valuable hunting-knife, and turned back in search of it, thinking that he had left it at the camp. The day was dark and gloomy. The ashes of the fires were still smoking by the river-side; the grass around them was trampled down by men and horses, and strewn with all the litter of a camp. Our departure had been a gathering signal to the birds and beasts of prey. Scores of wolves were prowling about the smoulder-ing fires, while multitudes were roaming over the neighboring prairie; they all fled as Shaw approached, some running over the sand-beds and some over the grassy plains. The vultures in great clouds were soar-ing overhead, and the dead bull near the camp was completely blackened by the flock that had alighted upon it; they flapped their broad wings, and stretched upwards their crested heads and long skinny necks, fearing to remain, yet reluctant to leave their disgusting feast. As he searched about the fires he saw the wolves seated on the hills waiting for his departure. Having looked in vain for his knife, he mounted again, and left the wolves and the vultures to banquet undisturbed.

The Mountain Goat at Home

[WILLIAM T. HORNADAY, SC. D.]

John Phillips and I were scrambling along the steep and rough eastern face of Bald Mountain, a few yards below timberline, half-way up 'twixt creek and summit. He was light of weight, well-seasoned and nimble-footed; I was heavy, ill-conditioned, and hungry for more air. Between the sliderock, down timber and brush, the going had been undeniably bad, and in spite of numerous rests I was almost fagged.

Far below us, at the bottom of the V-shaped valley, the horse-bell faintly tinkled, and as Mack and Charlie whacked out the trail, the packtrain crept forward. We were thankful that the camping-place, on Goat Pass, was only a mile beyond.

Presently we heard a voice faintly shouting to us from below.

"Look above you—at the *goats!*"

Hastily we moved out of a brush-patch, and looked aloft. At the top of the precipice that rose above our slope, a long, irregular line of living forms perched absurdly on the skyline, and looked over the edge, at us. Quickly we brought our glasses to bear, and counted fourteen living and wild Rocky Mountain goats.

"All nannies, young billies, and kids," said Mr. Phillips. "They are trying to guess what kind of wild animals we are." I noticed that he was quite calm; but I felt various things which seemed to sum themselves up in the formula—"the Rocky Mountain goat—*at last!*"

For fully ten minutes, the entire fourteen white ones steadfastly gazed down upon us, with but few changes of position, and few remarks. Finally, one by one they drew back from the edge of the precipice, and quietly drifted away over the bald crest of the mountain.

For twenty years I had been reading the scanty scraps of mountain-goat literature that at long intervals have appeared in print. I had seen seven specimens alive in captivity, and helped to care for four of them. With a firm belief that the game was worth it, I had traveled twenty-five hundred miles or more in order to meet this strange animal in its own home, and cultivate a close acquaintance with half a dozen wild flocks.

At three o'clock we camped at timberline, on a high and difficult pass between the Elk River and the Bull. That night we christened the ridge Goat Pass. While the guides and the cook unpacked the outfit and pitched the tents, Mr. Phillips hurried down the western side of the divide. Fifteen minutes later he and Kaiser—in my opinion the wisest hunting-dog in British Columbia—had twenty-eight nanny goats and kids at bay on the top of a precipice, and were photographing them at the risk of their lives.

Rifle and glass in hand, I sat down on a little knoll a few yards above the tents, to watch a *lame* billy goat who was quietly grazing and limping along the side of a lofty ridge that came down east of us from Phillips Peak. A lame wild animal in a country wherein a shot had not been fired for five years, was, to all of us, a real novelty; and with my glasses I watched the goat long and well. It was his left fore-leg that was lame, and it was the opinion of the party that the old fellow was suffering from an accident received on the rocks. Possibly a stone had been rolled down upon him, by another goat.

Suddenly sharp cries of surprise came up from the camp, and I sprang up to look about. *Three goats were running past the tents* at top speed—a big billy, and two smaller goats.

"Hi, there! Goats! Goats!" cried Smith and Norboe.

The cook was stooping over the fire, and looking under his right arm he saw the bunch charging straight toward him, at a gallop. A second later, the big billy was almost upon him.

"Hey! You son-of-a-gun!" yelled Huddleston, and as the big snow-white animal dashed past him he struck it across the neck with a stick of firewood. The goat's tracks were within six feet of the campfire.

The billy ran straight through the camp, then swung sharply to the left, and the last I saw of him was his humpy hindquarters wildly bobbing up and down among the dead jack pines, as he ran for Bald Mountain.

The two smaller goats held their course, and one promptly disappeared. The other leaped across our water-hole, and as it scrambled out of the gully near my position, and paused for a few seconds to look backward, instinctively I covered it with my rifle. But only for an instant. "Come as they may," thought I, "my first goat shall *not* be a small one!" And as the goat turned and raced on up, my .303 Savage came down.

We laughed long at the utter absurdity of three wild goats actually breaking into the privacy of our camp, on our first afternoon in Goatland. In the Elk Valley, Charlie Smith had promised me that we would camp "right among the goats," and he had royally kept his word.

At evening, when we gathered round the camp-fire, and counted up, we found that on our first day in Goatland, we had seen a total of fifty-three goats; and no one had fired a shot. As for myself, I felt quite set up over my presence of mind in *not* firing at the goat which I had "dead to rights" after it had invaded our camp, and which might have been killed as a measure of self-defence.

Our camp was pitched in a most commanding and awe-inspiring spot. We were precisely at timberline, in a grassy hollow on the lowest summit between Bald and Bird Mountains, on the north, and Phillips Peak, on the south. From our tents the ground rose for several hundred feet, like the cables of the Brooklyn Bridge, until it stopped against a rock wall which went on up several hundred feet more. In a notch quite near us was a big bank of eternal ice. In that country, such things are called glaciers; and its melting foot was the starting-point of Goat Creek. Fifty paces taken eastward from our tents brought us to a projecting point from which we looked down a hundred feet to a rope of white water, and on down Goat Creek as it drops five hundred feet to the mile, to the point where it turns a sharp corner to the right, and disappears.

Westward of camp, after climbing up a hundred feet or so, through dead standing timber, the ridge slopes steeply down for a mile and a half to the bottom of a great basin half filled with green timber, that opens toward Bull River. It was on this slope, at a point where a wall of rock cropped out, that Mr. Phillips cornered his flock of goats and photographed them.

At our camp, water and wood were abundant; there was plenty of fine grass for our horses, spruce boughs for our beds, scenery for millions, and what more could we ask?

The day following our arrival on Goat Pass was dull and rainy, with a little snow, and we all remained in camp. At intervals, someone would stroll out to our lookout point above Goat Creek, and eye-search the valley below "to see if an old silver-tip could come a-moochin' up, by accident," as Guide Smith quaintly phrased it.

That gray day taught me something of color values in those mountains. As seen from our lookout point, the long, even stretch of house-roof mountain-slope on the farther side of Goat Creek was a revelation. In the full sunlight of a clear day, its tints were nothing to command particular attention. Strong light seemed to take the colors out of everything. But a cloudy day, with a little rain on the face of nature, was like new varnish on an old oil-painting.

During the forenoon, fleecy white clouds chased each other over the pass and through our camp, and for much of the time the Goat Creek gorge was cloud-filled. At last, however, about noon, they rose and drifted away, and then the mountain opposite revealed a color pattern that was exquisitely beautiful.

For a distance of a thousand yards the ridge-side stretched away down the valley, straight and even; and in that distance it was furrowed from top to bottom by ten or twelve gullies, and ribbed by an equal number of ridges. At the bottom of the gorge was a dense green fringe of tall, obelisk spruces, very much alive. In many places, ghostly processions of dead spruces, limbless and gray, for-lornly climbed the ridges, until half-way up the highest stragglers stopped. Intermixed with these tall poles were patches of trailing juniper of a dark olive-green color, growing tightly to the steep slope.

The apex of each timbered ridge was covered with a solid mass of great willow-herb or "fireweed" (*Chamaenerion anguistifolium*), then in its brightest autumn tints of purple and red. The brilliant patches of color which they painted on the mountainside would have rejoiced the heart of an artist. This glorious plant colored nearly every mountainside in that region during our September there.

Below the fireweed, the ridges were dotted with small, cone-shaped spruces, and trailing junipers (*Juniperus prostrata*), of the densest and richest green. The grassy sides of the gullies were all pale yellow—green, softly blended at the edges with the darker colors that framed them in. At the bottom of each washout was a mass of light-gray sliderock, and above all this rare pattern of soft colors loomed a lofty wall of naked carboniferous limestone rock, gray, grim and forbidding.

It seemed to me that I never elsewhere had seen mountains so rich in colors as the ranges between the Elk and the Bull in that particular September.

The rain and the drifting clouds were with us for one day only. Very early on the second morning, while Mr. Phillips and I lay in our sleeping-bags considering the grave question of getting or not getting up, Mack Norboe's voice was heard outside, speaking low but to the point:

"Director, there's an old billy goat, lying right above our camp!"

It was like twelve hundred volts. We tumbled out of our bags, slipped on our shoes, and ran out. Sure enough, a full-grown male goat was lying on the crest of the divide that led up to the summit of Bald Mountain, seventy-five feet above us, and not more than two hundred and fifty yards away. The shooting of him was left to me.

I think I could have bagged that animal as he lay; but what would there have been in that of any interest to a sportsman? I had not asked any goats to come down to our camp, and lie down to be shot!

Not caring greatly whether I got that goat or not, I attempted a stalk along the western side of the ridge, through the dead timber, and well below him. But the old fellow was not half so sleepy as he looked. When finally I came up to a point that was supposed to command his works, I found that he had winded me. He had vanished from his resting-place, and was already far up the side of Bald Mountain, conducting a masterly retreat.

After a hurried breakfast, we made ready for a day with the goats on the northern mountains. Although there are many things in favor of small parties—the best consisting of one guide and one hunter—we all went together—Mr. Phillips, Mack, Charlie and I. Our leader declared a determination to "see the Director shoot his first goat," and I assured the others that the services of all would be needed in carrying home my spoils.

As we turned back toward camp, and took time to look "at the sceneries," the view westward, toward Bull River, disclosed a cloud effect so beautiful that Mr. Phillips insisted upon photographing it, then and there. To give the "touch of life" which he always demanded, I sat in, as usual.

By Mr. Phillips' advice, I put on suspenders and loosened my cartridge-belt, in order to breathe with perfect freedom. We wore no leggings. Our shoes were heavily hobnailed, and while I had thought mine as light as one dared use in that region of ragged rocks, I found that for cliff-climbing they were too heavy, and too stiff in the soles. Of course knee-breeches are the thing, but they should be so well cut that in steep climbing they will not drag on the knees, and waste the climber's horsepower; and there should be a generous opening at the knee.

In those mountains, four things, and only four, are positively indispensable to every party: rifles, axes, fieldglasses and blankets. Each member of our hunting party carried a good glass, and never stirred from camp without it. For myself, I tried an experiment. Two months previously Mrs. Hornaday selected for me, in Paris, a very good opera-glass, made by Lemaire, with a field that was delightfully large and clear. While not quite so powerful a magnifier as the strongest binoculars now on the market, its field was so much clearer that I thought I would prefer it. It was much smaller than any regulation fieldglass, and I carried it either in a pocket of my trousers, or loose inside my hunting-shirt, quite forgetful of its weight.

It proved a great success. We found much interest

in testing it with binoculars five times as costly, and the universal verdict was that it would reveal an animal as far as a hunter could go to it, and find it. I mention this because in climbing I found it well worthwhile to be free from a dangling leather case that is always in the way, and often is too large for comfort.

From our camp we went north, along the top of the eastern wall of Bald Mountain. Two miles from home we topped a sharp rise, and there directly ahead, and only a quarter of a mile away on an eastern slope lay a band of eleven goats, basking in the welcome sunshine. The flock was composed of nannies, yearling billies and kids, with not even one old billy among those present. Two old chaperons lay with their heads well up, on the lookout, but all the others lay full length upon the grass, with their backs uphill. Three of the small kids lay close against their mothers.

They were on the northerly point of a fine mountain meadow, with safety rocks on three sides. Just beyond them lay a ragged hogback of rock, both sides of which were so precipitous that no man save an experienced mountaineer would venture far upon it. It was to this rugged fortress that the goats promptly retreated for safety when we left off watching them, and rose from our concealment. Their sunning-ground looked like a sheep-yard, and we saw that goats had many times lain upon that spot.

Nearby, behind a living windbreak, was a goat-bed, that looked as if goats had lain in it five hundred times. By some curious circumstance, a dozen stunted spruces had woven themselves together, as if for mutual support, until they formed a tight ever-green wall ten feet long and eight feet high. It ranged north and south, forming an excellent hedge-like shield from easterly winds, while the steep mountain partially cut off the winds from the west. On the upper side of that natural windbreak, the turf had been worn into dust, and the droppings were several inches deep. Apparently it was liked because it was a good shelter, in the center of a fine sky-pasture, and within a few jumps of ideal safety rocks.

From the spot where the goats had lain, looking ahead and to our left, we beheld a new mountain. Later on we christened it Bird Mountain, because of the flocks of ptarmigan we found upon its summit. Near its summit we saw five more goats, all females and kids. At our feet lay a deep, rich-looking basin, then a low ridge, another basin with a lakelet in it, and beyond that another ridge, much higher than the first. Ridge No. 2 had dead timber upon it, but it was very scattering, for it was timberline; and its upper end snugged up against the eastern wall of

Bird Mountain. Later on we found that the northern side of that ridge ended in a wall of rock that was scalable by man in one place only.

"Yonder are two big old billies!" said someone with a glass in action.

"Yes sir; there they are; all alone, and heading this way, too. Those are your goats this time, Director, sure enough."

"Now boys," said I, "if we can stalk those two goats successfully, and bag them both, neatly and in quick time, we can call it genuine goat-hunting!"

They were distant about a mile and a half, jogging along down a rocky hill, through a perfect maze of gullies, ridges, grassplots and rocks, one of them keeping from forty to fifty feet behind the other.

Even at that distance they looked big, and very, very white. Clearly, they were heading for Bird Mountain. We planned to meet them wherever they struck the precipitous side of the mountain ahead of us, and at once began our stalk.

From the basin which contained the little two-acre tarn, the rocky wall of Bird Mountain rose almost perpendicularly for about eight hundred feet. As we were passing between the lake and the cliff, we heard bits of loose rock clattering down.

"Just look yonder!" said Mr. Phillips, with much fervor.

Close at hand, and well within fair rifle-shot, were four goats climbing the wall; and two more were at the top, looking down as if deeply interested. The climbers had been caught napping, and being afraid to retreat either to right or left, they had elected to seek safety by climbing straight up! It was a glorious opportunity to see goats climb in a difficult place, and forthwith we halted and watched as long as the event lasted, utterly oblivious of our two big billies. Our binoculars brought them down to us wonderfully well, and we saw them as much in detail as if we had been looking a hundred feet with the unaided eye.

The wall was a little rough, but the angle of it seemed not more than 10 degrees from perpendicular. The footholds were merely narrow edges of rock, and knobs the size of a man's fist. Each goat went up in a generally straight course, climbing slowly and carefully all the while. Each one chose its own course, and paid no attention to those that had gone before. The eyes looked ahead to select the route, and the front hoofs skillfully sought for footholds. It seemed as if the powerful front legs performed three-fourths of the work, reaching up until a good foothold was secured, then lifting the heavy body by main strength, while the hindlegs "also ran." It seemed that the chief function of the hind limbs was to keep what the forelegs won. As an exhibition of strength of limb, combined with sure-footedness and nerve, it was marvelous, no less.

Often a goat would reach toward one side for a new foothold, find none, then rear up and pivot on its hindfeet, with its neck and stomach pressed against the wall, over to the other side. Occasionally a goat would be obliged to edge off five or ten feet to one side in order to scramble on up. From first to last, no goat slipped and no rocks gave way under their feet, although numerous bits of loose sliderock were disturbed and sent rattling down.

It was a most inspiring sight, and we watched it with breathless interest. In about ten minutes the four goats had by sheer strength and skill climbed about two hundred feet of the most precipitous portion of the cliff, and reached easy going. After that they went on up twice as rapidly as before, and soon passed over the summit, out of our sight. Then we compared notes.

Mr. Phillips and I are of the opinion that nothing could have induced mountain sheep to have made that appalling climb, either in the presence of danger or otherwise. Since that day we have found that there are many mountain hunters who believe that as a straightaway cliff-climber, the goat does things that are impossible for sheep.

As soon as the goat-climbing exhibition had ended, we hurried on across the basin, and up the side of Ridge No. 2. This ridge bore a thin sprinkling of low spruces, a little fallen timber, much purple fireweed and some good grass. As seen at a little distance, it was a purple ridge. The western end of it snugged up against the mountain, and it was there that we met our two big billy goats. They had climbed nearly to the top of our ridge, close up to the mountain, and when we first sighted them they were beginning to feed upon a lace-leaved anemone (*Pulsatilla occidentalis*), at the edge of their newly found pasture. We worked toward them, behind a small clump of half-dead spruces, and finally halted to wait for them to come within range.

After years of waiting, Rocky Mountain goats, *at last*! How amazingly white and soft they look; and how big they are! The high shoulder hump, the big, round barrel of the body, and the knee-breeches on the legs make the bulk of the animal seem enormous. The whiteness of "the driven snow," of cotton and of paper seem by no means to surpass the incomparable white of those soft, fluffy-coated animals as they appear in a setting of hard, gray limestone, rugged sliderock and dark-green vegetation. They impressed me as being the whitest living objects I ever beheld, and far larger than I had expected to find them. In reality, their color had the effect of magnifying their size; for they looked as big as two-year-old buffaloes.

Of course only Mr. Phillips and I carried rifles; and we agreed that the left man should take the left animal.

"It's a hundred and fifty yards!" said Mack Norboe, in a hoarse whisper.

My goat was grazing behind the trunk of a fallen tree, which shielded his entire body. I waited, and waited; and there he stood, with his head down, and calmly cropped until I became wildly impatient. I think he stood in one spot for five minutes, feeding upon *Pulsatilla*.

"Why don't you shoot?" queried Phillips, in wonder.

"I can't! My goat's hiding behind a tree."

"Well, fire when you're ready, Gridley, and I'll shoot when you do!"

It must have been five minutes, but it seemed like twenty-five, before that goat began to feel a thrill of life along his keel, and move forward. The annoying suspense had actually made me unsteady; besides which, my Savage was a new one, and unchristened. Later on I found that the sights were not right for me, and that my first shooting was very poor.

At last my goat stood forth, in full view—white, immaculate, high of hump, low of head, big and bulky. I fired for the vitals behind the shoulder.

"You've overshot!" exclaimed Norboe, and

"Bang!" said Mr. Phillips' Winchester.

Neither of us brought down our goat at the first fire!

I fired again, holding much lower, and the goat reared up a foot. Mr. Phillips fired again, whereupon his goat fell over like a sack of oats, and went rolling down the hill. My goat turned to run, and as he did so I sent two more shots after him. Then he disappeared behind some rocks. Mack, John and I ran forward, to keep him in sight, and fire more shots if necessary. But no goat was to be seen.

"He can't get away!" said Norboe, reassuringly.

"He's *dead*!" said I, by way of an outrageous bluff. "You'll find him down on the sliderock!" But inwardly I was torn by doubts.

We hurried down the steep incline, and presently came to the top of a naked wall of rock. Below that was a wide expanse of sliderock.

"Thar he is!" cried Norboe. "Away down yonder, out on the sliderock, dead as a wedge."

From where he stood when I fired, the goat had run back about two hundred feet, where he fell dead, and then began to roll. We traced him by a copious stream of blood on the rocks. He fell down the rock wall, for a hundred feet, in a slanting direction, and then—to my great astonishment—he rolled two hundred feet farther (by measurement) on that ragged, jagged sliderock before he fetched up against a particularly large chunk of stone, and stopped. We expected to find his horns broken, but they were quite uninjured. The most damage had been inflicted upon his nose, which was badly cut and bruised. The bullet that ended his life (my second shot) went squarely through the valves of his heart; but I regret to add that one thigh-bone had been broken by another shot, as he ran from me.

Mr. Phillips' goat behaved better than mine. It rolled down the grassy slope, and lodged on a treacherous little shelf of earth that overhung the very brink of the precipice. One step into that innocent-looking fringe of green juniper bushes meant death on the sliderock below; and it made me nervous to see Mack and Charlie stand there while they skinned the animal.

As soon as possible we found the only practicable route down the rock wall, and scrambled down. The others say that I slid down the last twenty feet; but that is quite immaterial. I reached the goat a few paces in advance of the others, and thought to divert my followers by reciting a celebrated quotation beginning, "To a hunter, the moment of triumph," etc. As I laid my hand upon the goat's hairy side and said my little piece, I heard a deadly "click."

"Got him!" cried Mr. Phillips; and then three men and a dog laughed loud and derisively. Since seeing the picture I have altered that quotation, to this: "To a hunter, the moment of humiliation is when the first sees his idiotic smile on a surreptitious plate." It is inserted solely to oblige Mr. Phillips, as evidence of the occasion when he got ahead of me.

The others declared that the goat was "a big one, though not the very biggest they ever grow." Forthwith we measured him; and in taking his height we shoved his foreleg up until the elbow came to the position it occupies under the standing, living animal. The measurements were as follows:

ROCKY MOUNTAIN GOAT

Oreamnos montanus

Male, six years old. Killed September 8, 1905, near the Bull River,-British Columbia.

	Inches
Standing height at shoulder	38
Length, nose to root of tail	59.25
Length of tail vertebrae	3.50
Girth behind foreleg	55
Girth around abdomen	58
Girth of neck behind ears (unskinned)	18
Circumference of forearm, skinned	11.25
Width of chest	14
Length of horn on curve	9.75
Spread of horns at tips	5
Circumference of horn at base	5.60
Circumference of front hoof	10.50
Circumference of rear hoof	7.75
Base of ear to end of nostrils	10.50

Front corner of eye to rear corner	9
nostril opening	7
Widest spread of ears, tip to tip	15

Total weight of animal by scales, allowing 8 lbs. for blood lost	258 lbs.

The black and naked glands in the skin behind the horn were on that date small, and inconspicuous; but they stood on edge, with the naked face of each closely pressed against the base of the horn in front of it.

On another occasion I shot a thin old goat that stood forty-two inches high at the shoulders, and Mr. Phillips shot another that weighed two hundred and seventy-six pounds. After we had thoroughly dissected my goat, weighed it, examined the contents of its stomach, and saved a good sample of its food for close examination at camp, we tied up the hindquarters, head and pelt, and set out for camp.

And thus ended our first day in the actual hunting of mountain goats, in the course of which we saw a total of forty-two animals. The stalking, killing and dissecting of our two goats was very interesting, but the greatest event of the day was our opportunity to watch those five goats climb an almost perpendicular cliff.

• • •

This day, also, was the eleventh of September . . .

Mr. Phillips, Charlie Smith and I descended the steep side of Goat Pass, crossed the basin and slowly climbed the grassy divide that separates it from the source of Avalanche Creek. When half way down the southern side of that divide, we looked far up the side of Phillips Peak and saw two big old billy goats of shootable size. They were well above timberline, lying where a cloud-land meadow was suddenly chopped off at a ragged precipice. The way up to them was long, and very steep.

"That's a long climb, Director," said Mr. Phillips; "but there are no bad rocks."

I said that I could make it, in time—as compared with eternity—if the goats would wait for me.

"Oh, they'll wait! We'll find 'em there, all right," said Charlie, confidently. So we started.

As nearly as I can estimate, we climbed more than a mile, at an angle that for the upper half of the distance was about 30 degrees—a very steep ascent. At first our way up led through green timber, over smooth ground that was carpeted with needles of spruce and pine. That was comparatively easy, no more difficult, in fact, than climbing the stairs of four Washington monuments set one upon another.

At climbing steep mountains, Mr. Phillips, Charlie Smith and the two Norboes are perfect friends. They are thin, tough and long-winded, and being each of them fully forty pounds under my weight, I made no pretence at trying to keep up with them. As it is in an English workshop, the slowest workman set the pace.

In hard climbing, almost every Atlantic-coast man perspires freely, and is very extravagant in the use of air. It frequently happened that when half way up a high mountain, my lungs consumed the air so rapidly that a vacuum was created around me, and I would have to stop and wait for a new supply of oxygen to blow along. My legs behaved much better than my lungs, and to their credit be it said that they never stopped work until my lungs ran out of steam.

As I toiled up that long slope, I thought of a funny little engine that I saw in Borneo, pulling cars over an absurd wooden railway that ran from the bank of the Sadong River to the coalmines. It would run about a mile at a very good clip, then suddenly cease pulling, and stop. Old Walters, the superintendent, said:

"There's only one thing ails that engine. The bloomin' little thing can't make steam fast enough!"

I was like that engine. I couldn't "keep steam"; and whenever my lungs became a perfect vacuum, I had to stop and rest, and collect air. Considering the fact that there was game above us, I thought my comrades were very considerate in permitting me to set the pace. Now had someone glared at me with the look of a hungry cannibal, and hissed between his teeth, *"Step lively!"* it would have made me feel quite at home.

In due time we left the green timber behind us, and started up the last quarter of the climb. There we found stunted spruces growing like scraggy brush, three feet high, gnarled and twisted by the elements, and enfeebled by the stony soil on which they bravely tried to grow. Only the bravest of trees could even rear their heads on that appalling steep, scorched by the sun, rasped by the wind, drenched by the rains and frozen by the snow. But after a hundred yards or so, even the dwarf spruces gave up the struggle. Beyond them, up to our chosen point, the mountain-roof was smooth and bare, except for a sprinkle of fine, flat sliderock that was very treacherous stuff to climb over.

"Let me take your rifle, Director!" said Charlie, kindly.

"No, thank you. I'll carry it up, or stay down. But you may keep behind me if you will, and catch me if I start to roll!"

On steep slopes, such as that was, my companions had solemnly warned me not to fall backward and start rolling; for a rolling man gathers no moss. A man bowling helplessly down a mountainside at an angle of 30 degrees quickly acquires a momentum which spells death. Often have I looked down a horribly steep stretch, and tried to imagine what I would feel, and *think*, were I to overbalance backward, and go bounding down. A few hours later we saw a goat carcass take a frightful roll down a slope not nearly so steep as where we climbed up, and several times it leaped six feet into the air.

To keep out of the sight of the goats it was necessary for us to bear well toward our left; and this brought us close to the edge of the precipice, where the mountainside was chopped off. In view of the loose stones underfoot, I felt liked edging more to the right; for the twin chances of a roll down and a fall over began to abrade my nerves. Mr. Phillips and Charlie climbed along so close to the drop that I found myself wondering which of them would be the first to slip and go over.

"Keep well over this way, Director, or the goats may wind you!" said Charlie, anxiously.

"That's all right, Charlie; he's winded now!" said John.

I said we would rest on that; and before I knew the danger, Mr. Phillips had taken a picture of me, resting, and smiling a most idiotic smile.

At last we reached the pinnacle which we had selected when we first sighted our game. As nearly as we could estimate, afterward, by figuring up known elevations, we were at a height of about nine thousand feet, and though not the highest, it was the dizziest point I ever trod. Except when we looked ahead, we seemed to be fairly suspended in mid-air! To look down under one's elbow was to look into miles of dizzy, bottomless space.

The steep slope had led us up to the sharp point of a crag that stuck up like the end of a man's thumb and terminated in a crest as sharp as the comb of a houseroof. Directly in front, and also on the left, was a sheer drop. From the right, the ragged edge of the wall ran on up, to the base of Phillips Peak. Beyond our perch, twelve feet away, there yawned a great basin-abyss, and on beyond that rocky gulf rose a five-hundred-foot wall at the base of the Peak. A little to the right of our position another ragged pinnacle thrust its sharp apex a few feet higher than ours, and eventually caused me much trouble in securing my first shot.

We reached the top of our crag, and peered over its highest rocks just in time to see our two goats quietly walk behind a ragged point of rock farther up the wall, and disappear. They were only a hundred and fifty yards distant; but they had not learned of our existence, and were not in the least alarmed. Naturally, we expected them to saunter back into view, for we felt quite sure they did not mean to climb down that wall to the bottom of the basin. So we lay flat upon the slope, rifles in hand, and waited, momentarily expecting the finish. They were due to cross a grassy slope between two crags, not more than forty feet wide, and if not fired at within about *ten seconds* of their reappearance, they would be lost behind the rocks! The chance was not nearly so good as it looked.

But minutes passed, and no goats returned. It became evident that the dawdling pair had lain down behind the sheltering crag, for a siesta in the sun. We composed ourselves to await their pleasure, and in our first breath of opportunity, looked off southeasterly, over the meadow whereon the two goats had been feeding. And then we saw a sight of sights.

Rising into view out of a little depression on the farther side of the meadow, lazily sauntering along, there came ten big, snow-white billy goats! They were heading straight toward us, and there was not a nanny, nor a kid, nor even a young billy in the bunch. The air was clear; the sun was shining brightly, the meadow was like dark olive-brown plush, and how grandly those big, pure-white creatures did loom up! When first seen they were about four hundred yards away, but our glasses made the distance seem only one-third of that.

For more than an hour we lay flat on our pinnacle, and watched those goats. No one thought of time. It was a chance of a lifetime. My companions were profoundly surprised by the size of the collection; for previous to that moment, no member of our party ever had seen more than four big male goats in one bunch.

The band before us was at the very top of a sky-meadow of unusual luxuriance, which climbed up out of the valley on our right, and ran on up to the comb of rock that came down from Phillips Peak. In area the meadow was five hundred yards wide, and half a mile long. Afterward, when we walked over it, we found it was free from stones, but full of broad steps, and covered with a dense, greenish-purple matting of ground verdure that was as soft to the foot as the thickest pile carpet. The main body of this verdure is a moss-like plant called mountain avens, closely related to cinquefoil, and known botanically as *Dryas octopetala*. It has a very pretty leaf measuring about 7/16 by 3/16 inches, with finely serrated edges. In September a mass of it contains a mixture of harmonious colors: olive-green, brown, gray and purple. On this the goats were feeding. This plant is very common in those mountains above timberline, especially on southern slopes; but it demands a bit of ground almost exclusively for itself, and thrives best when alone.

Along with this there grew a moss-like saxifrage (*Saxifraga austromontana*), which to any one not a botanist seems to be straight moss. It grows in cheerful little clumps of bright green, and whenever it is found on a mountain-pasture, one is pleased to meet it.

I record these notes here, because our ten goats had been in no hurry. They were more than deliberate; they were almost stagnant. In an hour, the farthest that any one of them moved was about one hundred yards, and most of them accomplished even less than that. They were already so well fed that they merely minced at the green things around them. Evidently they had fed to satiety in the morning hours, before we reached them.

As they straggled forward, they covered about two acres of ground. Each one seemed steeped and sodden in laziness. When out grazing, our giant tortoises move faster than they did on that lazy afternoon. When the leader of this band of weary Willies reached the geographical center of the sky-meadow, about two hundred yards from us, he decided to take a sunbath on the most luxurious basin possible to him. Slowly he focussed his mind upon a level bench of earth, about four feet wide. It contained an old goat-bed of loose earth, and upon this he lay down, with his back uphill.

At this point, however, he took a sudden resolution. After about a minute of reflection, he decided that the head of his bed was too high and too humpy; so, bracing himself back with his right foreleg, like an ancient Roman senator at a feast, he set his left leg in motion and flung out from under his breast a quantity of earth. The loose soil rose in a black shower, two feet high, and the big hoof flung it several feet down the hill. After about a dozen rakes, he settled down to bask in the warm sunshine, and blink at the scenery of Avalanche Valley.

Five minutes later, a little higher up the slope, another goat did the same thing; and eventually two or three others laid down. One, however, deliberately sat down on his haunches, dog-fashion, with his back uphill. For fully a quarter of an hour he sat there in profile, slowly turning his head from side to side, and gazing at the scenery while the wind blew through his whiskers.

So far as I could determine, no sentinel was posted. There was no leader, and no individual seemed particularly on the alert for enemies. One and all, they felt perfectly secure.

In observing those goats one fact became very noticeable. At a little distance, their legs looked very straight and stick-like, devoid of all semblance of gracefulness and of leaping power. The animals were very white and immaculate—as were all the goats that we saw—and they stood out with the sharpness of clean snow-patches on dark rock. Nature may have known about the much overworked principle of "protective coloration" when she fashioned the mountain goat, but if so, she was guilty of cruelty to goats in clothing this creature with pelage which, in the most comfortable season for hunting, renders it visible for three miles or more. Even the helpless kidling is as white as cotton, and a grand mark for eagles.

That those goats should look so stiff and genuinely ungraceful on their legs, gave me a distinct feeling of disappointment. From that moment I gave up all hope of ever seeing a goat perform any feats requiring either speed or leaping powers; for we saw that of those short, thick legs—nearly as straight as four Indian clubs—nothing is to be expected save power in lifting and sliding, and rocklike steadfastness. In all the two hundred and thirty-nine goats that we saw, we observed nothing to disprove the conclusive evidence of that day regarding the physical powers of the mountain goat.

While we watched the band of mountain loafers, still another old billy goat, making No. 13, appeared across the rock basin far to our left. From the top of the northern ridge, he set out to walk across the wide rock wall that formed the western face of Phillips Peak. From where we were the wall seemed almost smooth, but to the goat it must have looked otherwise. Choosing a narrow, light-gray line of stratification that extended across the entire width of the wall, the solitary animal set out on its promenade. The distance to be traversed to reach the uppermost point of our sky-pasture was about fifteen hundred feet, and the contour line chosen was about four hundred feet above our position. The incident was like a curtain-raiser to a tragic play.

That goat's walk was a very tame performance. The animal plodded steadily along, never faster, never slower, but still with a purposeful air, like a postman delivering mail. For a mountain goat, not pursued or frightened, it was a rapid walk, probably three miles an hour. Its legs swung to and fro with the regularity and steadiness of four pendulums, and I think they never once paused. The animal held to that one line of stratification, until near the end of its promenade. There a great mass of rock had broken away from the face of the cliff, and the goat was forced to climb down about fifty feet, then up again, to regain its chosen route. A few minutes later its ledge ran out upon the apex of the sky-meadow. There Billy paused for a moment, to look about him; then he picked out a soft spot, precisely where the steep slope of the meadow ended against the rocky peak, and lay down to rest.

Up to that time, Mr. Phillips and I had killed only one goat each, and as we lay there we had time to decide upon the future. He resolved to kill one fine goat as a gift to the Carnegie Museum, and I wished two more for my own purposes. We decided that at a total of three goats each—two less than our lawful right—we would draw the line, and kill no more.

The first shot at the pair of invisible goats was to be mine; and as already suggested, the circumstances were like those surrounding a brief moving target in a shooting-gallery. Before us were two rocky crag-points, and behind the one on the left, the animals lay hidden for full an hour. Between the two crags the V-shaped spot of the meadow, across which I knew my goat would walk or run, looked very small. If he moved a yard too far, the right-hand crag would hide him from me until he would be three hundred yards away. I was compelled to keep my rifle constantly ready, and one eye to the front, in order to see my goat in time to get a shot at him while he crossed that forty feet of ground.

And after all, I came ever so near to making a failure of my vigil. I was so absorbed in watching that unprecedented band of billies that before I knew it, the two goats were in the center of the V-shaped stage, and moving at a good gait across it. Horrors!

Hurriedly I exclaimed to Mr. Phillips, "There they are!" took a hurried aim at the tallest goat, and just as his head was going out of sight, let go. He flinched upward at the shoulders, started forward at a trot, and instantly disappeared from my view.

The instant my rifle cracked, Mr. Phillips said, imperatively,

"Don't move! Don't make a sound, and those goats will stay right where they are."

Instantly we "froze." All the goats sprang up, and stood at attention. All looked fixedly in our direction, but the distant eleven were like ourselves, frozen into statues. In that band not a muscle moved for fully three minutes.

Finally the goats decided that the noise they had heard was nothing at which to be alarmed. One by one their heads began to move, and in five minutes their fright was over. Some went on feeding, but three or four of the band decided that they would saunter down our way and investigate that noise.

But what of my goat?

John slid over to my left, to look as far as possible behind the intercepting crag. Finally he said,

"He's done for! He's lying out there, dead."

As soon as possible I looked at him; and sure enough, he lay stretched upon the grass, back uphill, and apparently very dead. The other goat had gone on and joined the ten.

The investigating committee came walking down toward us with a briskness which soon brought them within rifle-shot; and then Mr. Phillips picked out his Carnegie Museum goat and opened fire, at a range of about three hundred yards. The first shot went high, but at the next the goat came down, hit behind the shoulder. This greatly alarmed all the other goats, but they were so confused that three of them came down toward us at a fast trot. At two hundred yards I picked out one, and fired. At my third shot, it fell, but presently scrambled up, ran for the edge of the precipice and dropped over out of sight. It landed, mortally wounded, on some ragged rocks about fifty feet down, and to end its troubles a shot from the edge quickly finished it.

Mr. Phillips killed his first goat, and before the bunch got away, broke the leg of another. This also got over the edge of the precipice, and had to be finished up from the edge.

But a strange thing remains to be told.

By the time Mr. Phillips and I had each fired about two shots of the last round, in the course of which we ran well over to the right in order to command the field, to our blank amazement my first goat—*the dead one!*—staggered to his feet, and started off toward the edge of the precipice. It was most uncanny to see a dead animal thus come to life!

"Look, Director," cried Charlie Smith, "your first goat's come to life! Kill him again! Kill him again, quick!"

I did so; and after the second killing he remained dead. I regret to say that in my haste to get those goats measured, skinned and weighed before night, I was so absorbed that I forgot to observe closely where my first shot struck the goat that had to be killed twice. I think however, that it went through his liver and other organs without touching the vital portions of the lungs.

My first goat was the tallest one of the six we killed on that trip, but not the heaviest. He was a real patriarch, and decidedly on the downhill side of life. He was so old that he had but two incisor teeth remaining, and they were so loose they were almost useless. He was thin in flesh, and his pelage was not up to the mark in length. But in height he was tall, for he stood forty-two inches at the shoulders, with the foreleg pushed up where it belongs in a standing animal.

Mr. Phillips' Carnegie Museum goat was the heaviest one shot on that trip, its gross weight being two hundred and seventy-six pounds.

Charlie decided to roll the skinned carcass of my goat down the mountain, if possible within rifle-shot of the highest point of green timber, in the hope that a grizzly might find it, and thereby furnish a shot. He cut off the legs at the knees, and started the body rolling on the sky-pasture, end over end. It went like a wheel, whirling down at a terrific rate, sometimes jumping fifty feet. It went fully a quarter of a mile before it reached a small basin, and stopped. The other carcass, also, was rolled down. It went sidewise, like a bag of grain, and did not roll quite as far as the other.

By the time we had finished our work on the goats—no trifling task—night was fast approaching, and leaving all the heads, skins and meat for the morrow, we started for our new camp, five miles away.

We went down the meadow (thank goodness!), and soon struck the green timber; and then we went on down, down, and still farther down, always at thirty degrees, until it seemed to me we never would stop going down, never reach the bottom and the trail. But everything earthly has an end. At the end of a very long stretch of plunging and sliding, we reached Avalanche Creek, and drank deeply of the icy-cold water for which we had so long been athirst.

After three miles of travel down the creek, over sliderock, through green timber, yellow willows, more green timber and some down timber, we heard the cheerful whack of Huddleston's axe, and saw on tree-trunk and bough the ruddy glow of the new campfire.

The new camp was pitched in one of the most fascinating spots I ever camped within. The three tents stood at the southern edge of a fine, open grove of giant spruces that gave us good shelter on rainy days. Underneath the trees there was no underbrush, and the ground was deeply carpeted with dry needles. Grand mountains rose on either hand, practically from our campfire, and for our front view a fine valley opened southward for six miles, until its lower end was closed by the splendid mass of Roth Mountain and Glacier. Close at hand was a glorious pool of icewater, and firewood "to burn." Yes, there was one other feature, of great moment, abundant grass for our horses, in the open meadow in front of the tents.

To crown all these luxuries, Mr. Phillips announced that, according to mountain customs already established, and precedents fully set, that camp would then and there be named in my honor—"Camp Hornaday." What more could any sportsman possibly desire?

The Quest of the Ptarmigan

[**REX BEACH**]

S ell Keno? No—guess not. Need Money? Oh yes—but. No—you can't buy him. That's a big price, I know, and I could buy lots of dog teams for that, but I may as well tell you I would as soon sell my brother—my best friend, or, if I had one, my wife. May be sentiment, but he saved my life, and no other man while he lives shall ever curl the lash of a dog-whip across his shaggy back. He's not a dog to me; he's my friend.

Want to hear about it?—Well—I don't mind. It's cold outside and nothing to do. Better light up. It's mostly a story of a ptarmigan hunt. Kind of a peaceful pastoral prelude, with merry guns cracking, ending up with a dash for life accompanied by a full fledged howling of the storm chorus under the baton of the spirit of the North.

Did you ever have the meat hunger so strong in your vitals that you would wake at night dreaming of the fried chicken that mother made, or could picture the grill-marks on a broiled steak? Just in from the states, eh?

Well, after a continuous diet of bacon, ham and the poorly-embalmed beef that made Chicago famous, the longing for something fresh becomes unbearable, so when McMillan, another old timer, dropped in at the bunk house one night and said that Nome River was "alive with ptarmigan" my partner Jack and I decided to take the dog team and drive over for a day's sport—and a week's grub.

The heavy snows had driven the birds down from the mountains to the coast where the willows were still uncovered. That was the year I had the great team, considered the best on the coast; fifteen as fine dogs as ever stole a ham; kept me broke, too, with dog-feed at 35 cents. Yes, that's the team we rescued the Cooper party with, after the big storm. I brought two of the frozen men to a doctor ninety-six miles in twelve hours, with Keno, here, in the lead. Good drive, eh?

Well, the next morning found us up, not bright and early, as daylight doesn't come till about eight o'clock and isn't any too bright when it does get around, but early nevertheless, and after a breakfast of oatmeal, bacon, evaporated potatoes and "sour dough" flap jacks warranted to stick to your ribs for a week, I slipped the harness over ten of the best dogs, and as the stars began to dim and fade we heard the "swish-swish" of McMillan's twelve-foot skis as he came down the creek. He looked ghostlike and unreal in his long white parka, or hooded shirt, with beard, mustache and eyebrows white from his frozen breath.

"How cold is it by your thermometer?" said he, "The 'quick' in ours is frozen up."

Our spirit thermometer registered 44 degrees below, but as there wasn't a breath of air stirring we anticipated a fairly comfortable day. My "malam-oots" had shaken off their sleepiness and seated shivering on the snow with heads to the stars saddened the air with dismal complaints.

Jack took his seat in the bottom of the long basket-sled, behind McMillan. There was a crack of the whip and a "Mush boys" and as the dogs leaped into their collars we were whisked around the cabin and out onto the main trail at railroad speed. Then a word to old Keno here and the pack settled down to the even run which eats up distance and which well-trained dogs maintain for hours.

When we reached the bunch of willows at the mouth of Osborne Creek we slipped into the snow-shoes and started back toward the foothills, keeping about a hundred yards apart.

I had been straining my eyes to detect some object on the monotonous expanse of white, when suddenly a spot of snow which I had scanned, broke up under my eyes into four animated, squawking snowballs, which went whizzing in as many different directions. I wasn't sure on my snow shoes and missed with both barrels.

While the birds remained above the skyline they were readily visible, offering a splendid target, but as they settled lower they were merged into the whiteness of the snow and instantly disappeared.

I heard McMillan's 10-bore explode and concluded he was doing business in his usual way. Then a double from Jack, followed by a peculiarly easy and melodious flow of profanity, showing at least three years' continuous residence "north of 53," explained perfectly the result of his two shots.

Near me I noticed a black dot like a small shoe-button against the field of white, and straining my eyes until the tears came and froze on my cheeks, I detected the outlines of a bird. With shoes well under me I advanced on the enemy's right wing, as it were. This time when my bird rose I cut short his derisive squawk, and with my right barrel knocked the tail out of another which had followed, and saw him wabble off for a hundred yards before giving up the fight.

Again I heard the report of Jack's Parker, and then

upon the still air there floated to me a bunch of the most earnest and sincerely heartfelt profanity that an active brain and facile tongue could master, interspersed with recurring prophesies as to the eventual destiny of the individual who invented smokeless powder, the corporation which made it, the store that sold it, and the infernal idiot who would attempt to use it in cold weather. I judged that he had attempted to use frozen nitro-powder and found that it would hardly clear the gun barrel of shot.

When I returned to the sled, the dogs were sleeping peacefully, curled up in the snow like round fur balls. While I straightened them out of the tangle of harness they had formed before lying down, Jack and McMillan cleaned the birds, distributing feathers and refuse impartially among the members of the team. The craving for fresh meat among the inner circles of the dogs is probably more acute than among us and certainly less often gratified.

Having put them in a good humor we were off again up the river in the direction our birds had gone. Jack had turned to ask me something when he interrupted himself to tell me that my nose was frozen. This particular feature is unduly prominent with me and its isolation from the base of supplies renders it "shy" on circulation, so that it grows chill and clammy in Indian summer and has been frozen stiff by Thanksgiving. These frost bites result in an exceedingly red-looking and painful member which later peels off like a boiled potato. After a few moments of vigorous rubbing and pinching I succeeded in restoring animation and thereafter by wrinkling my nose like a cow I could tell whether the circulation had "made good" or was laying off. If the part felt stiff and difficult to move, off would come the mittens and the osteopathy recommence, continuing until the organ became sensible to muscular control.

I had been sitting on the sled rail, engaged in working my nose up to a fever heat, when suddenly, with a jerk that nearly unseated me, the team leaped into a sharp run. Glancing ahead the cause was apparent in the shape of a big Arctic hare that had hopped from the deep snow in the willows to the bare ice of the river and was leisurely working the kinks out of his legs a short distance ahead of us.

The dogs quieted almost instantly, and with noses to the trail began to run madly, making our sled sing over the smooth ice, which allowed them a sure footing and offered no resistance to the sled. In fact, here lay the danger, for with the accelerated speed, our sled, striking the little inequalities of the ice surface, was veering wildly, sometimes sliding nearly broadside on. Striking an obstacle, with a string of sparks from the steel shoe, it would tilt on one runner, nearly hurling us headlong onto the ice, then back again to the other side.

To control a team with the smell of game in their nostrils is impossible, yet a spill on the ice at this rate of speed meant painful results, if not serious ones, while a runaway team would mean loss of outfit and a long trip home on foot.

The duties of the "chauffeur" of the team in addition to "dog punching" consists of preventing an upset, if possible, so bidding the boys keep their seats, I balanced my 200 pounds of avoirdupois on the upper rail of the sled, changing from side to side as it began its erratic flights. This method of shifting ballast was working admirably and we were enjoying our dizzy ride, when our pacemaker, thinking the excitement too tame, increased his speed, and turning abruptly, made for the willows on the river bank.

This particular curve was not graded for our rate of speed, and when the dogs turned the sled swung, skimming around broadside and striking an ice hummock upsetting with such violence as to hurl me flying through the air like a frog. I believe a parabola is the most beautiful curve in geometry, yet although I feel that the one I described was geometrically perfect, its beauty did not appeal to me. Experience on a bicycle track, from the days of the high wheel onward, had taught me a valuable thing about falling, and I rejoiced in the knowledge that unlike a board track there were no splinters here.

I landed amid a rain of dead birds with the breath knocked out of me and a mental photograph of Jack and McMillan in positions absolutely defying the laws of nature. Mac was evidently attempting to rise at the critical moment, and with his long legs curled beneath him, had added to his momentum by jumping at random—so I caught a fleeting glimpse of a giant, red-headed Scotchman apparently seated at ease on the ice, but progressing with surprising rapidity in the direction we had been going. I had never before seen a practical demonstration of the Scotch game of "curling." I believe I would enjoy watching a game.

Jack's early training on the deck of a cattle pony asserted itself, and clinging tightly to the sled he was dragged up the bank through the snow, and into the bushes where the dogs, becoming entangled, came to a stop and awaited us with wagging tails, lolling tongues and an expression plainly saying: "We gave him the run of his life, didn't we?" We found Jack with pipe still clenched between his teeth, gingerly testing his knee caps.

"They were my only points of bearing for fifty yards," said he, "and if they weren't good, thick Missouri knee caps, they'd be looking like a glass of toothpicks, now."

An excited team will tie knots in its harness that

would defy a sailor to attempt to straighten out the tangle.

Busied in this way I suddenly became conscious of an ominous movement of the air which till now had been deathly still. Glancing north up the valley I saw that which caused me to snatch the struggling dogs out on the ice with a curse, and utter a cry of warning to my companions. The mountains, towering on either hand, had changed, and instead of standing clear-cut and white in the marble stillness, a dim haze had veiled the landscape while from the peaks flew gossamer streams of whirling snow, like thin smoke of many fires. As yet the air of the valley was scarcely stirring, but as we gazed, the twin walls of mountains gleaming miles northward up the valley were silently blotted out by the gray clouds of snow that swept down upon us. We were in the icy grip of the "Terror of the Northland," the sudden breath of the Arctic which sweeps south without warning over this desolate wilderness.

"We'll have to run before it," said Jack, as we hurriedly donned the fur "parkis" which till now had remained unused. "No living thing could face a wind in this cold."

As we threw the birds in the sled, a puff of snow whirled past, enveloping us in a stinging cloud of frost crystals, while the dogs whined uneasily and strained against the harness.

The storm did not break suddenly, nor did it sweep down upon us with the roar and violence of a hurricane, but rather with a darkening of the heavens there came a restless stirring of the air which rapidly quickened and brought with it a moaning flurry of snow. This writhed along the ground as though loathe to part from its drifts.

McMillan's hooded figure floated ahead of us, visible only above the waist, his long legs invisible in the swirling snow, which clinging close to the earth, hid the dogs from view and seemed to buoy us up on a drifting sea of white. Soon the familiar landscape faded out and we were hurried on through a thick, gray, biting atmosphere, trusting to our general sense of direction.

Given a good sleeping-bag, the proper course to pursue in an extremity of this kind is to free the dogs from the harness and seeking the shelter of the sled, crawl inside the bag and wait for the storm to abate. This is no beauty sleep which one enjoys inside a deerskin sack during the two or three days that a blizzard rages, but with sufficient food to sustain bodily heat, it is a safe resource.

Totally unprepared as we were, the anxiety I saw in Jack's countenance was mirrored in mine, but I thanked my stars for not having a little wife waiting for me back at the claim, as he had.

McMillan paused until we blew up to his side, and

speaking through ice-burdened whiskers said, "Either my direction is wrong or the wind is changing. If we keep this course we'll be out on the ice of the Bering sea by night-fall."

"We don't need to complicate this pleasant situation by getting onto the ice-pack with an offshore gale," shouted Jack. "We'd better take the consensus of opinion and strike for the point we think is home."

The plain lying between the foothills and the ocean is devoid of vegetation and makes it extremely easy to wander out upon the ice-floe. Confused by the approaching darkness and the blinding snow, I feared for the result in such a case.

It seemed to our strained imaginations that we had travelled for hours before the early darkness, hastened by the gloom of the storm, settled upon us, and the dogs, wearied by constant plunging through soft snow and heavy with ice-matted coats, stopped, panting and exhausted.

There is no rest for man or beast on the frozen trail, and after cleaning the ice from their faces, with a cheering word to each, we forced them on.

Moving among them, and with hoarse cries of encouragement we plodded onward.

Suddenly with a shout Jack halted us. "We're out on the pack" said he, and stopping he dimly showed us the ragged point of an up-ended ice cake from which the snow had been blown.

With my sheath knife I chipped a piece off and the briny taste told me that we were indeed upon the ice of Bering Sea and perhaps headed for open water a few miles off shore. Fortunately we had not encountered a crevice, for had we done so nothing would have prevented our plunging into it, blinded and driven by the gale and with no question as to the result, for even though regaining the solid ice, the excessive cold would have instantly congealed our heavy clothes into icy armour impossible to bear.

Turning, we fought our way back again into the storm, but the dogs refused to face the cutting sleet. The heavy butt of the dog whip only produced whines of pain, so heading as closely to the wind as possible we changed our course back toward the shore.

I was faint from hunger and very tired. We had traveled for an endless time in this direction when McMillan staggered back to the sled and throwing himself upon it said, "I'm afraid I can't make it much farther. One of my skis is broken and I'm too far gone to travel without it."

Jack listlessly rubbed his cheeks with snow as he sank behind the sled.

"Fellows, my face has started to freeze," said he. "We might as well try to walk around till morning.

We may go it till daylight if we keep moving and don't let each other go to sleep."

I was glad to yield to an overpowering desire to stop. Rest was what I wanted and a little doze. It seemed many days since I had slept, and a few moments' sleep now would fix me finely.

Too drowsy and exhausted to answer, I went forward to cut the harness from the dogs, thinking that they at least would sleep the storm out and return safely to the claim.

Immediately upon stopping every animal save one, had curled up and was sleeping in its tracks. "Keno," the leader, sat up and with quivering nostrils was casting the wind for a scent. Three winters on the trail with this shaggy veteran had taught me the significance of his every move and had bred absolute confidence in his instinct.

"He smells a camp!" I shouted, and fell to madly pulling, beating and kicking the weary brutes onto their feet. We yelled and coaxed and entreated, careful not to confuse the leader who, given his head, started rapidly into the very teeth of the storm, occasionally raising his nose to the wind.

Soon one of the big gray wheel-dogs whined eagerly and strained into the harness, and with a chorus of sharp cries the team broke into a run while we clung stubbornly to the sled and plunging heavily were dragged up over a bank where the blizzard howled down from the hills above, and tearing the hoods from our faces, froze our wet streaming hair. Then the dogs were suddenly swallowed up in a dark hole which pierced the depths of a large drift, and with a crash the sled struck the log forming one side of the entrance, throwing us partially into the low black tunnel of an "egloo."

Almost instantly a blaze of light appeared at the end of the passage as a door swung open disclosing the rough interior of a roadhouse, while a man's tall figure was silhouetted against the square of welcome brightness. A ravishing steam of hot cooking assailed our nostrils, and as he waded towards us through the struggling mass of smoking wolf-dogs he cried, "My God, strangers! Who hits the trail on a night like this?"

Sources

"The Hunt for the Man-Eaters of Tsavo," by Lt. Col. J.M.
Patterson, D.S.O., from *The Man-Eaters of Tsavo*, 1907.

"An Elk Hunt at Two-Ocean Pass," by Theodore Roosevelt, from *The Wilderness Hunter*, 1893.

"De Shootin'est Gent'man," by Nash Buckingham,
Recreation, 1916.

"That Twenty-Five Pound Gobbler," by Archibald
Rutledge, *Outing*, 1919.

"Tige's Lion," by Zane Grey, *Field & Stream*, 1908.

"Red Letter Days in British Columbia," by Lieutenant
Townsend Whelen, *Outdoor Life*, 1906.

"The Alaskan Grizzly," by Harold McCracken, *Field &
Stream*, 1920.

"The Plural of Moose Is Mise," by Irwin S. Cobb, *Field &
Stream*, 1921.

"Brant Shooting on Great South Bay," by Edwin Main
Post, *Field & Stream*, 1910.

"Some Tiger Stories," by Sir Richard Dane, from *Sport in
Asia and Africa*, 1921.

"Bear Hunting in the Smokies," by Horace Kephart, *Field
& Stream*, 1909.

"The Forest and the Steppe," by Ivan Turgenev, from *A*

Hunter's Sketches, 1852. Sometimes called *A Sportsman's Sketches*. Three chapters added in 1872 editions.

"Bob White, Down 't Aberdeen," by Nash Buckingham, *Field & Stream*, 1913.

"Hunting on the Oregon Trail," by Francis Parkman, from *The Oregon Trail*, 1847.

"The Mountain Goat at Home," by William T. Hornaday, Sc. D, from *Camp-Fires in the Canadian Rockies*, 1906.

"The Quest of the Ptarmigan," by Rex Beach, Outdoor Life, 1903.